DLT Malta

DLT Malta

Thoughts from the Blockchain Island

Edited by

Patrick L Young

&

Joseph Anthony Debono

DV Books

Valletta

Legal disclaimer

Contents

Part I. Humanitas

Part II. Negotium

Part III. Lex

Part IV. Scientia

Part V. Epilogue

Sponsors

The Blockchain Malta Association thanks its generous sponsors for supporting the publication of this book.

zeta.

Dedication

Beatae Christinaeque, mulieribus dilectissimis,
quarum virtutes tam plurimae quam nitidae.
Eadem enim virtus et viro et feminae.

Foreword: Prime Minister Joseph Muscat

There can be no doubt this is a world prone to volatility and change. However, we do not have any time to waste on pessimism. A world of digital opportunity awaits us.

Malta is a small state that registers one of the highest rates of economic growth in Europe and in the world. Positioned in the centre of the Mediterranean, juxtaposed in the middle of a very historic trade route between North Africa, the Middle East and mainland Europe, we have enjoyed the fruits of physical trade for many centuries. Millennia in fact. Nevertheless, in a digital world, geography can become significantly less important. Finding a productive place on the silicon equivalent of the Spice Road is a challenge, particularly in an era of increasingly competitive global trade. Closing ourselves off to the forces of technological change would not only leave us excluded from global dialogue, it would be denying our citizens the rich tapestry of opportunity that awaits all citizens in the digital world. At the same time, we cannot advocate a single, simplistic solution to the complex phenomenon of economic growth. Moreover, while we may be small in area and modest in population, Malta is a nation with a hearty appetite to play an active role in the world as a member of the Commonwealth, the European Union, and the United Nations.

A way forward that Malta advocates is the harnessing of new

technologies, which pose endless possibilities. We are currently in exciting technological times: with the lightning pace of current technological advance, each incredible piece of new innovation can hold a new solution to a problem persisting for decades, from advanced robotics and artificial intelligence, to 3D printing and the Internet of Things.

Yes, there are challenges in this fast and obvious transition to the digital economy. These challenges have to do with the very nature of concepts that we have believed would stay with us forever. One of them is the nature of work, how we envisage it, how we compensate it, how we maximize its efficiency, and how the state creates new safety nets. It is a conversation that has just started globally, but one that will shape public debate during our lifetime.

We can take the antagonistic view that technological progress is bad for us, that it will lead to new types of poverty, that it will outstrip people of their rights, or even take decisions out of their hands. While this may sound appealing as a short-term strategy for some politicians, and even sensible to well-meaning people frightened that progress will cost them their jobs, it would be as myopic as those advocating to prevent the replacement of horse carts by motor vehicles.

Be it for immigration or technology, solutions do not come from closing doors. The digital economy needs to be seen as an opportunity, without nevertheless thinking that we can best harness its opportunities without evolving the current social contracts in place.

Those who will be able to pair the digital economy with a new state, the digital state, will be best poised to have a futureproof society where change does not galvanize extremes, but provides for other decades of sensible, mainstream policymaking and prosperity.

Then there are the other big questions that the dawn of this digital age will need to see answered. Can we solve stalemate diplomatic negotiations by applying algorithms that can avoid war? Can we disarm terrorists using the latest technology? Is it possible to know immediately which remote parts of our planet need international humanitarian assistance? Can we create new organs for people so that no one may die on a donor list? Can we live for the day when humanity can be told that there is a cure for all cancers?

Only time will tell. But it is the accessibility to advanced technologies that will lead to solutions. Hopefully for the whole world.

I passionately believe technology revolutionizes and improves systems.

Which is why, in Malta, we have launched ourselves as the Blockchain Island by becoming the first jurisdiction to regularize a new technology that had previously existed in a legal vacuum. We took a decision, and have become the centre of such an important discussion on important technology.

Blockchain makes cryptocurrencies, the inevitable future of money, more transparent since it helps filter good business from bad business. But these distributed ledger technologies can do much more. They can provide new solutions to healthcare systems by which patients have real ownership of their medical records. Emissions trading systems can be taken to the next level. We can help verify that humanitarian assistance is reaching its intended destination. We can make sure that nobody is deprived of their legitimate property because of compromised data. Corporations will be able to become more accountable to their shareholders. States will need to move from hoarding information on citizens to regulating an environment in which citizens trust the handling of their data.

Whether you are a digital native, a recent convert to the power of the blockchain, or this is your first encounter with this incredible technological advance, I believe you will find this book of interest. It is a reflection of the rich Maltese tradition of debate and science, of diligence and innovation. Just as our islands were shaped by events and people around us, so too this book is a reflection of how our nation has embraced a digital transformation to become the Blockchain Island in what is less than a blink of an eye in the history of our archipelago.

The Malta Blockchain Association has, under the editorship of Joseph Anthony Debono and its chairman Patrick L. Young, compiled a fascinating anthology of chapters that reflect many diverse factors in the construction and development of the Blockchain Island strategy my government instigated in 2017. Encapsulated in this book is the Maltese message that we like to do things the right way in clear and sensible parameters, not in a hurried rush. Our philosophy is to be honest brokers.

We have built a legal framework, and are working to fine-tune the best regulatory mix that protects investors as well as delivering employment locally while serving users of this ground-breaking technology across the world. In essence this book serves as a repository of work done and a laboratory for stimulating ideas on how we may move the island and this technology forward. The applications of this technology are unlimited, from healthcare to banks, to the environment, to financial services. While mindful that blockchain is a decentralized technology, Malta serves as a perfect laboratory of ideas to power the immutable progress of the distributed ledger. The sky is the limit as long as the law is observed. That is how we earned the epithet of the Blockchain Island.

The rise of cryptocurrencies can be slowed but cannot be stopped. Some financial institutions are painstakingly accepting the fact that the system at the back of such transactions is much more efficient and transparent than the classical ones. My point is that rather than resist, European regulators should innovate and create mechanisms with which to regulate cryptocurrencies, in order to harness their potential and better protect consumers, while making Europe the natural home of innovators.

At the same time, facing this incredible technological transition, I do not blame anyone for sometimes feeling a bit lost and numb. The world as we know it is changing so rapidly, and more often than not we find ourselves breathless, hardly keeping up with the pace.

People's lives cannot wait for politicians to get their act together. It is we who have to keep pace with the changes happening in our societies.

Living in an era of technological disruption is indeed a challenging prospect. The industrial revolution brought about by technological advancements, simplifying the nature of work, made it accessible to lesser trained persons. This access to work in turn led many previously disenfranchised persons to start earning a decent living and benefit from social mobility. It was the biggest boost ever to the global middle class, an essential component of any democracy, and part and parcel of our electorate.

Inversely, we must acknowledge that the new industrial revolution we are facing, spearheaded by artificial intelligence, risks depriving the working and middle class of what it has achieved. The instinct of many is thus to resist, if not oppose, change.

At the dawn of the Industrial Revolution in the nineteenth century, there was a group of textile workers, the Luddites, who would go to factories to smash machinery they blamed for depriving them of their jobs. Their successes were brief, their victories Pyrrhic. We must be progressive. We cannot afford to be the Luddites of the new industrial revolution. In this progressive spirit, we were always about change not against it.

Rather than ignore or hope to postpone this change, we should embrace and harness it. We need to seek the answers to the issues that will define the next generations.

We should not fear to do so in all areas, outside our comfort zones. While we must be defined by our core human values, our embrace of technology, of the distributed ledger and cryptocurrency, is an opportunity we must exploit to power a future wave of social mobility across our society. Our vision is to see this sector grow in volume, and find new ways in which tech can improve people's lives.

True, the pace of technological change is daunting. We simply cannot hope people will revert to using cassette tapes and the Walkman, a gadget my tech-savvy 11-year-old daughters examined with archaeological fascination when they found one in an attic box a year ago.

In the smallest member state of the European Union we are making the case for embracing technological change and the opportunity it delivers. This book is not a manifesto, it is a tool to help further understanding of why Malta is at the heart of this technological revolution. If you are uncertain, I encourage you both to relax in a comfortable armchair and then to ease your way out of your comfort zone while reading this thought-provoking book, born on the Blockchain Island, and embracing its core values – innovation and organization with strong and coherent legal precepts to enable the technology to flourish in every kind of application. The blockchain seed landed on fertile soil here. We began watering it to ensure it grows in an organic way, building the blocks to ensure that it will bear fruit when the time is right. We are telling everyone that we are open for business, within the parameters we designed with all stakeholders. Our playing field is designed and laid now. Now we are inviting people to come and play in our fields. Hopefully this book will encourage you to come and see the Blockchain Island for yourself.

We are not done yet. Of course not. What's next is the question we ask every day. Like every company we can only find opportunities if we are out there on the lookout. Who knows, perhaps that will prove fertile ground for the agile minds of the Blockchain Malta Association to distribute another volume of their thoughts.

I believe there is a sea of opportunity waiting for us. And our bark has barely set sail.

In the meanwhile, I commend to you this book as a useful meditation on the genesis of Malta as the Blockchain Island.

The Honourable Dr Joseph Muscat MP
Prime Minister of Malta
Auberge de Castille
Valletta

Parliamentary Secretary Silvio Schembri

There are four things about Malta that immediately strike the visitor – its tiny size, the immense architecture of thousands of years of civilization, the glittering sea, and the bustling streets of its booming economy. These things are connected. History shows that the challenges of an unfavourable or insular environment can be turned into golden opportunity by hard work and responsible policies, For this combination generates economic growth, and trade, which together incentivize the innovation that keeps this cycle going. This is what Malta has done for centuries and is still doing to date, Malta's nimble and agility puts it at an advantage to continue to innovate the economy, from a manufacture based economy to the one based on services as we are witnessing today.

The current stage in the development of Malta as an economic centre in the middle of the Mediterranean is the establishment of a regulated environment for blockchain and distributed technologies, home to a new emergent sector likely to shape the upcoming years. There is much scepticism about these technologies, but we have to be pragmatic. These technologies exist, and they are disruptive. The solution is to regulate the field, and nurture it in such a way that its innovative qualities, and creative energies will make a net contribution to human well-being and economic growth whilst providing the legal certainty operators and consumers within this industry demand. This is what Malta has managed to provide.

The Government of Malta became increasingly interested in supporting and nurturing this new environment as early as 2016. In fact, on April 2017, Prime Minister Dr Joseph Muscat announced in Parliament that the Cabinet had approved the first draft of Malta's Blockchain Strategy.

It was then when later that year I was appointed Parliamentary Secretary for Financial Services, Digital Economy and Innovation, the first time in the history of the Maltese Government that a specific secretariat for the digital economy was appointed, that the importance this legislature is giving to new economic niches was made apparent. With immediate effect, a Blockchain Taskforce was established, later followed by the public consultation of the document 'Malta-A leader in DLT Regulation' which presented our vision for this sector. This Government sees blockchain.as a golden opportunity to create new value for the Maltese economy and investors therein. Initiatives followed thick and fast.

Our vision and the holistic approach in the way we look at regulating this industry without stifling innovation earned Malta the nickname of The Blockchain Island. Soon after publication, key players in the blockchain and crypto sphere announced their decision of relocating or establishing their presence in Malta.

The crown jewel of our efforts was born when the Maltese Parliament, in July 2018, enacted the three Acts that serve as the triple columns of our DLT legislative framework. These three Acts are the Malta Digital Innovation Authority Act (MDIAA), the Innovative Technology Arrangements and Services Act (ITASA), and the Virtual Financial Assets Act (VFAA). The MDIAA establishes an authority to oversee the sector, the ITASA establishes a certification regime, not just for DLT technologies, but one sufficiently flexible to regulate future innovative technologies. The VFAA regulates virtual financial assets, including initial coin offerings, that do not fall under any other Maltese legislation, and it also regulates service providers in the field. With these Acts, therefore, Malta now has the first fully fledged legislative framework that brings together legislative and technological innovation into a single infrastructure designed to bring regulatory oversight, security, peace of mind, innovation and prosperity to every stakeholder; which Acts came into effect on November 1st. We set the ball rolling and now we have the first Virtual Financial Asset Act certified by the Malta Financial Services Authority and the first System Auditors certified by the Malta Digital Innovation Authority. This was a crucial step awaited by many which finally came about after a rigorous due diligence process. Both VFA Agents and System Auditors will act as the gatekeepers of this industry and be the main point of reference for the Authorities during the licensee process. We looked at establishing the highest standards in the best interest of the Maltese jurisdiction and elevate the prestige amongst companies that acquire a Maltese license.

Undoubtedly, Malta, a small nation in the middle of the Mediterranean, is leading the pack. From a lone voice possibly in the world, to now the focal point of a thriving sector.

Whilst we're providing a regulatory framework that appeals to the industry's needs, we're enhancing the skills of current and future generations by the introduction of DLT related courses at the University of Malta as well as offering scholarship programmes for students to pursue their studies in DLT, both at Masters and Phd level. We have come this far and successfully we have placed Malta at the forefront of this digital revolution.

Finally, I express my heartfelt thanks for the invitation by the Blockchain Malta Association to contribute in the first edition of this book, which will offer a wide spectrum of the leading figures and some of the greatest minds in Malta's DLT industry. By way of introduction, this book will showcase what the Maltese jurisdiction has to offer to the global industry in this sector.

The Honourable Silvio Schembri MP
Parliamentary Secretary for Financial Services,
Digital Economy and Innovation

Patrick L Young

"I can't understand why people are frightened of new ideas.
I'm frightened of the old ones."

— John Cage

Everybody in this book has their own story about how the Blockchain Island became tangible. While the stories may differ, they all concur on one point. This upheaval occurred with the sort of page turning rapidity more often seen in potboiler fiction than reality. Indeed, when Tintin inadvertently strikes oil on a native American reservation in Herge's magnificent comic strip, he goes to sleep in a wigwam only to awake the next day to discover that a vast metropolis has emerged around his discovery of Black Gold. There are days when it has felt like this on the Blockchain Island! I have the feeling that our charismatic pug Toby, on his morning constitutional around the streets of Valletta, has been looking at the many DLT pioneers passing by and musing that they seem to be maturing at a pace that exceeds even dog years for accelerated development!

In 2016, some time after a trajectory had been set for my wife and me to move to Malta, I had already completed a round of key conferences when I was invited to address a meeting of the JCI (Junior Chamber of Commerce) at Malta Enterprise on the topic of fintech. Having written Capital Market Revolution! the original bestselling book on the topic in 1999 (a decade before the word 'fintech' was even deployed!) I was happy to provide insights into all aspects of the subject, including the brave 'new' world of blockchain and cryptocurrency.

At that event, around 80 cheery souls sat through an afternoon presentation. I am minded to say with hindsight that I think many did so more out of loyalty to the JCI and a mild sense of curiosity as opposed to a deep desire to embrace the deployment of DLT or smart contracts, or even buy a few bitcoins.

From 1 February 2016 let us fast forward barely 18 months to the evening of Friday 29 September 2017. By then a sea change had swept through the archipelago, most notably in April when addressing a conference on the future of the economy, the Prime Minister, Dr Joseph Muscat set the stage for the national blockchain revolution. This marked the high-water mark of speeches outlining a radical rethink of Malta's innovation strategy that had been mentioned en passant for some weeks in other addresses.

During the summer of 2017, correspondence from the Gozo-Malta Bitcoin Club earnestly explained that they hoped to break the three-figure mark for meeting attendance, and wondered if I might like to address the September event with a view to setting a new benchmark.

By the time I arrived at the Gozo-Malta Bitcoin Club I was already aware that the room had been upgraded from the compact 100-seater semi-circular 'theatre' of Le Meridien hotel to the much larger ballroom, so I was optimistic we would see the prerequisite three-figure target achieved. However, I was rather unprepared for the remarkable scene at registration. Fully 365 people were registered, and it may be that more actually attended the event (along with one Bitcoin ATM). As I was speaking, the first ten minutes were punctuated by amusing scenes at the back of the room. A rather stressed hotel porter rolled in trolleys stacked with chairs.

When it was clear that despite the dispersal of a third stack, many folks were still left standing, he offered a rather theatrical series of shrugs inferring a mix of hopelessness and frustration akin to a vexed Charlie Chaplin before taking his trolley and storming off never to be seen again.

Anyway, there I was on a Friday night, in Le Meridien's ballroom in the trendy entrepôt of St Julian's, an area surrounded by bars and nightclubs and yet... and yet, there was an audience equivalent to around 0.1% of the entire population of Malta entirely riveted to my presentation on how the crypto/DLT industry was likely to play out locally and across the world. Clearly something had happened in the intervening time: 80 JCI members (perhaps not so fussed on fintech but supporting their fine organisation) had essentially metamorphosed into a full ballroom of crypto/DLT enthusiasts on a Friday night! All within 18 months! Since then, larger gatherings still have brought 8500 or more people to Malta, but the indigenous record for a single club meeting remains that September evening in 2017.

That was how I witnessed at first-hand the Blockchain Island trajectory take hold across the archipelago of Malta from mild Bitcoin curiosity to a DLT frenzy within a year and a half!

The aim of this book was to galvanize and to record some history and forward thought, all in one readable tome. Early in the genesis of the Blockchain Island, it was clear that the industry needed an association to represent, and indeed consider how best to help the great progress made by the Government of Malta in the passing of the laws.

Actually, rewind and reconsider that last sentence. For the embryonic Blockchain Island concept that was reported in the media in April 2017 was at that stage in its first trimester of development.

From those embryonic points early in 2017, consider that by 4 July 2018 – a digital independence day for Malta no less! – the government had enacted three laws creating a first truly comprehensive regulatory framework for the operation of Malta's DLT centre. You will learn more of these laws in several subsequent chapters.

If you in any way think that this is not a sublime achievement for a modern democracy to go from adopting a semblance of an idea to delivering a comprehensive legal framework for a new technology in 18 months, bear in mind that there was even a pulsating month-long general election campaign during 2017 before the re-elected government sat down to fully map out the Blockchain Island strategy backed by a hefty electoral mandate.

With the laws in situ, our association has been working, often behind the scenes, to help drive the Blockchain Island forward. In public we have enjoyed a hugely successful partnership with Finance Malta to deliver 'BlockFinance' a series of workshops that delve into the key areas where better understanding is required to truly deliver on the digital promise of DLT.

This book was my idea at an early board meeting of the Association. "DLT Malta – Thoughts from the Blockchain Island" has come to fruition since I was elevated to chairman. The time-consuming nature of presiding slowed book progress to a trickle for some months until I was able to co-opt the excellent offices of my good friend Joseph Anthony Debono. I hugely appreciate the hard work and great initiative Joe has placed into this volume by increasing its original scope and contributor list. All the while, moreover, Joe has ensured a better gender balance of contributors too.

I hope you find this book stimulating and a useful resource while we are all getting to grips with exploiting the blockchain revolution for the betterment of society. As a passionate technophile and a fintech pioneer, I see enormous opportunity that can deliver an incredible series of 'win-win' outcomes for Malta and the rest of the world. Our association stands for an open approach to solving problems and building profitable endeavours. Testament to this stand our many contributors that have helped bring this book to fruition. Moreover, I hugely appreciate the support of our sponsors in helping us make the 'Blockchain Malta Association' viable for future iterations of the Blockchain Island.

With those key thanks (and more in the acknowledgement section), I will leave you with one final thought: my wife and I are relatively recent arrivals in Malta albeit we still pre-date the Blockchain Island strategy. For all its many achievements to date, that strategy is still in its relative infancy. When you are considering your blockchain initiatives, do consider Malta in your plans. To all other associations in this space promoting the industry, whether in whole or part, we look forward to dialogue with you. Come and visit these enchanting islands. Sit down to discuss business with us in whatever sector you are active, however you may be deploying blockchain or cryptocurrency. Before coming to Malta, we explored over 40 jurisdictions and found Malta to be a fabulous place at the intersection of so many intriguing opportunities – of which blockchain is just the latest in a 4000-year-old mercantile culture. Even before Malta became the Blockchain Island, we felt it offered a compelling choice for residence and the building of business. The addition of the national blockchain and AI strategies are just a couple of the many steps being made here to blend a fabulous, business-friendly, and innovative working environment with a historic and delightful lifestyle.

However, let me step aside (we'll meet again in a subsequent chapter). For this book is a team volume contributed by a unique group of people – key thinkers and executives – who have been working hard to create and shape the Blockchain Island. This book reflects their thoughts. All I can add is that while statisticians will note that a genius is a one in a million, the Maltese archipelago with a population of under 500,000 residents is clearly substantially 'over quota' with regards to DLT.

These are their thoughts.

I hope you enjoy their insights.

Patrick L. Young
Patrick@RevolutionMarket.Capital
Chairman
Blockchain Malta Association
Valletta
20 May 2019

Kenneth Farrugia

Never static, Malta's financial services industry is going through a particularly interesting period of development. While the domestic-focused market has been internationalising to a regional financial centre, we are also focused on technological developments.

Of course, IT is at the epicentre of new developments in finance, and the Blockchain Island seeks to maximize the use of DLT while AI is also becoming a key element in our national drive for innovation across all sectors of Malta's diverse economy.

Physically Malta is a gateway to Europe, inside the Eurozone and the EU, while geographically we are in the centre of the Mediterranean strategically close to the Middle East and Africa. This EuroMed location is also feeding financial interest in blockchain thanks to our robust regulatory framework, accessible financial services regulator, strong operational infrastructure, overall cost competitiveness and skilled labour force. These differentiating factors that have thus far enabled the industry to stand out, are now enhanced by our unique and highly detailed blockchain laws that encompass the world's first truly comprehensive framework for cryptocurrency and distributed ledger applications operating in Malta.

I believe that our Blockchain Island strategy, allied with our responsiveness and 'can-do' mindset will continue to attract new operators to our growing regional financial centre.

Having worked with the Blockchain Malta Association since its foundation, I am delighted as Chairman of Finance Malta to add my moniker to this book that reflects the depth of thought from the public and private sector that went into creating the Blockchain Island strategy. It is a holistic strategy that meshes elegantly with the overall aims for the development of skills and commerce within our islands.

Finance Malta is at your disposal if we can assist you in any way to do business with the Blockchain Island.

Kenneth Farrugia
Chairman
Finance Malta

Kenneth Farrugia is Bank of Valletta plc (BOV) Chief Business Development Officer and sits on the Group's Management Board. Kenneth is Chairman of Finance Malta, Malta's national promotional body for financial services.

Preface

The purpose of the book is to encourage the Blockchain economy while showcasing Malta: a cutting-edge jurisdiction in the sector of blockchain. The contents were created by leading figures active on the island before the first glimmers of the Blockchain Island strategy became apparent. Individual contributors were invited to contribute a chapter on anything involving thinking and blockchain, not necessarily to what is happening in Malta. The result is a collection of truly eclectic chapters that reflect all the dynamism, colour, innovation and expertise that are driving forward Malta as a leading digital jurisdiction.

The eclectic mix of chapters has been divided into four sections. In Humanitas (loosely: "The Humanities") Leonard Bonello and Simon Mercieca take different approaches to the history of the blockchain initiative in Malta. Joseph Anthony Debono considers the historic impact of blockchain, while Sophia Tillie examines the potential of blockchain for charity organizations. The second section, Negotium ("Business"), groups together chapters related to finance, business and economics. Ramona Azzopardi and Rachel Vella Baldacchino outline the tax regime in Malta related to ICOs and Cryptoassets, Jean Paul and Stephanie Fabri examine the economics of blockchain, Patrick L. Young talks about how double-entry book-keeping and the third dimension of accounting meet in Malta, while David Zammit discusses whether cryptocurrencies are money or assets. The third section Lex ("Law") contains contributions by leading Maltese legal practitioners. Diane Bugeja focuses on the use of DLT in the financial sector, while Christopher Buttigieg and Gerd Sapiano give an overview of the VFA Agent. Max Ganado considers the provision of legal personality to innovative technology arrangements. Lara Tanti and Max Ganado write about regulatory considerations for smart contracts, with Joshua Ellul, Ian Gauci and Gordon Pace musing about the need for hybrid programmer-lawyers to support smart contract drafting. The final section Scientia ("Knowledge" or "Science"), is more focused on technical matters. Tyron Baron says that privacy has had its day but that the future is bright. Charlene Cassar is not so sure about the death of privacy, as she writes in her chapter on Zero-Knowledge proofs while Ian Gauci discusses about the change from putting trust into individuals into moving to trust inbuilt into systems.

Bringing up the rear of these four sections is an epilogue in which Joseph Anthony Debono and Lida Sherafatmand discuss how the cover art relates to blockchain and Malta, while Gordon Pace explores the possible future through a tantalising glimpse of science fiction. We hugely appreciate the effort made by all contributors none of whom (including the editors) was remunerated.

Malta is an ancient civilization, famous in history for trade, architecture, and the ability to adapt to the challenges of the changing wind of history. Once more, it is poised to make its mark on the oncoming wave of change having developed an innovative and extremely promising legislative framework for this new technology. Above all, its greatest asset, as ever in its history, is its human resources. This book is an excellent showcase of the calibre of thinkers and actors in this space in Malta. All that is left is for you to take it up, read, and find out just how many benefits this island holds out to anyone interested in taking advantage of all that it has to offer. You may read from start to finish or in any order you prefer!

Patrick L. Young
Joseph Anthony Debono
Valletta
Malta
20 May 2019

PART I

HUMANITAS

Human Affairs

1. Genesis

Leonard Bonello

'Begin at the beginning,' the King said, very gravely,
and go on till you come to the end; then stop.'
— Lewis Carroll, Alice in Wonderland, chapter XII.

Ganado Advocates partner Dr Leonard Bonello leads the fintech practice at the firm. Leonard is also a founding member and a board member of the Blockchain Malta Association.

Over the past 15 months, Malta has gone through a radical transformation in the sector of financial technology. From a jurisdiction that came late to fintech, Malta leapfrogged the whole queue to land at the very forefront of those jurisdictions engaging with cryptocurrencies and Distributed Ledger Technology (DLT). The change in culture, attitude, and vision was indeed as radical as the difference between day and night. It is not easy to determine the precise moment when the current Maltese DLT Framework was conceived. Some of the seeds had already been sown towards the end of the previous legislature with 'Fintech', 'Blockchain' and 'DLT' forming part of the everyday vocabulary in the run-up to the general election that was held on 3 June 2017.

In August of 2017, the Parliamentary Secretariat for Financial Services, Digital Economy and Innovation issued a consultation document for the strengthening of the Malta Financial Services Authority (MFSA). Although this document makes no reference to blockchain or DLT, the document specifically referred to 'challenges and opportunities that are likely to emerge in the coming years'.

The first official reference to virtual currencies came in October 2017 when the MFSA issued a consultation document on the proposed regulation of collective investment schemes investing in virtual currencies.

It was only in February of 2018 that Malta produced a fully fleshed-out articulation of its intention to turn into 'Malta – A Leader in DLT Regulation'. This vision of leadership in the field of DLT was set out in a consultation document outlining the principles underlying the intended Maltese framework. Malta was not the first jurisdiction to publish its vision. Other jurisdictions had already made public statements to that effect. One of these jurisdictions was Gibraltar. Since 1 January 2018, any firm carrying out by way of business, in or from Gibraltar, the use of DLT for storing or transmitting value belonging to others, needs to be authorized by the Gibraltar Financial Services Commission as a DLT provider.

Legislative Innovation

Malta's legislative history has a track record of adopting and adapting existing models to suit its needs. Malta's Civil Code is based on the Corpus Iuris Civilis of Justinian and on the Code Napoléon. Our Companies Act owes its existence to the 1985 UK Companies Act. As a jurisdiction, Malta has excelled at identifying innovative and business-friendly concepts, and adapting them within its body of laws. The Trust and Trustees Act, the Arbitration Act, and the Securitisation Act are simply a handful of such examples. This notwithstanding, in the past decade, Malta has been so bombarded with the constant onslaught of EU directives that needed transposition into Maltese legislation that it seemed to have put aside its innovative instincts to focus predominantly on the herculean labour of aligning its legislation with the directives of the EU.

In the light of the overwhelming labour of transposing EU legislation into national law, the DLT initiative was a unique outburst of legislative innovation in this rather mundane landscape. Malta not only had to rediscover its innovative instinct, but it had to conceive and engineer from scratch a legislative framework for the DLT industry – one that would be sufficiently detailed to give the necessary legal certainty to operators while at the same time retaining the necessary level of flexibility to suit a sector that is by nature highly dynamic. Easier said than done.

The importance of legal certainty is often understated, but it is indeed crucial to attract business towards a jurisdiction. Global banks tend to prefer lending to borrowers set up in jurisdictions where the legal remedies available to creditors are more favourable. Pharmaceutical companies and technology companies set up in jurisdictions that grant them the greatest protection for their intellectual property. Likewise, DLT operators are most likely to flock towards those jurisdictions that do not merely tolerate them and allow them to operate in a legal vacuum but rather create a regulatory framework to allow them to grow and flourish under the regulator's umbrella.

At the same time, such laws also require a huge amount of flexibility. Ex-UK Prime Minister Harold Wilson is supposed to have coined the saying that 'a week is a long time in politics', but he clearly never imagined the speed at which things change in the DLT industry. The pace of changes requires a principles-based framework to ensure that the legal framework remains current notwithstanding such explosive growth.

The only other industry remotely resembling the DLT industry is the online gaming industry. As it would later do with the DLT sector, Malta had set out to create a legislative framework for the online gaming industry through trailblazing work in a legal vacuum. In fact, it is not a coincidence that some of the early advocates of DLT came from the Island's thriving online gaming community. Like the pioneers in DLT, these were used to treading where no one else had trodden before.

Malta was not the first jurisdiction to adopt a DLT strategy. Gibraltar was one of the first jurisdictions at the starting blocks of the DLT sprint. One of the key elements of the Gibraltar strategy was to place the responsibility for DLT providers under the Gibraltar Financial Services Commission. This approach communicated the message that DLT is a sub-set of Financial Services. Malta's approach is radically different to this. Malta wanted to acknowledge the use of DLT by existing financial services while recognizing that DLT was not a sub-set of financial services but rather a new category that transcended practically all industries. By placing the responsibility within the Malta Digital Innovation Authority (MDIA), a new purposely set up authority, Malta wanted to send a different message. DLT is not a vertical pillar, but rather it is horizontal in nature. DLT is larger than any one single industry, and can be applied to practically any existing major industry in Malta, be it tourism, land ownership, financial services, pharmaceuticals, gaming, intellectual property, shipping, or aviation.

This underlying thought is the principle upon which were founded the three acts: the Malta Digital Innovation Authority Act (MDIAA), the Innovative Technology Arrangements and Services Act (ITASA) and the Virtual Financial Assets Act (VFAA).

A Play in Three Acts

The Maltese Parliament enacted these three Acts, the MDIA, ITAS, and VFA Acts, in July 2018, with the MDIAA coming into force almost immediately on 15 July 2018, while the ITASA and VFAA came into force on 1 November 2018.

Virtual Financial Assets

One cannot deny that DLT has substantial uses in financial services, and that this is indeed the raison d'être for the Virtual Financial Assets Act. Although Bitcoin was envisaged as a means of payment, and as a substitute for traditional fiat currencies, to date it has acted much more as a store of value rather than a medium of exchange or unit of account. Bitcoin (and many other cryptocurrencies) have been predominantly purchased for investment purposes, and therefore acted as a substitute for financial instruments. It is for this reason that the Maltese legislator chose to model the Virtual Financial Assets Act largely on the Investment Services Act insofar as service providers are concerned. By service providers we are referring to the various crypto-brokers, crypto-exchanges, custodians, crypto-investment advisors, market-makers, and the like that have developed over the past couple of years. One common regulatory trend is to regulate the gatekeepers, and the service providers are in most cases the gatekeepers of the crypto industry. They will be the ones setting standards, providing investor protection and safekeeping clients' crypto assets. The Second Schedule of the VFAA provides a list of service providers that are licensable.

Insofar as Initial Coin Offerings (ICOs) issuers are concerned, the model adopted was that set out by the EU in terms of the Prospectus Directive. The Virtual Financial Assets Act may be deemed to have created a MIFID-light, and a Prospectus Directive-light regime for service providers and issuers respectively. The First Schedule of the VFAA provides a list of disclosures that an ICO issuer is required to disclose in the white paper for it to be registered with the MFSA. Once again, the VFAA is clearly aiming to set the necessary standards in this sector. Far too many white papers have been published with little or no information on the entity issuing the tokens. The First Schedule creates a list of compulsory information requiring disclose to ensure that token purchasers are adequately informed throughout the decision-making process.

Malta Digital Innovation Authority Act

One of the big issues that was debated was whether the country needed the Malta Digital Innovation Authority. Was a new authority really necessary? Would it have been possible to allocate those responsibilities to existing authorities? Would it not have been easier to rope in an existing authority with an existing structure and existing set-up? This was quite a tough question to answer and a rather philosophical one. On the one hand, the creation of yet another centralized authority was an ironic outcome within an industry based on decentralized technology. On the other hand, the creation of the MDIA shows the commitment of the jurisdiction and the focus of the Authority on this particular industry. At the same time the MDIAA sets out a mechanism through which a lead regulator is selected when a particular project relates to more than one local authority. Furthermore, it also sets up a committee entrusted with furthering the digital innovation agenda of the country.

Innovative Technology Arrangements and Services Act

In its infancy the DLT industry was propelled forward by anarchists, individuals that wanted to bypass the banks, and governments, and create a new paradigm. Anarchists however remain a relatively fringe part of the population. There are still many people taking comfort from authorization or certification issued by a central authority. It is indeed this desire for security, and the legislation to meet it, which will allow DLT to go mainstream.

While the VFA Act is an authorization regime, it is not possible or desirable to create an authorization regime for innovative technology arrangements such as DLT platforms or smart contracts.

For this reason, a certification regime was felt to be more appropriate. In the same way that ISO standards impart a certain level of comfort about the quality standards relating to a particular good or service, the ITAS certification will provide equal comfort to users on the tests that the particular innovative technology arrangement is required to satisfy. At this point in time, the ITAS is limited to the certification of DLT platforms and smart contracts. However, the ITASA is intended to allow the flexibility to certify further innovative technology arrangements as they develop in the future.

Linking the Acts

The link between ITASA and MDIAA is quite evident. This is the same link between the Malta Financial Services Authority Act and the Banking Act, the Investment Services Act, the Financial Markets Act, and so on. One Act establishes the authority while the other focuses on the subject matter.

The link between the VFAA and the other two Acts is slightly less obvious. One important thing to keep in mind is that while the VFA is mandatory law (i.e. failure to comply with this Act would create a breach of law), the ITAS regime is, as a general rule, a voluntary regime (i.e. submission of the innovative technology arrangement to MDIA certification in terms of ITASA is a choice). Having said that, when a VFA is utilizing an innovative technology arrangement, the MFSA is likely to impose MDIA certification as a minimum requirement. Certification would therefore be a licensing prerequisite. For example, a securities depository utilizing DLT would require licensing in terms of the VFA, but, in turn, the MFSA would impose MDIA certification as a prerequisite to licensing.

The Last Word

'Begin at the beginning,' the King said, very gravely,
and go on till you come to the end; then stop.'
– Lewis Carroll, Alice in Wonderland, chapter XII.

While it is difficult to identify the beginning of DLT regulation for Malta, it is clearly even more difficult to predict the end of this road. The outcome of this journey will depend on how flexible the framework proves to be, and how proactive the authorities will be to ensure that the framework remains as relevant in the future as it is today. This is by no means an easy feat, but the initiative and the vision in evidence in the establishment of this legislative framework bode well for the future continuous development of this industry.

2. Prometheus Onchained

Joseph Anthony Debono

"...there is a secret known
To thee, and to none else of living things,
Which may transfer the sceptre of wide Heaven,
The fear of which perplexes the Supreme."
– Percy Bysshe Shelley,
Prometheus Unbound, Act 1, verses 371-374.

Co-editor of this book, Joseph Anthony Debono, is a highly qualified historian and classicist who since 2016 has increasingly focused on cryptocurrencies and Distributed Ledger Technology.

One of the most symbolically potent figures of Greek mythology is the titan Prometheus. The story of Prometheus is that of conflict between a trickster deity and the supreme divinity, Zeus himself. Prometheus had cheated the gods to the benefit of mankind by deceiving Zeus. He presented Zeus with a choice between the bones and fat of a butchered animal, and its tender flesh. Zeus, deceived by the wrapping, chose the bones as the portion falling to the gods, while the tender flesh fell by default to humanity for all time. More significantly, Prometheus stole fire from the gods and handed it over to humanity that had been wilfully deprived of its great benefits by the decree of Zeus. In rage, therefore, Zeus had Prometheus chained to a rock with an eagle devouring the tormented titan's regenerating liver every day. At length, Prometheus was saved by the divine hero Herakles, who shot the eagle and unchained the titan from his bonds.

The story of Prometheus pits an absolute hegemon against a subversive trickster. Prometheus is the champion of man against the indifferent omnipotence of Zeus. He provides them with sustenance through the most nutritious parts of cattle, and to access to technology through the theft of fire. And for this he pays a terrible price. In early Greek literature, such as Hesiod, the advancement of mortal interests happens in just the two outlined episodes, but in later literature, starting from Aeschylus, he is seen as a general benefactor, and also creator and saviour of mankind. Later traditions grow dramatically in complexity but the essence is that of a champion striking a blow against hegemonic authority, and it is in this essence that the figure of Prometheus features in art and literature in the post-classical world.

The global financial crisis that started in 2007, lasting into 2009, was terrible in itself. But quite apart from the destruction of wealth, and of lives dependent on that wealth, there came dramatic loss of faith in the current financial and economic systems, and in the political system with which they are interlinked. For decades, the current system, with states in firm control of monetary policy, and with banks that had become virtually branches of government, together with a global network of blocs and alliances, had assumed the crown of an omnipotent hegemon. But the crisis of 2007-2009 shook that crown to the core. And it was in the white heat of that crisis that an unknown individual released the first blockchain-driven virtual currency. Prometheus is about innovation, rebellion, and disruption of established hegemonies. And for this very reason, there is no more fitting symbol for this technology and the changes yet to come.

Forging the chain

The first virtual currency is Bitcoin. Late in 2008, an unknown individual, going by the pseudonym of Satoshi Nakamoto, published a paper on a cryptography mailing list entitled 'Bitcoin: A Peer-to-Peer Electronic Cash System'. The abstract of the paper defines the nature of this new technology so well, and is likely to prove so historically significant, that it is worth quoting in full. Satoshi Nakamoto proposes that:

"A purely peer-to-peer version of electronic cash would allow online payments to be sent directly from one party to another without going through a financial institution. Digital signatures provide part of the solution, but the main benefits are lost if a trusted third party is still required to prevent double-spending. We propose a solution to the double-spending problem using a peer-to-peer network. The network timestamps transactions by hashing them into an ongoing chain of hash-based proof-of-work, forming a record that cannot be changed without redoing the proof-of-work. The longest chain not only serves as proof of the sequence of events witnessed, but proof that it came from the largest pool of CPU power. As long as a majority of CPU power is controlled by nodes that are not cooperating to attack the network, they'll generate the longest chain and outpace attackers. The network itself requires minimal structure. Messages are broadcast on a best effort basis, and nodes can leave and rejoin the network at will, accepting the longest proof-of-work chain as proof of what happened while they were gone."[1]

Bitcoin is therefore a system of electronic or digital cash that can be used for online payments by sending it directly from one user to another without needing to send it through a central authority such as a bank. It is difficult to understand why this is so revolutionary, and the nature of the technologies involved, without understanding the challenges to create such a system of cash. These challenges boil down to two fundamental ones, the double-spend problem, and the Byzantine Generals' problem. These two problems had been bedevilling attempts to create a reliable digital cash system long before Bitcoin was invented, and it was their solution by Nakamoto that laid the foundations for the virtual currency revolution.

The double-spend problem is inherent in digital assets. Digital assets, given their nature as arrangements of 1s and 0s on a storage device, can be copied very easily indeed. This problem has plagued many industries, especially the software, music, and movie industries for a long time. Anyone who buys such a digital asset can easily make a copy and pass that copy on to someone else. In fact, there is no limit to how many copies of a digital asset that one can make, unlike with analogue media, copies of which degrade with every iteration. It is a sobering thought that although legislative developments have severely hindered digital piracy, this problem still remains acute. Now since a virtual currency is, at the end of the day, a string of digital information, then it is susceptible to the same problem. Imagine owning a unit of digital cash and copying it over and over and over again, and spending it for as many times as you have copied it. In effect, you have eliminated the quality of scarcity and destroyed any demand for your asset, since demand is contingent on scarcity. Obviously, therefore, without a solution to the double-spend problem, no virtual currency is possible.

The Byzantine Generals' Problem was described by Leslie Lamport, Robert Shostak and Marshall Pease in 1982 and it is a challenge in distributed computing to find a solution to the risk of malfunctioning components that give conflicting information to different parts of a computer system. It is commonly phrased thus: a group of Byzantine generals are besieging a city. They can only take the city if they launch a co-ordinated attack, but they are not in personal contact with each other and they have no means of secure and real-time communication. They can only communicate by messenger. Their predicament is complicated by the existence of traitors in their ranks. Any messages passed around may be compromised by the traitors. How do these generals plan a co-ordinated attack in which the ratio of loyal officers to traitors is 2:1, thus enabling a successful assault on the city? In terms of a virtual currency such as Bitcoin, the Byzantine generals are the participants in the virtual currency's network, the messages are the transactions in the virtual currency, and the challenge of co-ordinating a majority attack on the city is the challenge of ensuring that the transactions are sanctioned and recorded by the system.

Satoshi Nakamoto solved these two problems in a way as titanic as any achievement of Prometheus, for in doing so he created one of the most disruptive watersheds in the history of money, and arguably the history of technology. Nakamoto's Bitcoin consists of four technologies: (A) The Bitcoin protocol, (B) The blockchain, (C) Consensus rules, and (D) The Proof-of-Work algorithm. In a nutshell, the Bitcoin protocol creates a network of individual users transacting in a digital asset, in this case a digital cash system called Bitcoin.

The protocol makes use of consensus rules to govern independent transaction validation and currency issuance across the entire network without the need for a central authority. The proof-of-work algorithm forces participants to expend CPU power (therefore electrical energy, arguably a commodity) to achieve global decentralized consensus for transactions, and then these transactions are added to a block that is then linked to subsequent blocks through hashing cryptography. This chain of blocks, the blockchain, is the ledger of this system, and it is distributed, synchronized and guaranteed across the whole network, once again removing the need for a central authority to guarantee a central ledger. This creates a decentralized system that is tamper-evident, immutable, and does not depend on trusting any individual or single system. It is responsible for the issuance of the (limited) units of its own currency. Moreover, it deals with the possibility of bad actors, the traitors of the Byzantine Generals' Problem, by forcing them to expend more power, through the proof-of-work algorithm, than the bona fide actors on the network. Since bad actors usually act alone, or in small groups, the chances of a co-ordinated attack by bad actors strong enough to overwhelm the rest of the system are vanishingly low.

This is the system at the heart of Bitcoin, Satoshi Nakamoto's watershed innovation. However, Bitcoin is not the only virtual currency. Operating on these principles, anyone can develop his own virtual currency, and, as of present, there are hundreds of different types (such as Litecoin), and there is no limit to how many can be developed with a little adaptation of the rules and principles of the Bitcoin protocol.

Smart Contracts and Tokenisation

Nakamoto's proposal is a true revolution in the way it decentralizes the transmission of value securely and without the need for gatekeepers and central authorities. Currency, such as bitcoin, is only one application. This technology can be applied to many other applications, such as voting, registries of all sorts and so on, that are currently managed by central authorities, and to applications that still have to emerge from the potential offered by this system. One such application, which has already had enormous impact, is smart contracts.

A traditional contract, drawn up by a notary, and deposited in an archive, outlines the terms of a particular agreement between parties. The contracting parties are then expected to adhere to this agreement, and the courts enforce this agreement if the terms of the contract are not honoured. The notary serves as the gatekeeper of the contract, which is then secured in an archive and protected by the force of law. Moreover, if the contract is a public one, the notary must register it with the public registry otherwise it binds only the contracting parties. A smart contract is software that encodes the terms of an agreement and executes them automatically once these terms are met. It is software that encodes the terms of an agreement and executes them automatically once these terms are met. There are no notaries involved, and there is no need for a court to arbitrate between parties because the smart contract executes automatically once the set conditions are met. And there certainly is no need for a public registry for smart contracts because an open decentralized blockchain is by definition as open to public scrutiny as possible. Smart contracts are deployed on a blockchain that keeps track of the state of all the smart contracts deployed on it, much like the Bitcoin blockchain keeps tracks of the current and historic state of all transactions of each unit of its currency. Smart contracts on a decentralized blockchain are immune to fraud, censorship, downtime, or interference by third parties.

Such is the power of the Bitcoin structure that it has potential to be used even for smart contracts though it was designed primarily for the transmission of its proprietary currency. However, for a long time, the most advanced blockchain for smart contracts was Ethereum. Ethereum was built from scratch for the purpose of creating decentralized applications using smart contracts. Ethereum infrastructure is similar to Bitcoin and it comes with its own currency, ether, that people can use to make use of services on Ethereum. Essentially, Ethereum is a computation engine running on a decentralized blockchain, like Bitcoin's, to allow decentralized applications that are not under the control of a central authority or corporation. Imagine a traditional web application like Facebook or Twitter. Now imagine a similar application that is not generated and controlled by such a corporation but runs on a decentralized blockchain. Instead of being generated by Facebook's software, this decentralized application is generated by smart contracts running on that blockchain. Anything that can be done on the internet can henceforth be done through a decentralized application, thus eliminating central authority. The implications are beyond imagination.

While it is still far too early to see anything but the faintest glimmer of such potential, one area in which smart contracts have been truly revolutionary is that of tokens. Tokens are digital assets registered and tracked on a blockchain. One type of token is a cryptocurrency, like Bitcoin, but another is the most popular and lucrative use of smart contracts right now, which is that of a token backed by an asset and issued by means of an Initial Coin Offering (ICO) through a smart contract on a blockchain like Ethereum's. The assets may be of many kinds, but currently, an ICO is usually a swap of newly created tokens with a cryptocurrency (such as bitcoin, or ether itself) to raise funding for start-ups, originally in the cryptocurrency community, but now increasingly in other areas. It is essentially a form of fundraising that is globalized and decentralized and has very low barriers of access. The most common way of creating an ICO is to create it as a smart contract on Ethereum by which contributors of the requested cryptocurrency receive a certain amount of the new token created by the ICO. Once the investors receive their tokens, they may trade it on exchanges that list it, or hold them until a profit is realized and then exchanged for some other cryptocurrency on an exchange. ICOs offer investors easy access to investment opportunities and an increasingly large choice of such. For start-ups, ICOs offer easy and cost-efficient fundraising without giving up equity or control over companies.

All tokens are strings of data on a blockchain. However, classification is necessary for the purpose of regulation and taxation. Currently, we can distinguish between three broad categories of tokens. These are pure equity tokens, security tokens, and utility tokens, and all three of them may be offered through an ICO. Pure equity tokens offer equity or stock in a company without giving up equity or control over companies. A utility token allows an investor to make use of the services of a company through its products or services. Security tokens are tokens that are backed by a security, which is a tradeable asset. Traditional securities are either equities or debts. A security token is a token based on such an asset, currently a new start-up but it is not difficult to foresee traditional securitization moving to blockchain-based tokens sooner rather than later. However, the potential of security tokens is truly gigantic. For with this technology, it is possible to tokenise any asset imaginable very easily, thus providing new liquidity to the owners of the asset without forcing them to relinquish control.

Status Quo Ante Bellum

The decades of the late 20th century were marked by increasing prosperity. But many were those who observed that this prosperity was based on 'excessive build-up of debt, imbalances in trade and capital flows, and the financialization of the economy, which underpinned a social and political structure reliant on debt-driven consumption and increasing levels of borrowing to fund social entitlements'[2].

Nakamoto's proposal appeared in the dying months of the financial crisis that broke out in 2007. In brief, this happened because financial institutions became far less careful about providing mortgages to riskier borrowers because they could package these risky mortgages (called subprime mortgages) with other mortgages in complex securities that were then sold on to other investors, many of them institutional. When the riskier borrowers started having problems keeping up with their payments, the shock ran through the system, affecting the price of anything from securities to housing, and from there it spiralled across the whole economy. Thus, the housing crisis and subprime mortgage started a chain reaction that ran through most financial institutions in the world, leaving them with massive liquidity problems and debt. The interbank market itself, a foreign exchange market where banks trade in currencies, was on the verge of collapse, with huge ramifications for global equities and financial markets. In the end, the only thing that stopped the crisis from spiralling totally out of control was the Emergency Economic Stabilization Act of the US government in October 2008 by which the government bailed out a number of major banks, financial institutions and other companies. The case of Lehman Brothers taught the US that some institutions under the current system were too big to fail, indeed could not be allowed to fail, thus justifying government interference in the markets. But this can only be a temporary solution, because the tremendous debt caused by this financial crisis has not been paid off. The balance sheet of the US government currently shows a debt north of $21 trillion dollars as of April 2018, roughly equivalent to its annual GDP. Instead of reducing debt, reversing imbalances and bringing about major changes in policy, governments preferred to take on private debt, increase public spending financed by yet more government debt, and to expand the money supply to increase demand. After the initial government bailouts, further such activities were carried out by central banks, including the Bank of England, leading to massive problems with their balance sheets, problems compounded by quantitative easing. We have yet to see the consequences of this mess.

The subprime mortgage crisis was caused by many factors but the most ominous part of the story is the cure, which may very well be worse than the disease itself. Taking bad debts, and putting them on the government's balance sheets, and attempting to stimulate the economy through quantitative easing (essentially expanding the money supply) is only a natural consequence of financial policies that have been prevailing for decades. It is the story of exchanging commodity money for what is essentially a promissory note, making that promissory note a global reserve currency, engaging in a debt-driven economy, managed by inflation and quantitative easing, while using the privileged position of the US dollar as the global reserve currency to enforce US political hegemony across world and shut countries and individuals out of the global financial system at will, in the process making banks virtually agents of its enforcement, and central banks virtually a branch of government. The world carries out its business through a global reserve currency that can be inflated at will, through an international financial system that is at the mercy of legislation governing that currency, and enforced by the full weight of the strongest military in the world. The entire issue boils down to the US's control of the global reserve currency and the fact that this currency is a piece of paper with no intrinsic value beyond the promises of the US government to back it. Arguably, there is nothing behind the global financial and economic systems but the idea of America. There has been no greater hegemon, and more effectively centralized power, in history. Zeus is on Olympus and all's right with the world.

Disruption

Perhaps one of the most important inventions in history is that of writing. Writing is a system for recording information and transmitting it through time and space, allowing for the recording and transmission of far more complex information than prevailing hitherto. Writing did not emerge out of the blue, but is the result of pre-existing processes undergoing change over a long period of time. There are numerous theories about the emergence of complete writing, but perhaps the most interesting for the subject of this chapter is the theory of the token. In the Middle East, goods were tallied for thousands of years using small clay tokens. These 'early tokens were counters in a rudimentary book-keeping system; that their form indicated the product counted; that one token equalled one counted unit; and that these tokens led directly to complete writing'[3]. This idea has its detractors, but it does appear that tokens made a substantial contribution to the emergence of a complete writing system. Be it as it may, it is generally acknowledged that the earliest evidence of a complete writing system emerged in the alluvial plain of Southern Iraq towards the middle of the Fourth Millennium B.C. With just one exception, the earliest records of writing consist of lists of assets and individuals, essentially records of account and identity. The exception consists of lists drawn up for learning. This system was pictographic (cuneiform), but, eventually, the alphabet made its appearance through a process starting from the Egyptians and going through the Phoenicians to the Greeks.

Whether writing produced the state, or the needs of the state led to the invention of writing is unclear. What is certain is that writing alone is insufficient for the purposes of running a state. What is needed is authenticated writing, or immutable records. The state therefore acquired the role of authenticating documents and storing them in its archives, ensuring that claims were brought forward on the basis of authenticated documents. However, since documents are fragile, and easily forged, the only solution available for the necessity of authentication was centralization. The only archives that could be trusted were those held by a strong gatekeeper or central authority. Hence, the need of civilized societies to record assets and debts, and keep track of their transfers on authenticated documents led to ever increasing power of the state, which alone could command the trust required by all parties involved.

Writing has been probably the most transformative technology ever invented. The ability to record assets and information, and file these records away is really the infrastructure of civilization. It begets states bigger in space and time than the immediate environment of a few hundred individuals. It permits ownership, the accumulation of wealth and knowledge, and its transmission over space and time, and for this reason it has been responsible for the exponential explosion of progress since its invention. When, in the 2nd Millennium B.C., the Phoenicians developed a consonantal alphabet that was later perfected into a full alphabet by the Greeks, civilization took off at an accelerating rate. And the ability to record assets and debts from one year to another, to record the transfer of such assets and debt, and to transmit these records through time and space, is what underpins civilization as we know it. This is why antiquity, the period after the emergence of writing, is marked by the tendency of small states to coalesce into increasingly larger empires, such as the Babylonian, Egyptian, Persian, Hellenistic and Roman Empires.

The story of centralization is indeed the story of writing and its authentication. This tendency did not come to an end with the fall of the Roman Empire as a state. For although the barbarian tribes that divided up the old territories of the Roman Empire did represent a counter-tendency to that of centralization, the Roman Catholic Church stepped in to preserve many of the infrastructures of the Roman Empire, including its legal traditions and its religious orthodoxy. The barbarian tribes that carved up the Roman Empire were soon converted to Catholicism, generally between the 5th and 10th century A.D., and, though Western Europe in that period was fractured into a patchwork of petty kingdoms and fiefs, the pervasion of Catholicism throughout this area brought a cultural, religious, institutional and linguistic unity to the continent. And if kings of the period were fractious, and from time to time clashed with Church and Pope, they were excommunicated for their pains, and brought to heel. Thus, religious, intellectual and cultural centralization was the prevailing tendency of the Middle Ages as it had been in antiquity. Despite the achievements in art and architecture, the net result is that in science and philosophy, little was achieved beyond what could be erected upon the surviving Greek and Roman texts of the time without disrupting the prevailing orthodoxy.   But orthodoxy would not survive the 15th century.

In around 1450, Johannes Gutenberg, a German, produced one of the most important technological innovations in history, the printing press. Gutenberg's press was not the first type of printing in history. The Chinese had been there before. But Gutenberg's breakthrough, much like Nakamoto's, was the development of an original process through the combination of pre-existing technologies. In the case of the printing press, these technologies included the Roman wine-press, the goldsmith's punch, and impressionable paper. Gutenberg's press also benefited immensely from the Latin alphabet because this permits the printing of any text with only around twenty-four characters, give or take a few depending on the language. This innovation made it possible to replicate and disseminate books, once a tremendously laborious and expensive task, tremendously easily and cheaply. Some insight into the scale of this revolution may be gained from the comparison between the collections of Humphrey, Duke of Gloucester, a very rich landowner, just before the invention of the Gutenberg Press and the fictitious collection of Don Quixote de la Mancha, an impoverished landowner, in the eponymous novel published in 1605. It is calculated that the Duke of Gloucester had 500-600 books, an immense library relative to the expense of writing and illuminating books by hand[5]. On the other hand, barely 150 years after Gutenberg started operations, the subject of Cervantes's celebrated novel, an impoverished minor noble, could afford over a hundred volumes. That impecunious individuals could afford significant collections of books so soon after the invention of the Gutenberg Press carries considerable implications for the dissemination of knowledge as a result of printing. Indeed, the cheap and easy dissemination of knowledge made possible by the printing press transformed universities from bastions of orthodox theology, philosophy, and law, into laboratories of research and higher education. This led to the scientific and industrial revolutions, later to the political revolutions of the late 18th century onward. Likewise, in 1517, Luther ignited the Protestant Revolution against the Catholic Church, and one of the tools in its arsenal was sola scriptura, the doctrine that only the Christian scriptures are the sole infallible authority of Christianity. And, of course, such a doctrine was impossible without the easy availability of cheap Bibles. It is therefore entirely thanks to the printing press that there has been such an exponential explosion in intellectual and general progress since the mid-15th century due to the easy availability of media of information, and the widespread literacy that is the inevitable consequence of this. But the printing press, though it shattered Catholic orthodoxy, did not shatter the need of a centralized state for even with the printing press, the need to maintain records and guarantee their authenticity remained. Significantly, accounts and contracts were still drawn up by hand, and deposited in state-sanctioned and guaranteed archives. Still, the printing press permitted the cost-effective diffusion of knowledge to the point at which in barely 500 years from its invention, the world leapt from the Middle Ages to the Computer Age and the Internet.

The printing press disrupted, it is true. But the printing press disrupted the cultural monolith of the Middle Ages, not the state per se. Ironically, the printing press in its way paved the way for modern states, not in the same way that writing did, by providing strong grounds for the emergence of these organizations, but by producing the technology permitting a government to exercise increasing control over large swathes of space, and then time. The printing press produced the Scientific and Industrial Revolutions, and new technologies such as steel foundries, the steam engine, and increasingly sophisticated weaponry. With these technologies, small states like Britain, the Netherlands, Spain, Portugal and France, could quell restless nobles, and acquire global empires far bigger than the world had ever seen. With steamships, and railways, even enormous territories like Asia and Africa were brought under the comfortable control of these states. Later on, flight, the automobile, and electronic communications shrank the world to the point at which any government can easily administer huge territories without serious trouble. And the culmination of this process is the current system of globalization through a global reserve currency and financial system controlled by a single country that is the most powerful in history. And yet, though this system has brought undeniable benefits, it hinges on the strength of the United States to keep maintaining this system. Still, the US dollar is backed by nothing but faith in the United States, and the United States keeps racking up unprecedented foreign debt and record trade deficits, managing it by expanding the money supply and enforcing its laws against those countries and individuals that want out of this system, or cannot meet the requirements to participate in it. It is arguable that this system has reached both the maximum of centralization and the maximum of sustainability.

Enter Prometheus, or rather Satoshi Nakamoto, who in the thick of the financial crisis of 2007-2009, swept away in one fell swoop many of the justifications for the existence of the state. For the Nakamoto proposal provides a decentralized system for immutably recording and transmitting data, including currency, without the need for a gatekeeper and authenticator. The modern state has lost its privileged position in the issuance of currency, in maintaining and guaranteeing registries and records, and the ability to censor, control and intercept this technology in carrying out the tasks that were hitherto its prerogative. The existence of public blockchains with the rest of the Nakamoto infrastructure, such as Bitcoin and Ethereum, means that people no longer depend on the state, and its officers, for their means of exchange, for their transactions, for their contracts and their enforcement, and for the registries in which all the records on which transaction and administration are necessary. With Bitcoin, for example, individuals can earn the currency through working for it, through exchanging it for other currencies, or by participating in the system. Then they can transact in it and transmit it across the world, with no intermediaries, in a very short time and for very minor costs. With Ethereum, they can do the same with smart contracts, and even its own form of currency, if they so wish. There is no need for third parties to monitor, register, safeguard, reverse and lockout any transaction whatsoever. As a consequence, even banks themselves stand to lose much of their current functions beyond that of providing loans.

The consequences of this disruption are impossible to predict but some are more obvious than others. With technologies that allow individuals to circumvent the services and functions of the state, that permit currencies not in control of the state, that make it immensely difficult for states to collect taxation given that individuals will no longer need to transact in legal tender, it is not difficult to envision states finding it increasingly difficult to raise money, especially if their legal tender is a currency backed by nothing but weighed down by immense liabilities, while their citizens become increasingly reluctant to pay taxes in a currency that cannot be easily confiscated or controlled by the state, if at all. For the first time in history, technology rips power out of the hands of the state, rather than strengthens it. The state will no longer be needed to run many of its services. Most of them can run very well on this new infrastructure without the need of the state to provide its services to do so. In this scenario, is it so outlandish to predict that states whose functions have been severely curtailed and their sources of income dramatically limited, will shrink as rapidly as they grew after the invention of the printing press and the subsequent revolutions it engendered? Although we have grown used to the form of the modern state, it is in fact a very recent invention that goes back to the early modern period. There is no reason why future states, stripped of many of their functions and sources of income, should not shrink dramatically, perhaps to the size of city-states such as Athens and Rome were before they rose to empire.

There are other more or less obvious consequences. The financial crisis of 2007-2009 may have been replaced by another round of prosperity. But the problems have not gone away. An enormously powerful hegemon effectively is in control of the financial and commercial interactions of the globe through the use of its currency, which is backed by nothing except its promises, weighed down by enormous debt, and struggling to maintain the system by sanctioning any country and individual that does not want to, or cannot, play ball with its system. Many governments are weighed down by massive bailouts, and so are central banks. Priceless energy and resources, which are desperately needed elsewhere in the system, are going into compliance and regulation, the inevitable consequence of gatekeeping and centralization. There are two billion people without a bank account, many of them in Third World countries because they are too poor, or because they do not have documentation sufficient to pass the extensive Know-Your-Client and other compliance and regulation checks that centralized gatekeeping mandates. This means that these people are cut off from the global financial system, that as consequence, live in terrible misery, and that any work, goods and services they produce do not go into the system. This imbalance between states concentrating power into their own hands for self-preservation and self-perpetuation regardless of the consequences on the vast majority of people helpless in front of such concentrated power is a massive injustice, one that we are not the first to observe. The Nakamoto proposal, not only blockchain but the recording and transfer of value across a global, public, permissionless blockchain carried out peer-to-peer, will connect these people into the global economy, and provide it with a huge stimulus, desperately needed given the challenges it is facing, and give these people access to all the facilities they need. It is very likely that the consequence of all this will be a system that replaces the creaking current system and bring an unprecedented new wave of prosperity, this time including the world's poorest people, those who have suffered the most from a centralized global economy. Essentially for the first time in history, since the emergence of writing, a technology decentralizes power, disenfranchises the centralized state, and redresses the huge imbalance of power between the state and the individual citizen. This new technology, which is the biggest revolution in recording and authenticating technology since the invention of writing, therefore has historically unparalleled implications for politics, economics, finance, organization, and social relations. It is truly Prometheus Onchained.

It is easy to foresee a withdrawal in state power, new models of decentralized societies, and new waves of prosperity as a consequence of the Nakamoto proposal. it is far more difficult to foresee the consequences if this new technology goes exponential. Speculation is usually most useful as a thought experiment, so one example of the potential will suffice to illustrate how unpredictable are the consequences of this technology. A smart contract blockchain like Ethereum enables Decentralized Autonomous Organisations (DAOs). These are organizations the entire infrastructure of which is powered by smart contracts running on the Ethereum blockchain and they are currently stateless, subject to no state or legislation beyond the rules encoded in the smart contract. It is possible to create an organization that runs itself, carrying out its functions, producing goods and or services, raising money, spending that money on upgrading itself, modifying the smart contracts that are its DNA and evolving over time. Perhaps it may be possible for such a DAO to eventually achieve that state that we might define as 'artificially intelligent', at least insofar as it is fully functional independent of human intervention, and evolving to acquire goals and purposes that are completely independent of human interest, purpose, interaction, control, jurisdiction and sovereignty. Prometheus did not just steal fire. In some myths, he is also said to have created man. Perhaps Nakomoto has not just torn power from the hands of the state. Perhaps his proposal will lead to ends that are wilder than... myth.

Prometheus Onchained

The myth of Prometheus expresses the divine role that the centralized state acquired in human affairs, and it also represents the tension between this centralization, and the Promethean struggle for its subversion. Writing, and then printing, have always been at the service of the state, and have, indeed, supported the claims of the state to absolute sovereignty – such as by providing legal tender, the recording of assets and information, the authentication of these records, and the need to provide secure repositories for these records. Printing put still more powerful tools into the hands of the state. Contemporary states have simply become too big and too concerned with their own self-perpetuation to successfully tackle the global problems that their bulk has created. The lesson of 2007-2009 is clear – policymakers will do anything to preserve the status quo at all costs. This is the importance of the Nakamoto proposal. For this technology is impossible for any state, no matter, how powerful to control. It provides the very tools needed to bypass the gatekeepers and central authorities of the state. It renders most of the functions of the state unnecessary and irrelevant and is perhaps the greatest political revolution in history. In the same way that Prometheus stole fire from the gods, Nakamoto stole control of value from the state. History will never be the same.

Endnotes

1. Satoshi Nakamoto, Bitcoin, 2008, bitcoin.org
2. Vivek Kaul, Easy Money: Volume 1, (Harper Business, 2019), Kindle Locations 25-32.
3. Steven Roger Fischer, A History of Writing, (Reaktion Books, 2011), Kindle Locations 310-31.
4. Cyril J. Gadd, "The Cities of Babylonia", in The Cambridge Ancient History – Vol. 1 Part 2 (CUP, 2006), pp. 93-94.
5. David Rundle, "Good Duke Humfrey (Part I)", Bonæ Litteræ, 2013, wordpress.com.

3. A Maltese History of Blockchain and Cryptocurrency

Simon Mercieca

Cryptocurrencies and blockchain are the greatest revolution that the world has experienced since the invention of the printing press. Like the printing press, they have the potential to revolutionize the way society interacts.

Dr Simon Mercieca is senior lecturer in the Department of History at the University of Malta specializing in Demography.

A historian's usual brief is to write about events that took place decades, if not centuries, ago. The history of cryptocurrency and blockchain in Malta is still young and ongoing. It is a history of the present, a present that only started when Satoshi Nakamoto published his famous proposal in 2008[1]. This chapter will therefore look at the development of the cryptocurrency and blockchain industry in Malta from Nakamoto's publication to the end of 2018.

Once the author began his research, it became apparent that many in Malta conflate all cryptocurrencies with Bitcoin. Equally, many people in Malta do not understand the link between Bitcoin and blockchain, missing the fact that a blockchain is the underlying distributed ledger on which the possession and the transfer of bitcoins are recorded. More importantly, while experts understand and discuss this essential link between blockchain and cryptocurrencies, the public debate in Malta during the first years focused on cryptocurrencies rather than on blockchain. This research has also revealed that in Malta the term 'Bitcoin' started to be used as a catch-all phrase for all cryptocurrencies even though Bitcoin is only one such type. Besides Bitcoin, there are other forms of cryptocurrencies such as Ethereum, Dash, Litecoin or Dogecoin. These cryptocurrencies all feature heavily in the debate about this type of currency but Bitcoin became the most popular[2]. Despite this, the author will be referring to Bitcoin only with specific reference to this particular cryptocurrency[3].

The First Years: 2008 – 2015

The history of cryptocurrencies and blockchain in Malta can be traced back to a few years after Nakamoto introduced the idea in 2008[4]. By 2011, Bitcoin had gained traction as the most popular cryptocurrency[5]. This stimulated interest on the island, and the Library of Congress reported that 'in October 2012, a Maltese company launched the first Bitcoin hedge fund. The fund was incorporated as a Bermuda-exempted company and was registered as a segregated account company receiving funds at Citibank London'[6]. It is to be noted that in this report the term 'Bitcoin' was used and not 'cryptocurrency' because of the type of currency used in this hedge fund. The first company to trade in this form of currency began trading in bitcoins in 2012. But this hedge fund, and Bitcoin trading, did not hit the general media. Bitcoin only started to make its mark forcefully in the local media in 2017. As often happens in such cases, Bitcoin hit the media for negative reasons. First, Malta started reacting to international reports that defined Bitcoin as a bubble[7]. In a small community like Malta, these reports continued to strengthen the perception that this was the only form of this type of currency in Malta. This was not the case.

The first social categories in Malta that began to take an interest in this sector came from two specific fields: the legal and the financial. Then there were outliers that became interested in the digital mechanics of this system. Among legal companies that started to show an interest in blockchain, the most prominent were Ganado Advocates, GTG Advocates and WH partners. The name of Ian Gauci starts to crop up repeatedly during the course of this research with a significant footprint in most media. In finance, Chris Vassallo and Patrick L. Young appeared with comparable frequency.

Other companies took an interest from the word go. The law firm of Chetcuti Cauchi deserves special mention. But more significantly for the long-term prospects of the industry, a number of foreign individuals started to settle down in Malta. Some of these were engaged in digital technology. Two that would come to play a special role in the blockchain industry of Malta were Leon Siegmund and Steve Tendon.

What comes across strongly in this analysis is that some of the first persons in Malta behind these initiatives were neither seeking personal nor financial success. At the same time, they did not suffer from the social malaise that afflicted 17th century society in Holland, which Simon Schama describes as the embarrassment of riches[8]. What transpires is more a sense of altruism; they wanted to share their success with others so that they too might participate in the economic and financial potential of this new technology.

However, the lesson that history teaches us is that revolutions need a demographic element to be truly successful. The first element is that of education. No revolution can be successful, whether in finance or society, if it does not take root in a highly-educated section of the population. More importantly, these individuals were willing to invest in themselves. Some even went abroad to the UK for further training.

But for the purpose of historiography, the intention of this chapter is to go beyond this narrative. The fertile soil for the debate in Malta on these ground-breaking technologies was laid down by the progressive economic evolution that started taking place around the time of Independence in 1964. For a country that had a mere few years before been a British Colony with depressingly negative hopes for its future economic well-being, Malta in the 1960s started to attract the first global names in manufacturing[9]. This was the corner-stone for the country on which to build an increasingly prosperous future, one that, in time, would start to adopt new technologies and evolve a mind-set ready to embrace, with great maturity, the most advanced technologies in the field of economy and finance.

What to many appeared as mysterious as science fiction, to others seemed feasible. Yet, a study of the individuals entering this sector reveals the presence of a number of individuals not from the world of finance or economics. Indeed, the author, during the course of his research, formed the impression that the most sceptical of these new forms of finance were those whose original background was finance. Their scepticism about this new technology was also reflected in the local media.

A number of investors in Bitcoin came from the Humanities. These individuals were the most vociferous and possibly even the most adventurous. Those studying the Humanities tend to have such a trait. But the Maltese are not idiosyncratic in this respect. A similar pattern is in evidence globally. Around the world, numerous accounts emerge of individuals entering this field from other, perhaps even incompatible, fields. However, there are plenty of actors coming from a background in finance and economics. Patrick L. Young is one of these. Interested in financial technology since 1994[10], his interest and activities in the field are so extensive that he is an internationally lauded blockchain expert[11]. In 1999, he published a book wherein he expressed seminal ideas about digital money[12]. Therefore, when Satoshi Nakamoto published his famous proposal, he realized the potential that was opening up to the world of finance and that the future lay within this new revolution.

In contrast, Leon Siegmund is a migrant to the world of finance. He comes from the world of computing. He is German by birth but a citizen of the world by profession, and fully qualifies as a digital nomad. He is one of those digital gurus who conducts his professional life all over the world. Coming to Malta, he took up residence in Gozo, Malta's sister island. Indeed, the study of the onset of cryptocurrencies in Malta starts with Gozo. Siegmund was working in bitcoins. It was a natural step for Siegmund to set up on the sister island what he called Bitcoin Club Gozo. There then followed the Bitcoin Club Malta.

The obvious question that follows is how is it possible that individuals who have not been trained in finance or economics to become successful in this sector. The first answer lies in the structure of liberal arts courses. They are designed to train students to ask questions and thereafter give answers. Some liberal art students showed an interest in this sector for philosophical reasons. Bitcoin and blockchain challenged many of the positions associated with current political propositions.

The initial approach of these individuals from a liberal arts background was to implement these new technologies outside the structures of government and regulations. This approach is still favoured by a number of early adopters. This was a generation that dreamed of a world without frontiers and governments. This is the generation that on a demographic level embraced concepts of diversity and different gender identities. It began envisaging the nation-state as an entity that possesses more than one identity. The identity of every government today is based on the identity of the nation-state, one based on territory. Digital technology is changing all this. Identity is not congruent with frontiers. People can move and carry their skills with them. What is needed are favourable legal structures through which people can operate without problems.

The first operations were carried out in a legal void. As always happens with new economic factors, there are some advantages in having no regulations. This allows pioneers to act freely without any legal hindrances. In January 2014, the Library of Congress published an interesting entry about Bitcoin in Malta. This is what it had to say about this sector:

"Malta currently does not have any regulations pertaining specifically to bitcoins, nor does there appear to be any official government statement on the recognition or policy towards the bitcoin. According to news reports, the bitcoin is not deemed as a regulated instrument under the EU's Markets in Financial

Instruments Directive 2004/39/EC (MiFID), thus there are no licensing requirements for companies that deal in Bitcoins to obtain a license from the Malta Financial Services Authority."[13]

Picking up Steam: 2016-2017

The lack of any regulation or legislation in Malta to regulate business in Bitcoin continued in the following years. Reflecting on the situation, Stephen O'Neal wrote that the situation in Malta continued to be 'immature' with regards to cryptocurrency infrastructure. The leading company back then was the Bitcoin & Auto Trader located in Qormi where one could buy a Lamborghini, among other vehicles. O'Neal also hinted at the presence of a crypto-friendly sushi restaurant [14].

Yet, this state of bliss and immaturity could not continue for ever. Those wishing to work in this sector realized that soon they would need laws to regulate these operations. A stroke of luck was that the government of the day was open to discussion. In general, governments are slow to act and adapt in the face of revolutionary technology. Foremost among those reaching out to government were Steve Tendon and Chris Vassallo. These two played a key role in promoting the technology with the local authorities. Their interlocutor was Minister Chris Cardona who, at the time, was Minister of Economy, Investment and Small Businesses. These contacts started in 2016. Eventually, Steve Tendon became strategic adviser to Minister Cardona and was appointed to design the National Blockchain Strategy for Malta.

In August 2016, the first draft of Malta's National Blockchain Strategy was drawn up. The document outlined a plan to implement the technology across multiple sectors, not just finance, and to develop a strategy to serve and benefit the Maltese economy as a whole. In October of that same year, a draft strategy was presented to Minister Cardona and subsequently, deemed strategically important, it was then turned into a memorandum and presented to Cabinet[15]. Malta's National Blockchain Strategy was approved unanimously by the Cabinet in April 2017[16].

As always, universities tend to provide the most solid expertise to government. In the case of Malta, the earliest published news about the involvement of the University of Malta in this sector goes back to 2016[17]. The names of Gordon Pace[18] and Joshua Ellul[19] become increasingly prominent due to their courses on this subject. The Faculty of Laws proposed a related course in 2017. The course, on Legal Futures and Technology, was launched in 2018 by Dr Ian Gauci.

Dr Jonathan Galea, a lawyer, was particularly interested in this field, and by the end of 2016, had set up Malta's first Association, Bitcoin Malta, to campaign in favour of blockchain technology and cryptocurrencies among the general public. It went public at the beginning of 2017 when, on 3rd January, it launched a Twitter account and next day its website was activated[20].

A similar initiative would follow when a number of individuals, some of whom have been mentioned above, got together to set up the Blockchain Malta Association. These were Chris Vassallo, Ian Gauci, Max Ganado, Leonard Bonello, Patrick L. Young, Leon Siegmund, and Louis Mercieca[21]. According to Chris Osborne, a few months after its inception the Association had succeeded in becoming 'the most influential organization' in this sector in Malta. Osborne stated this when he included this Association on the list of the 15 most important cryptocurrency companies in Malta. Though strictly speaking the Association is not a company, Osborne included it because in his words, this Association 'consults regularly with

Malta's Government on how the country can continue attracting more crypto companies to its shores, and also plays a significant role in influencing the development of crypto regulations within the country'[22].

At first, the Government's idea was to turn Europe into a 'Bitcoin continent'. For this reason, Prime Minister Joseph Muscat approved what was back then called a blockchain strategy[23]. Intriguingly, once the Government began to consider embarking on this road, a new political controversy, with a small bank at its epicentre, hit Malta. The operations of this small bank were linked to the Panama Papers. This episode seems to have distracted the Government from going public about its intent. One suspects that there was a concerted international effort to ensure that the banking sector in Malta would be put in a bad light. The presence of this small bank, by the name of Pilatus Bank, would prove useful in this attempt. The political controversy centred around the presence of such a bank and included accusations of money laundering. This served the wider strategy of putting spokes in the wheels of the Government's initiatives regarding its new vision.

Evidence points towards a connection between the criticism that was levied against Pilatus Bank and the projects in the blockchain sector. Clearly, the coincidence is a subtle one. The attack on Pilatus Bank reached new heights when Minister Cardona started private discussions on a cryptocurrency and blockchain strategy for Malta. The person who started criticizing Pilatus Bank was Daphne Caruana Galizia on her blog. The accusations levied against Pilatus Bank were that of money laundering and facilitating suspicious transactions linked to politically exposed persons[24].

After a series of articles, in which she accused Pilatus Bank of money laundering, on 1 March 2017, Caruana Galizia wrote a blog attacking cryptocurrency and blockchain[25]. Then, in April 2017,

Carauna Galizia alleged that the Prime Minister's wife held declarations of trust showing that shares in Egrant Inc., one of the offshore shell companies featured in the Panama Papers, were held at this bank[26]. Eventually, the Prime Minister's wife was cleared of this allegation following an inquiry[27]. Caruana Galizia wrote another article against cryptocurrency on 13 September 2017[28], that is after the Government started launching a number of positive initiatives in favour of this sector.

This controversy brought Malta under the full glare of the international limelight with the result that eventually Bank of Valletta blocked client-transactions to purchase bitcoins[29]. Later on, other banks in Malta were accused of money laundering, including SATA Bank[30] and HSBC[31]. These incidents are indicative of the effectiveness of the strategy adopted at the time, and the author of this chapter reiterates his views that this was not just an internal political controversy but an attempt by international players with a vested interest to bring about the demise of the cryptocurrency and blockchain strategy.

What is incontrovertible is that Muscat bided his time and waited for his second mandate. It was only after winning its second mandate, in June 2017, that the Maltese Government began to go public with its plans for this sector. Interestingly enough, although the Government had been working for more than a year on this project, not a word about these intentions was leaked during the electoral campaign, or mentioned in the electoral programme of the Labour Party.

Immediately after receiving its second mandate, the Labour Government sent its first positive signals regarding this budding sector. While, as expected, the Minister of Finance, Edward Scicluna, was reappointed, a junior minister, Silvio Schembri, was chosen to head a new ministry to oversee the new sector. The Government set up a Parliamentary Secretary for Financial Services, Digital Economy and Innovation. It was the first time in the history of the Maltese Parliament that there was to be a specific parliamentary secretary for digital economy. What was also innovative was that this junior ministry would not fall under the Minister of Finance but would be accountable directly to the Prime Minister. This was a very strong signal of the Government's favourable intentions for this sector.

The Labour Government's economic successes between 2013 and 2017 allayed political fears amongst a section of the electorate, in particular that section inclined towards economic investment. Such fear emanated from previous Labour administrations, in particular those between 1971 and 1987. Back then, digital technology was perceived and described as a threat to jobs by the Labour Government[32]. Prime Minister Joseph Muscat kept his political pledge after winning the 2013 election. He had clearly stated before then that he would play safe with business. This helped him move more confidently into this new economic area, and his pledges were taken seriously.

The votes had not all been counted before the Government of Malta was presented with a blockchain project in June 2017. The recommendations presented to Government were that it needed to act swiftly as other more determined countries were also interested in this field. The advice to the Government was to eliminate any intermediate stages. Was this the reason why a junior minister for this sector was appointed directly under the Prime Minister?

Joseph Muscat did not see digital technology as a threat, despite the current narrative that blockchain and Bitcoin threaten to undermine the nation-state. In an important political message that the Prime Minister delivered in his New Year's speech in 2018, he said that citizens should learn to turn threats into opportunities[33]. It is difficult to overlook a reference to SWOT analysis. The word he used in Maltese was sfidi, 'challenges', but the challenges that he had in mind were those representing a threat to the individual.

Therefore, it may not come as a surprise that a government of a small nation-state embraces an economic and financial agenda that is perceived to undermine the model of the state[34]. The counter-argument here is that Muscat perceived these new technologies as challenges that can be turned into benefits for a small nation-state such as Malta. The truth is that small nation-states have a better chance of succeeding in this area than bigger states[35].

However, beyond issues of purely political and philosophical import, there is an underlying demographic factor. Malta is still a small island-state in demographic expansion. While Malta's fertility has declined, the population is still expanding, partly thanks to migration and partly to high fertility in particular periods in the past. The crux here is that the island still has a relatively strong and young population and, somehow, this has had an impact on the sector.

If one delves deeper, one may notice that, in Malta, those vociferously in opposition to this sector tend to be of a certain age. The author has met individuals holding senior positions in finance asserting that this sector is doomed to failure. It is also no coincidence that most of the stakeholders in this sector are young; the majority below the age of forty. This, in itself, is indicative of the age gap. Normally, those in the financial sector, who are critical of blockchain and cryptocurrencies, are, in general, over the age of forty.

On the other hand, the gender barrier is less pronounced this time. Even if males appear to be still higher in number, the rate of female participation is encouragingly positive. From a demographic point of view, the recent history of Bitcoin and blockchain has overcome gender barriers. Normally, gender plays an important role in government initiatives as jobs tend to be biased in favour of men. In this case, the participation of women is exceedingly high, which is again a confirmation of the silent revolution that is taking place in employment locally. As the leading French demographer, Emmanuel Todd shows, the success of any revolution lies in education[36].

Another factor is the Prime Minister's age. He is still young[37] and this has made him more open to what may appear as audacious initiatives. As Prime Minister, Muscat is open to innovation. His own vision of society is one built on multinationalism. This goes beyond issues of diversity. Finally, the Government's goal is an identity based on the idea of the bit-nation.

The vibes were so strong that this particular sector continued to expand rapidly[38]. In July, an ATM machine for the purchase of bitcoins was set up in Blanche Huber Street, Sliema. It was the brainchild of Gabriel Cretu Torica a Romanian entrepreneur. The idea was for people to buy bitcoins with their eWallet on their smartphones while Torica would earn an 8% transaction fee. While the idea was promising, the implementation was faulty. A month later, this ATM started having problems and making transaction errors. It had to be closed down[39].

Meanwhile, the news portal, Lovin Malta, reported that a local Bitcoin start-up, by the name of Ivaja had ordered its own Bitcoin ATM – partially through a crowdfunding campaign – that would allow people to both buy and sell bitcoins through it. This initiative was the brainchild of Jonas Abrahamsson from Sweden together with Leon Siegmund[40.]

On 29 August 2017, an important seminar on Blockchain was organized at Le Meridien Hotel in St. Julian's. It was chaired by Steve Tendon. Of the speakers, perhaps the most notable were Dr Ian

Gauci and Dr Max Ganado. Ian Gauci delivered a speech on the legislative challenges facing legislators and regulators in light of the imminent blockchain revolution. Dr Max Ganado spoke about Intellectual Property (IP) and how blockchain could develop into great relevance for the IP sector. It was the first seminar of its nature in Malta, and was organized by Blockchain Malta and Linkedin Group Malta in collaboration with Finance Malta[41].

In September 2017, Parliamentary Secretary Silvio Schembri set up the National Blockchain Strategy Taskforce. Its purpose was to review proposals and produce recommendations to the Government of Malta to implement its national blockchain strategy. These were Ian Gauci, MITA enterprise architect Wayne Grixti, blockchain experts Loui Mercieca and Steve Tendon, Malta Gaming Authority executive chairman Joseph Cuschieri, finance expert Carlo Stivala, and economist Mario Borg.

The Maltese public started to respond positively to blockchain but still remained a little more hostile to cryptocurrency[42]. These negative views on cryptocurrencies were in part due to a strong international media campaign against Bitcoin. Bitcoin has been described as a fraud and soon to disappear[43]. Should cryptocurrencies fail, blockchain still holds future promise as it can be used for systems other than cryptocurrency. However, with no data of value to record and transfer, it is a meaningless and inefficient database. What makes it revolutionary is the ability to record the possession and transfer of value data such as the Bitcoin system.

In November 2017, Bank of Valletta (BOV) stopped allowing its clients to buy cryptocurrencies. Bank clients making use of SEPA transfers to cryptocurrency exchanges or wallets had their transactions reversed. Public sentiment reacted to this news in different ways. For some, it was an indication that the banks had no faith in these types of currencies[44]. For others, it contradicted the Government's commitment to cryptocurrencies. The truth behind BOV's action was another. It feared that cryptocurrency would be used for money laundering, and that, because of the bank's limitations, large American banking institutions, like JP Morgan, would stop effecting SWIFT transfers.

Maturity: 2018

These controversies convinced the Government and the private sector of the urgent need to pass an act that regulated cryptocurrencies and blockchain. In this regard, the Maltese legal system has an advantage. Despite the fact that Malta inherited a British colonial system, through which laws are to be drafted by the office of the Attorney General, the Government can avail itself of legal firms to draft legislation. This system has the advantage that the Government can respond far quicker to demands for new forms of legislation as it can outsource expertise on specific matters. Conscious of the flexibility that the legal system offers the Government, in February, those interested in this sector started to lobby for the introduction of comprehensive legislation as had happened with Igaming, Aviation and Financial Services[45].

In that same month, the Prime Minister made his views on the subject explicitly clear in Brussels. Speaking at the CEPS Ideas Lab Conference on 'Reconstructing Europe', Prime Minister Muscat referred to cryptocurrencies. Rightly so, he said that cryptocurrencies could not be stopped, thus making a case for their regulation[46]. On his return, Joseph Muscat spoke in favour of blockchain, and stated that blockchain did not depend on the country's tax regime[47]. In brief, unlike Malta's tax regime, the use of blockchain cannot come under the control of governments or bankers. Although this may appear contrary to the interests of the nation-state, Prime Minister Muscat still wanted Malta to be a pioneer in these two sectors. From the beginning, the intention was for the island to pass ground-breaking legislation aimed at making Malta a cutting-edge hub for companies seeking growth in this sector[48].

The industry realized the importance of a good legal framework that could provide the quantum leap forward. It was at this stage that Dr Max Ganado came into the picture again. The importance of Dr Ganado's contribution is related to the fact that, in 2007, his firm had written the Trust and Foundation Law, a piece of world-class legislation. This act gave this firm international clout, and brought it into contact with the world's biggest law firms, firms on which one could rely to assist Malta in this sector. In 2014, Dr Ganado's firm promoted an important document on Intellectual Property Industries that later passed into law[49]. It consolidated and rationalized various registers of IP assets such as trademarks, patents and the like. It included recommendations to turn all these into a single centralized digital register for all IP categories and also create a digital trading platform for such assets[50].

Once more, in drafting this new legislation on cryptocurrency and blockchains, Dr Ganado, who has a particular interest in the philosophy of law, sought to gain a wider understanding of the bigger picture. Dr Ganado was not alone in this initiative. He led a stellar team comprising Dr Joshua Ellul, Dr Ian Gauci, Dr Abdalla Kablan, and Professor Gordon Pace. Another expert whose input was frequently sought and graciously given was Dr Jonathan Galea. Due credit must be given to Dr Christopher Buttigieg, the person who produced the first draft of the policy and the VFA law.

The Hon. Silvio Schembri called a press conference in February

2018 to announce the publication of a consultation document entitled 'The Establishment of the Malta Digital Innovation Authority; the Framework for the Certification of Distributed Ledger Technology Platforms and Related Service Providers; and a Virtual Currency Act'. This document outlines three separate but interlinked bills: the MDIAA, the ITASA, the VFAA. These bills outlined the plan to create a supervisory authority, as well as the world's first comprehensive legal framework to govern cryptocurrencies, DLT and ICOs. These bills laid down the foundations for the Blockchain Island.

Before adjourning for summer recess, on 26 June 2018, Parliament unanimously approved the first reading of these three bills to regulate DLT[51]. The MDIA bill came into force in July 2018, while the other two in November 2018, providing the much needed legal and regulatory protection for all stakeholders operating within the sector.

Thanks to these laws, Malta is now regulating ICOs, cryptocurrencies, the setting up of cryptocurrency exchanges, and service providers of Distributed Ledger Technology (DLT)[52]. Thus, Malta became the first country in the world to develop a regulatory system custom-made for blockchain-based businesses[53].

Even if this law did not come immediately into effect until November 2018, it soon started to attract companies working in cryptocurrencies and blockchain. Among these companies were Binance and OKEx[54]. Both moved from Hong Kong to Malta due to restrictions that the Hong Kong Government placed on cryptocurrency exchanges[55]. Another big name in this sector, Neufund, announced in April 2018 that it was moving its operations from Germany to Malta. Justin Sun, founder and CEO of TRON, the decentralized entertainment platform, also said his company was 'seriously considering' a move to Malta[56]. In September 2018, Bittrex bought a 10% stake in Palladium. Chaired by Paolo Catalfamo, Bittrex is a USA-based company working in cryptocurrency exchanges around the world. In August, Palladium launched one of the world's first fully regulated tokenised convertible warrant[57].

These companies availed themselves of the new legal framework now attracting foreign investors to Malta. Other benefits were similarly attractive. Malta has an efficient corporate tax. In Malta, whether foreign or local, any investor can incorporate a company in less than 48 hours. Furthermore, Malta-based companies enjoy primarily an efficient tax treatment. Corporate tax rate in Malta stands at 35% but the country has a tax refund system through which shareholders are refunded part of the tax paid on dividend distribution. Malta also enjoys tax incentives for Highly Qualified Persons. These individuals are offered a tax rate of 15% on their employment income generated in Malta[58]. The end result was that by September 2018, Malta registered the largest share of cryptocurrency trading volume in the world[59].

Finance Malta, a public-private initiative chaired by Kenneth Farrugia, joined forces with the Blockchain Malta Association to host seminars on the subject under the banner of BlockFinance. These events were aimed at exploring the effect of blockchain on different sectors in the financial services industry. The second seminar in this series was addressed by the executive head of BOV Asset Management, Mark Agius. He spoke about the way BOV was positively reacting to blockchain technology by investing in better resources to help integrate blockchain in banking. Moreover, the bank pledged that its asset managers would be collaborating with other market participants, and were prepared to share common infrastructures and common standards for blockchain to achieve the desired success[60]. It was a sign of détente from the bank after it had temporarily shunned this sector.

It was at this stage that the idea of a blockchain island came to the fore. As an idea, it was not new. It had surfaced in the Isle of Man, the first attempt to become a blockchain island that included passing laws seeking to regulate the cryptocurrency and blockchain space[61]. But the type of international jurisdiction that the Isle of Man has, and its particular dependence on UK banks, led to a sense of unease with respect to cryptocurrencies and blockchains.

It was in the light of this that Malta needed to act quickly and, to borrow the words of Dennis Mark Gauci, a partner with KSi Malta, to 'push forward a legal framework in which a business could operate in a way that is compliant with existing legislation and where certain safeguards are implemented particularly to ensure market integrity, consumer protection and financial stability'[62].

Government began to implement the bills passed by Parliament, first by setting up the Malta Digital Innovation Authority (MDIA) so that this new authority might start consultation with service providers, and register them, to certify blockchain applications. Joshua Ellul was appointed its first chairman, thus confirming the Government's interest in transparency and the highest standards of professionalism. Ellul is an academic at the University of Malta lecturing on blockchain, and is also the director of the Centre for Distributed Ledger Technologies. He has also worked on research and development projects at IBM Research Zurich and Imperial College London[63].

On Tuesday 18 September, the MDIA published four documents. The first document outlined the requirement for registration. The second is a consultation document listing the requirements for the certification of DLT Platforms and Smart Contracts. The third is a consultation document outlining the requirements for the entity responsible to maintain and oversee the Technology Arrangements to safeguard user protection. The fourth is a consultation document related to the Resident Agent Guidelines that obliged non-Maltese companies/individuals to engage a person residing in Malta for their operations[64].

But there was still a lot of work to be done. An international survey conducted by PwC, whose results were published in September 2018, showed that the main reason why one in three of those respondents did not get involved with blockchain was due to cost (31%). Uncertainty came second with 24%, and governance issues were of least concern at 14%[65].

Whether reacting to this survey or not, legal and financial firms once more started writing to the press to explain blockchain and cryptocurrencies. Lawyers at Ganado Advocates started writing in the Times of Malta to explain the benefits of blockchain technology[66]. Chetcuti Cauchi Advocates helped in fostering the feel-good factor by publishing a number of articles, penned by their senior managers and associates, in the Times of Malta. A case in point were the opinion pieces written by Nicholas Warren and Steve Muscat Azzopardi. Another contributor to the media was Dr Ian Gauci of GTG Advocates, who became particularly prolific from late 2017 onwards.

The efforts of the Maltese Government in this sector were laid out by Prime Minister Muscat at the Swiss Blockchain Leadership Summit. He discussed the efforts of the Maltese Government to prioritize transparency. Muscat spoke alongside industry shapers such as #cryptovalley ecosystem founder @johanngevers[67].

October and November were turning points in the history of cryptocurrency and blockchain locally. In October, the Maltese Government presented its budget. For the first time, specific reference to blockchain was made in the budget speech. Funds were allocated for the promotion and the use of this technology, as well as to create a Blockchain Laboratory and a Blockchain Startup Hub[68].

Soon after, the final regulations and rules for the VFA Act were issued[69]. According to these new regulations, those seeking to become cryptocurrency agents needed to obtain certification through an examination. It is reported that only 39% of those who sat for the first session in September passed. The exam was in the form of multiple-choice questions with negative marking. About 250 sat for this exam. Most were lawyers, accountants, and auditors[70]. Furthermore, the cost of obtaining a licence from the MFSA to work in this sector was made intentionally hefty, and abuse is punishable by heavy fines and imprisonment[71]. These measures by the MFSA are intended to hinder malfeasant operators from this business.

On the evening of 3 October, the Delta Summit on blockchain was inaugurated at the Intercontinental Hotel in St. Julian's. This summit attracted thousands of international industry experts and leaders in this sector. Top-notch speakers were brought over to speak about their inspiring experiences, and to debate on the potential emerging from this sector, as well as on disruptive technology in general.

Moreover, during this summit, entrepreneurs discussed the future of connectivity. A director of the E&S Group, Dr Christian Ellul, spoke on the first day of the event, discussing Malta's place in the world of blockchain and cryptocurrency technology, and its potential to lead the global industry despite the country's small size[72]. Companies such as Binance, Okex, Bitfury, Crypto.com, Cubits, Palladium were among the participants at this conference. Speakers included Parliamentary Secretary for Financial Services, Digital Economy and Innovation Silvio Schembri, Tim Draper, founder of Draper Fisher Jurvetson and Draper University, Binance founder and CEO Changpeng Zhao, Wikipedia co-founder and Everipedia CIO Larry Sanger, Mycelia founder Imogen Heap, and computer and venture capital entrepreneur Hermann Hauser. This was the first time that Malta was hosting such a conference. This summit was seen by everyone as a major opportunity for Malta to stake its claim as a centre for digital innovation[73].

Furthermore, on the first day of November, the Maltese Government brought into force the two remaining bills that were passed in June to secure DLT on the island. These were the VFAA and the ITASA respectively[74].

On that same day, the Maltese Commissioner for Revenue issued guidelines on the interpretation of income tax, duty on documents and VAT in connection with activities involving Distributed Ledger Technology assets. According to Dr Christina Scicluna, who published an article on the subject, these guidelines gave certainty and stability to investors and operators in the sector in Malta[75].

Moreover, on 1 November an international conference on blockchain was held in Malta. It was another step forward in the space of Distributed Ledger Technologies[76]. This event, part-conference/part-fair, was launched with a bang by Eman Pulis of SiGMA in February 2018[77]. The Malta Blockchain Summit was a resounding success and won euphoric coverage in the local media:

"The Malta Blockchain Summit lived up to its expectations with an incredible turnout of 8,500. Those attending had an opportunity to visit the vivid exhibition with more than 400 companies participating. They enjoyed the keynotes of the conference, witnessed the hackathon and attended workshops on investment, marketing, business development and many other topics."[78]

Extending Blockchain into Other Fields

The discussion in Malta was, till now, mainly related to finance. But debate on extending blockchain to healthcare, energy and industrial manufacturing[79], and entertainment now also started to take place.[80] While in February 2018, the private sector identified these four pillars of blockchain technology and expansion, in September the Government came out with the innovative idea of developing blockchain in another area – education. In education, the private sector is less visible as most of the schools in Malta are either run by the state or by the Roman Catholic Church. This initiative in education was on different levels and definitely a pre-emptive move. The Ministry of Education and Employment announced a new project that would put educational and academic records on blockchain[81].

The Malta College of Arts, Science and Technology (MCAST) was next to enter the field of blockchain. On 22 September, a press conference was held in which it was stated that MCAST was exploring educational courses that would lead to a diploma in this new technology[82]. The University of Malta published more than one initiative to provide teaching in this field. It teamed up with the Malta Information Technology Agency (MITA) to start training students in this new technology. A €300,000 blockchain and Distributed Ledger Technology (DLT) scholarship fund was set up for students with backgrounds in ICT, law, finance and engineering, and who wished to do their Master's and Ph.D. research dissertations in blockchain and DLT[83].

However, there is another area in which Malta can certainly make interesting proposals. This is also related to cryptocurrency and blockchain and it may lead to a revolution in the philosophy behind our legal system, which is coercive per se. In our current legal system, laws are passed through parliament to punish undesirable behaviour or to prevent it. But to date, no one has considered passing laws to promote and reward acts of good citizenship. Bitcoin may make this idea possible. A proposal of this sort cropped up in debate in Malta in 2017 though nothing came of it for various reasons. But still, as an idea, it was the first of its kind in Malta. The proposal showed how bitcoins could make a social contribution by rewarding desirable behaviour. In future, technology may devise the means to reward socially beneficial behaviour in the same way that Bitcoin awards its tokens to miners that enable transactions and other benefits to this system.

In July 2018, the Trust headed by the President of the Republic, Marie Louise Coleiro Preca, signed a MOU with Binance, the cryptocurrency exchange, to explore ways in which blockchain technology may be used by NGOs. Binance set up a Blockchain Charity Foundation with the mission to improve public awareness of blockchain technology. Sarah Borda Bondin, who was appointed to head the Trust, said that the Foundation and the Trust would kick-start their strategic collaboration with Project Educ8, and the Trust would co-ordinate with local NGOs to educate and empower young people to utilize blockchain for sustainable development[84].

In September 2018, it was again the turn of the President of the Republic, Marie Louise Coleiro Preca, to link blockchain to another benevolent social cause. Companies involved in this technology, such as Stasis, started collecting funds in support of the Malta Community Chest Fund.

More than once in her speeches, the President Coleiro Preca insisted that blockchain technology could be a catalyst to transform the way in which charitable organizations are created and regulated in the future. Such a transformation would ensure that the funds, resources and goodwill of our country, the private sector, and civil society had the best impact on most people[85].

Another area in which blockchain technology started spreading was that of iGaming. In March 2018, the Malta Gaming Authority (MGA) began exploring the possibility of introducing DLTs and virtual currencies in gaming. The Malta Gaming Authority became aware that iGaming needed to embrace this technology, and once the Malta Digital Innovation Authority was set up, it entered into discussions with a view to carrying out the necessary changes to the current iGaming laws. A consultation document was published containing new regulations that need to be enacted to cater for virtual currencies and DLTs. Once again, Malta is at the fore in regulating this area.[86]

Conclusion

This short historical analysis confirms that cryptocurrencies and blockchain are the greatest revolution that the world has experienced since the invention of the printing press. Like the printing press, they have the potential to revolutionize the way society interacts. Fear has been overcome in Malta through largely positive media coverage. Despite the fact that in early 2018 Bitcoin traders and owners registered a drop in the value of their holdings, the Maltese public remains positive.

It is clear that, in general, the Maltese investor keeps his eyes open on developments that are taking place abroad and keeps himself well informed. The general public reacted positively to the signals that the Government was sending, and continues to do so. On its part, the Government's vision was to turn Malta into a blockchain island. As this analysis shows, the Government at first had a vision of proposing to Brussels that Europe be turned into a blockchain continent. But instead the Government ended up re-dimensioning its views and focusing its strategy on Malta.

At the same time, while the account of blockchain and Bitcoin was unfolding locally, the Government got entangled in a controversy about the rule of law or the lack of it in Malta. This controversy appears to have somehow negatively affected progress in this sector, and distracted the Government from focusing on this vital sector. What this controversy shows is that the legal system can be coercive. This is the nature of its origin in the Ancient Greek world, and its development in the Roman. The law is there to control the behaviour of people. What the state seeks to control is undesirable behaviour and this control is exercised through punishment. Blockchain and Bitcoin are bringing about a revolution even in the legal sector, though this part of the debate is still missing in Malta.

The author believes that this sector is destined to grow, and through this research is now genuinely convinced that this is not a mere bubble. This is an area that is destined to expand and these digital platforms are here to stay. They are the future and, as this analysis shows, there are substantial gains to be made.

Endnotes

1. Satoshi Nakamoto.
2. James Catania, "The Block Behind the Coin", Times of Malta, 2018.
3. Bitcoin has passed into common parlance in Malta, as has happened in the rest of the world.
4. Satoshi Nakamoto.

5. "Malta And Blockchain", The Malta Independent, 2018.
6. Global Legal Research Center, Regulation of Bitcoin in Selected Jurisdictions(The Law Library of Congress, 2014), p. 15, loc.gov.
7. For example, many comments on blogs echoed this idea. The following is a case in point: Dominic Cortis, "A Bitcoin Crash or Dip?", Times of Malta, 2018.
8. Simon Schama, The Embarrassment of Riches. An Interpretation of the Dutch Culture in the Golden Age(University of California Press, 1987).
9. Salvino Busuttil, "The National Income Tax of the Maltese Islands 1946-1960", in Tribute to Alan Blondy(Fondation de Malte, 2017), p. 91.
10. "Patrick Young: Blockchain and Cryptocurrencies are Warming Up | Bitcoin Conference Malta", Malta.Bc.Events, 2017, malta.bc.events.
11. Ibid.
12. Patrick L Young and Thomas Theys, Capital Market Revolution (FT Prentice Hall, 1999).
13. Global Legal Research Center, Regulation of Bitcoin in Selected Jurisdictions p. 14.
14. Stephen O'Neal, "From Malta To Prague: What is the Most Crypto-Friendly Travel Destination?", Cointelegraph, 2018.
15. "Malta and Blockchain", The Malta Independent.
16. Ibid.
17. The University of Malta has given increasing importance to this field.
18. "Prof. Gordon Pace – Computer Science – University of Malta", University of Malta, 2018, um.edu.mt.
19. "Dr Joshua Ellul – L-Università ta' Malta", University of Malta, 2018, um.edu.mt.
20. "Bitmalta (@Bitmalta) On Twitter", Twitter, 2017, twitter.com.
21. "About", Blockchain Malta Association, 2018, blockchainmalta.org.
22. Chris Osborne, "15 Crypto Companies in Malta You Should Get

to Know", Chris Osborne, 2018, kintu.co.

23. Bertrand Borg, "BOV Turns Against Cryptocurrencies", Times of Malta, 2017.

24. Daphne Caruana Galizia, "Declarations of Trust in Pilatus Bank Safe: Egrant Inc Shares Held for Michelle Muscat", 2017.

25. Daphne Caruana Galizia, "Muscat Says Europe Should Become a "Bitcoin Continent", as the EU Fights Against the Rise of Money-Laundering and Terrorism Financing Through Bitcoins", 2017.

26. Daphne Caruana Galizia, "Declarations of Trust in Pilatus Bank Safe: Egrant Inc Shares Held for Michelle Muscat".

27. Neil Camilleri, "Egrant Inquiry Clears PM and His Wife, Finds that Signatures on Declarations Were Falsified", The Malta Independent, 2018.

28. Daphne Caruana Galizia, "Bitcoin: JP Morgan Boss Calls It "A Fraud That Will Blow Up"", 2017.

29. Bertrand Borg, "BOV Turns Against Cryptocurrencies".

30. Jacob Borg, "Financial Investigators Comb Through Satabank's Client Files", Times of Malta, 2018.

31. "Money Laundering: Greens MEP Tells HSBC to Quit Malta, PN MP Tells Him to 'F... Off'", The Malta Independent, 2018.

32. "Mintoff: On the Threshold of Grandness", The Malta Independent, 2018.

33. "The Prime Minister's Message for the New Year – TVM News", TVM, 2017, tvm.com.mt.

34. "The Stateless Society – Earn a Living", ARTE TV, 2018, arte.tv.

35. Jen Fifield, "Tiny Towns, Small States Bet on Bitcoin Even as Some Shun its Miners", Huffpost, 2018.

36. Sonya Faure and Cécile Daumas, "Emmanuel Todd : «La Crétinisation Des Mieux Éduqués Est Extraordinaire»", Libération, 2017, liberation.fr.

37. "Dr. Joseph Muscat", Office of the Prime Minister, 2018, opm.gov.mt.

38. Simon Mercieca, "Bitcoins and Blockchain", The Malta

Independent, 2018, and Simon Mercieca, "Is Malta Losing its Sovereignty?", The Malta Independent, 2018.

39.   Tim Diacono, "Malta's First Bitcoin ATM Runs into a Bit of Trouble", Lovin Malta, 2018.

40.   Ibid.

41.   "Dr Max Ganado Delivers Presentation at Blockchain Seminar", Ganado Advocates, 2018, ganadoadvocates.com.

42.   For example, slain journalist Daphne Caruana Galizia heavily criticized DLT and crypto. As she was an acerbic critic of the Labour Government, this was seen as an attack on the Labour Government.

43.   Nicky Woolf, "Bitcoin 'Exit Scam': Deep-Web Market Operators Disappear With $12M", The Guardian, 2015.

44.   Bertrand Borg, "BOV Turns Against Cryptocurrencies".

45.   Steve Muscat Azzopardi, "Setting Up a Blockchain Technology Company", Times of Malta, 2018.

46.   Simon Mercieca, "Bitcoin and the Return of Traditional Family Values", The Malta Independent, 2018.

47.   Ibid.

48.   Steve Muscat Azzopardi, "Setting Up a Blockchain Technology Company".

49.   "Dr Max Ganado Delivers Presentation at Blockchain Seminar", Ganado Advocates.

50.   Ibid.

51.   Jimmy Aki, "Malta Approves Favorable Cryptocurrency Bills in Next Step as a Blockchain Island", Bitcoin Magazine, 2018.

52.   Dennis Mark Gauci, "The Blockchain Island", Times of Malta, 2018.

53.   Bertrand Borg, "Hold Your Horses, MFSA Tells Blockchain Sector", Times of Malta, 2018.

54.   Dennis Mark Gauci, "The Blockchain Island".

55.   Chris Osborne, "15 Crypto Companies in Malta You Should Get to Know".

56.   Alexandre Dreyfus, "Malta: One Step Ahead in

Blockchain", Times of Malta, 2018.

57. "Top US Cryptocurrency Exchange Invests in Malta-Based Blockchain Company", Times of Malta, 2018.

58. Steve Muscat Azzopardi, "Setting Up a Blockchain Technology Company".

59. Ibid.

60. "Blockchain Opportunities in Asset Management", Times of Malta, timesofmalta.com.

61. Dennis Mark Gauci, "The Blockchain Island".

62. Ibid.

63. "Blockchain Academic to Be First Chair of Malta Digital Innovation Authority", Times of Malta, 2018.

64. "First Steps Towards Blockchain Applications Being Discussed", Times of Malta, 2018.

65. "84% of Executives Report Blockchain Initiatives – Pwc", Times of Malta, 2018.

66. James Debono and Michael Kelley, "Overhauling Industries Through Blockchain Technology", Times of Malta, 2018.

67. Joseph Muscat, Twitter, 2018, twitter.com.

68. "Malta and Blockchain", The Malta Independent.

69. "VFA Framework", MFSA, 2018.

70. Kevin Helms, "Only 39 Percent Pass Malta's Cryptocurrency Exam", Bitcoin News, 2018.

71. "MFSA Fees to Issue and Operate a VFA License", VFA Hub, 2018.

72. "Malta and Blockchain", The Malta Independent.

73. "Blockchain on the Agenda as Malta Delta Summit Opens", Times of Malta, 2018.

74. Steve Muscat Azzopardi, "Setting Up a Blockchain Technology Company".

75. Christina Scicluna, "Malta, the New Kid on the Blockchain", Times of Malta, 2018.

76. Steve Muscat Azzopardi, "Setting Up a Blockchain Technology Company".

77. "Positioning Malta as a Blockchain Destination", Times of Malta, 2018.
78. "Malta and Blockchain", The Malta Independent.
79. "84% Of Executives Report Blockchain Initiatives – Pwc", Times of Malta.
80. "Positioning Malta as a Blockchain Destination", Times of Malta.
81. "Malta And Blockchain", The Malta Independent.
82. Ivan Martin, "Malta Becomes First Country to Explore Blockchain Education Certificates", Times of Malta, 2017.
83. "€300,000 For Blockchain Scholarships At UOM", Times of Malta, 2018.
84. "President's Trust Teams Up with Crypto Giant Binance", Times of Malta, 2018.
85. "'Blockchain Can be Used for Social Good', President Says", Times of Malta, 2018.
86. Steve Muscat Azzopardi and Silvana Zammit, "A Blockchain-Based Future for the Malta Gaming Industry", Times of Malta, 2018.

4. Silver Bullet

Sophia Tillie

Blockchain is by no means the panacea to all the sector's ills. Yet, if successfully integrated, blockchain could engineer a more decentralized, inclusive, agile, and cost-efficient system.

Sophia Tillie, recently obtained an MA in Iranian Studies from the University of Tehran, where she wrote her thesis on the opportunities and threats of blockchain adoption in Iran. She works with multiple NGOs.

Despite a decade of system-wide reforms, the humanitarian sector continues to fall short in the world's most enduring crisis responses, and finds itself on, 'the cusp of a decisive moment in its history'[1.] As the gap between aspiration and achievable results continues to grow, the sector's fundamental architecture and tools are increasingly being called into question as the right way to address the multi-faceted needs in many of today's emergencies. In short, the formal humanitarian sector is facing a crisis of legitimacy.

Such deep-seated dilemmas concerning the sector's overall effectiveness have been amplified in its recent encounter with blockchain technology, whose greatest impact is said to be in its wider-trend of decentralization and disintermediation. While many insist that blockchain will trigger the sector-wide paradigm-shift necessary for its survival, others prophesize that within thirty years, blockchain could displace the humanitarian sector altogether.

Blockchain combines several existing technologies such as cryptography, distributed databases, consensus algorithms and decentralized processing. Information shared on the blockchain make it more transparent, tamper-proof, traceable, and secure, which increases its efficiency and accountability. It also cuts down third-party involvement, which in turn cuts down on fees and charges when moving money. While it was originally created to transfer financial value, second generation blockchain is now viewed as having the potential to be a more efficient and secure way to transfer or share any type of digital information or asset in sectors beyond the financial.

If applied to the humanitarian sector, blockchain has the potential to transform and improve the current system of information management including protected data-sharing, identification, co-ordination of aid delivery, management of crowdfunding, tracking supply chain, cash-transfer programming and improving humanitarian financing. It could also help the sector address existing challenges of corruption and fraud by providing cost savings and traceability of information flows, and by reducing transaction times.

With the sector's recent attempts at piecemeal reform proving an insufficient response to the volume and complexity of humanitarian needs[2], and with capacity and funds falling ever short, there is evidently a need to challenge the underlying structures and assumption under which the formal humanitarian system operates. The question remains, is blockchain that silver bullet? Can blockchain transform the system's architecture sufficiently for it to survive into a new era of multipolarism[5]? Or will the formal humanitarian sector simply be dismissed as an, 'intermediary', a relic of bygone Western hegemony?

The central contention of this chapter is that blockchain is by no means the panacea to all the sector's ills. Yet, if successfully integrated, blockchain could engineer a more decentralized, inclusive, agile, and cost-efficient system. As such, the sector's adoption of blockchain could well be the silver bullet needed for its survival.

Historical background

With its roots embedded in an age of European Colonialism, the formal humanitarian system institutionalized its growth after the end of the First and Second World Wars. Yet it was the era of decolonization fused with strategic Cold War geopolitics that stimulated a significant increase in non-governmental humanitarian action, along with the sharpening of the sector's double-edged sword; post-colonial states were seeking resource and infrastructural assistance in the vacuum left behind by the rapid withdrawal of the colonial powers. This combined with the geopolitical competition between the superpowers led some NGOs to form strategic alliances with some of these newly-independent states.

It was the period of unprecedented US power and reach, however, that witnessed the development and expansion of today's major Western NGOs, who for three-quarters of a century have seen themselves as the beating pulse of humanitarian action, indispensable to all elements governing the conduct of relief. But the formal system of international agencies, the Red Cross Movement and the large international NGOs is the product of this period of Western economic and political hegemony.

Yet since the Second World War there has also been significant expansion in the number, type, and size of humanitarian organizations laying claim to the humanitarian cause. These have taken the form of militaries, multinational corporations and private companies, diaspora groups, local NGOs, 'new' or 'rising' donors, and regional organizations. Often these other actors come with their own distinctive traditions and cultures that have informed and influenced humanitarian action more widely but do not necessarily subscribe to the historically evolved norms and principles that underpin Western humanitarianism. As such the rich history of the non-Western traditions in the humanitarian field is often obscured.

Modern Crisis

The problem that has arisen from the increase of 'non-system' actors, is that the humanitarian sector has become a crowded and competitive field. While evidence shows that local actors and organizations have become critical elements in driving significant areas of crisis response, with new technologies changing the way assistance is organized and delivered between these various groups, there is also evidence of a growing disconnect between the formal humanitarian sector and national and local organizations. According to Bennett, there clearly exist huge financial, cultural and regulatory barriers to closer engagement with the formal humanitarian system, its processes, structures and decision-making. The result, according to Gabaudan, is a lack of sufficient co-ordination between groups to meet the changing needs of the people they seek to assist, and a concurrent failure to create smooth transition between operations. And with the growing demands of more frequent and enduring humanitarian crises, and the changing nature of conflict, clearly the system is struggling to keep pace.

Yet, according to Gabaudan, and perhaps more significantly, such barriers and lack of efficient co-ordination between different groups have resulted in the system's failure to bridge the gap between Humanitarian Action and Development Assistance. This is at a time when there is ever greater need for an aid system of emergency assistance to respond quickly to the crisis, and then to 'seamlessly bridge' provision of effective development assistance that aims for longer-term change.

Root Problems

Before assessing how this might be achieved, an examination of the root causes of this fatal fault-line is needed. Whilst some dismiss it as merely being due to a continued lack of agreement between aid agencies and national leaders about how aid should be provided, other reports indicate that the problem lies within the system itself, within its arcane administrative and financial procedures, and more specifically in the donors' out-dated bureaucracies and budgets. It is this latter view that will now be examined.

Despite the fact that in 2005, the UN rolled out a new system designed to provide better co-ordination within, and to bring a measure of predictability and accountability to the humanitarian community, it fell short of expectation. Such failure, as pointed out by Gabuadan, was primarily due to the fact that efforts to co-ordinate humanitarian aid in disasters have not been matched with similar endeavours to link emergency relief with early recovery and development. This, he states, is itself due to the lack of successful integration of technology to co-ordinate the plethora of new actors.

On the other hand, Bennett points to current funding structures as being the root cause which she believes disincentivizes aid agencies to hand over responsibility to other actors, or to prepare local partners to drive forward a response in genuine medium-term or long-term initiatives. While there have been efforts to diversify the humanitarian funding base, and develop new financing mechanisms, to allow for the entry of some significant emerging players, the overall result is still heavy centralization of the entire, formal sector that remains dominated by five government donors and the EU. Together, alone, they disburse more than two-thirds of funds channelled through the formal system, and such a concentration of funding sources is also reflected in the parallel concentration of funding recipients. In short, there exists in the formal sector a serious problem of over-centralization.

Another major problem identified is, 'corporatization' of the aid sector, where the success of whole teams responsible for ensuring adequate financing of their operations, ranging from country directors to field-based programme managers right up to the UN and NGO fundraising and marketing teams, is assessed on the basis of how much money they bring in for their organization. Therefore, established aid agencies are prone to consider other actors as potential competition for funding resources, and as a result keep their funding networks closed. According to Bennett, such a dynamic perpetuates paternalism and drives a preoccupation with growth, competition and market share, which create powerful disincentives to diversification, devolution and systemic change.

These enduring power-imbalances and the structures that underpin them, according to Bennett simply, 'ring-fences the system', which has amplified into a situation where the global financing of humanitarian action has become 'bifurcated': on the one hand, the quantifiable, trackable funding passing through the UN and the main international NGOs, and on the other an unknown, but possibly much larger, flow of money from organizations, groups and individuals operating largely independently of, and more or less invisible to, the financial tracking and accounting mechanisms of the formal system.

With increasingly complex processes and procedures, and anti-corruption and counter-terrorism concerns, accountability requirements from donors and implementing agencies have also contributed to the exclusion of potential operational partners, particularly national governments and local NGOs. This tendency to exclude those who do not act like organizations within the formal system, and to side-line the new approaches that many of these actors can offer, means that other potential channels and sources simply do not figure in the financial architecture of the formal system, and often makes emergency preparedness and response less cost-effective. As the Humanitarian Policy Group report highlights, this creates unhelpful rivalries and inefficiencies within the formal sector, and erects high barriers that stand in the way of more constructive and fruitful engagement between those within and outside the current formal system.

The consequences of such a system, which lacks a single, easily accessible entry point for new actors, particularly at the national or subnational levels, means that many prefer to establish parallel systems, rather than navigate the web of international actors. The danger of this is a potential radicalization of the donor-recipient dynamic, and further fragmentation of the sector. But as Bennett insists, from a purely financial perspective, this is a missed opportunity to tap into hundreds of billions of dollars of potential funding at a time when there is broad acknowledgement that the humanitarian sector needs significantly more resources to address global need[3].

Aid theorists insist that a persistent performance gap will continue to exist as long the expectation is that the humanitarian sector is equipped to address highly uncertain and complex crises systems but remains centralized and bureaucratic, and while partnerships and interactions remain transactional and competitive, rather than reciprocal and collective. What is therefore needed is clearly a system where there exists greater transparency about the way the sector conducts its operations and greater openness to other actors within the humanitarian space – a system that enhances decentralization, and increases financial inclusion of emerging players. As currently structured, however, the incentives for such engagement do not exist. Could it be that the application of Blockchain to the sector would be the revelation of what a more inclusive, diverse and distributed sector could actually look like? A SWOT analysis will now follow.

SWOT Analysis

Strengths

Blockchain's main innovation is that it is distributed, which links users and organizations directly together through a shared ledger network. This enables actors to engage directly with each other on a peer-to-peer basis and eliminates the need for a third-party intermediary to oversee interactions. The fact that actors are able to transmit value without an intermediary removes many of the costs involved in facilitating exchanges through a third party, and therefore lowers transaction costs. It is in the smart contract, which is what enforces the negotiation and performance of a contract without the need for an intermediary, and which are trackable and irreversible, that the full potential of the technology is realized.

The fact that blockchain provides an unalterable public ledger facilitates the availability of open and transparent data, which increases transparency and accountability. Since the blockchain records, verifies and timestamps every action made on the network, actors can see exactly the source and time of each action. This would help share and understand patterns and trends found in transaction data, such as equality of usage and access among affected population groups.

In addition, smart contracts that run on a blockchain are nearly instantaneous, and compared to the existing technology of financial transactions in the banking system, the blockchain offers a much faster route. In summary, the key features of Blockchain are that it is distributed and enables lower transaction costs and faster transaction times. It also increases transparency and accountability, as well as offers improved management of information and traceability of transaction, and heightens data security due to encryption.

Opportunities

Such features create a host of opportunities within the sector, most obviously by facilitating new methods to improve co-ordination between a multitude of actors via information and data sharing, and in particular in methods of improved financing.

a) Information and Data Collection and Sharing

Blockchain can provide an information marketplace that is publicly accessible to all users while ensuring information security to maintain data privacy, when required. This can overcome the problem of unreliable information sharing. As such, blockchain will allow organizations to gather large quantities of data about vulnerable populations by using the distributed database component, whilst potentially using private blockchain to allow only certain networks to gain access to the data, in order to maintain data privacy of these populations.

b) Identification and Documentation

A lack of identity documentation is a key challenge in humanitarian response and early recovery systems. The blockchain can provide accessible and verifiable identification in humanitarian and disaster situations and makes it possible for an individual to prove their existence and identity through a distributed public ledger. Such basic documentation is often essential in order to obtain basic humanitarian assistance and reach areas of safety.

c) Supply Train Tracking and Transparency

Humanitarian supply chains are extremely dynamic, and logistic efforts account for eighty per cent of disaster relief, but current supply chain visibility and data tracing can often be poor. By providing a publicly visible ledger, a shared, secure record of exchange, the blockchain can be used as a data platform that traces the origins, use, and destination of humanitarian supplies, and therefore introduces transparency in humanitarian supply chains. Increasing supply chain transparency can greatly improve humanitarian operations by providing data to 'inform more effective and accurate decisions, enabling evidence-based interventions and management, exposing issues for effective remedy and increasing accountability'[4]. Such a system would save costs while potentially opening up the formal systems closed subcontractor networks to other actors.

d) Humanitarian Financing

As previously examined, there is a need for more flexible, efficient, transparent and effective donor financing. This is coupled with a call for greater visibility and transparency of financing, not only to address issues of corruption and misuse of funds, but also to enable actors to better identify funding gaps based on impact rather than institutional requirements. This could be most evident in the transformation it would provide to its Cash Transfer Programming (CTP).

Digital cash and payments technology is widely employed among humanitarian actors as they ensure greater transparency around how much aid reaches affected populations. They also make payments cheaper, increase security and accelerate financial inclusion. The aforementioned features of blockchain technology can be leveraged to address many of the challenges of using centralized databases. The same is true for crowdfunding and micro-financing in emergencies, where previously a centralized service was needed to enable a campaign. By providing a decentralized funding platform, using existing digital currencies, blockchain technology removes the need for an intermediary third party to monitor and disburse funds. Such use of blockchain technology would reduce transaction costs and enable rapid disbursement of micropayments.

As we have seen, a more open and transparent data, published on a single global platform, could help reduce the usual transaction costs associated with humanitarian financing and increase effectiveness by cutting out the traditional 'middleman', and instead go directly to communities in need. Its peer-to-peer features could facilitate localization efforts whilst tracing the distribution of aid, both of which would enable better co-ordination among humanitarian actors. The blockchain enables flexible and responsive financing system, directly dealing with the problem of architectural incompetence. Such methods of improved co-ordination could also encourage insurance, telecommunication and logistics companies to get involved in providing their relevant skills and capacity for delivering life-saving assistance. In short, a more inclusive system that would open up the domain to potentially better skilled actors' involvement, which would lift the bar on the quality of execution.

Weaknesses

Despite the fact that blockchain can offer an easy, more affordable and safer solution for cash transfers and data transaction during and after disaster management, which would quite clearly assist in bridging the gap, both between aid assistance and development, as well as between the formal sector and other actors that lie outside of its traditional remit, there are some significant challenges to its widespread adoption.

- New technology: Blockchain as a technology is still in its infancy, and as all new technology is still in an early stage of development. Whilst protocols are being developed, adoption and real use cases are limited and broadly untested. Whilst its potential is undoubted, the implications are still hard to estimate.
- Technical barriers in understanding blockchain technology: Despite the fact that the core blockchain fundamentals have existed for a number of years, there are countless competing protocols, servicing multitudes of different use cases. This complexity makes it hard to fathom for potential clients and people. It remains the case that user-friendly applications are still in their infancy.
- Reputation of Digital Currencies: There is a misconception that blockchain technology is fundamentally tied to Bitcoin and is not merely part of the infrastructure underpinning the currency. There is a reputation gap for potential clients and the general public, with Bitcoin and cryptocurrencies seen as speculative and unregulated. This has hampered universal adoption.
- Market Restriction: Cash-based transfers through blockchain are only effective when there is access to the markets. For example, there are limited fiat-to-crypto exchanges in regions where aid agencies operate. This restricts the potential flow at the grass roots.
- Internet access and infrastructure: As a given, using any internet-based technology requires access to the internet, electricity and other infrastructure. Many of these elements simply do not exist in crisis areas. The limited access to the digital world has also left a digital divide, which should not be underestimated as a barrier.

- Scalability limitations: Similarly, as the blockchain is still in its infancy, the technology can only be scaled within its current uses. It is worth remembering also the severe knowledge gap for potential actors attempting to implement blockchain protocols in real life use cases.

Risks

Arguably the greatest risk that the technology poses is in its ability to enhance neo-colonialist tendencies in the donor-recipient dynamic. This could be particularly dangerous in an era of multipolar, regional hegemons, vying for new alliances, influence, and resources. Such tendencies would be most evident in the executions of smart contracts and local NGOs' insufficient knowledge of how to protect their data, making local populations and resources more vulnerable to external manipulation and potential abuse.

With the peer-to-peer features of smart contracts, which bypass national legislation, local stakeholders could be left more vulnerable than ever to the power dynamic that already exists in the donor-recipient contract. The purest idea of a smart contract is the relationship between two parties, however there is potential danger that smart contracts are created with conditions that service the needs of donors not the recipients. This is exacerbated by the recipient aid agencies' lack of understanding of this new technology and any legal or technical support. This would be further enhanced if the sector were to splinter into parallel systems, each with their independent protocols, and answerable to nobody.

The involuntary sharing of private data is another such threat. While the consensus component in blockchain can determine whether the blockchain is public or private, privacy settings in blockchain are still not 100% fool-proof, and social, legal and regulatory frameworks, including applicable privacy norms, are developing at a relatively slower pace than the technology. A recent project by Microsoft, Blockstack Labs and ConsenSys is working on an 'open source, self-sovereign, blockchain-based identity system'[5]. This enables a decentralized personal data-management system that individuals own and control themselves. BitNation and OneName are also working in this space. While such privacy and data ownership apps are being developed, it is still in the early stages, and local NGOs should be aware of their options on how to be responsible for the data they are sharing with 'partners', especially data concerning vulnerable populations.

Strategy for Adoption

By highlighting the opportunities and potential risks of blockchain, the formal humanitarian sector, in its adoption, should strive to create a system that is more inclusive and collaborative, cost-efficient and effective in achieving its aims. This should be alongside the development of an international aid protocol that aims to protect the data of those that are most vulnerable. This might be achieved by establishing an agency foundation that assists local NGOs to better understand the possibilities of using smart contracts. This could also be achieved by developing necessary social, legal and regulatory frameworks for blockchain adoption within the sector and, in particular, in regard to privacy norms. This could be further enhanced through the promotion of working examples that seek to improve data protection, and which could act as a blueprint to other NGOs. Further dissemination of materials that highlight the opportunities and risks of blockchain adoption to all stakeholders would also be needed.

It must be noted that, in this early stage, the major blockchain innovations in the charity sector are currently being led by those at the top. While there will increasingly be a trickle-down of such technologies, the responsibility also lies with smaller NGOs, who need to sufficiently prepare themselves. It is the responsibility of local NGOs to monitor developments and stay on top of changes if they are to seriously consider adoption. They also need to take into account the threat that delayed adoption might entail.

Practitioners will need to determine whether blockchain technology is the right tool to apply to particular topic areas, or whether other tools may be more appropriate. From the above SWOT analysis, we can see that blockchains are most valuable when they are used to track ownership and supply chains, when there are multiple groups or actors involved, when groups or actors involved need to work collaboratively, and when a record or proof of transactions is desired. Perhaps more crucially is the importance of discussing how blockchain might be implemented with relevant stakeholders; trustees, senior executives, trusted advisers, major donors and beneficiaries. Implementing blockchain will take time, so keeping up to date with innovations would be needed. Investment in internal expertise might also be a consideration.

Conclusion

In conclusion, while blockchain technology is clearly no panacea to all the sector's ills, its adoption could well be a silver bullet to survival. Rather than the technology displacing the formal humanitarian sector, as an intermediary of a bygone era, blockchain could have a revolutionary impact on the way the sector handles information and data, as well as the distribution of funds. If adopted in a correct and discerning way, it could transform the financial and administrative architecture of the sector to become a more decentralized, diverse and efficient system that allows it to bridge the gaps where it currently falls short. Such adoption could be the first steps towards challenging and shifting the sector's more fundamental assumptions, the power dynamics and incentives that underpin its current operations and culture, and which have contributed to its recent fracturing. Survival could see the formal humanitarian sector play an increasingly, pivotal role in assisting the emergence of a new, global geopolitical landscape, as well as better assisting those who are most in need.

Endnotes

1. Christina Bennett, Matthew Foley and Sara Pantuliano, Time to Let Go, (ODI 2016).
2. Michel Gabaudan, "From Emergency Aid to Development Aid", The Guardian, 2012.
3. How Cash Transfers Can Transform Humanitarian Aid (ODI, 2015).
4. Asheem Singh, Nothing to Lose, (Charity Futures, 2018).
5. Josh Borenstein, "Microsoft, Consensys & The Blockchain Tackle Human Rights 2", Ethnews.com, 2016.

PART II

NEGOTIUM

Business Matters

5. Tax Me or Tax Me Not?

Ramona Azzopardi, Rachel Vella Baldacchino

The development of an appropriate and proportionate framework in Malta that comprehensively considers the fiscal consequences of cryptoassets across direct and indirect tax, as well as duty on documents, is proving immensely beneficial to an evolving industry.

Dr Ramona Azzopardi heads the Tax and Private Client Department of WH Partners. She is also Council Member at the Malta Institute of Taxation.

Dr Rachel Vella Baldacchino is an associate at WH Partners practising in the firm's M&A and corporate finance teams.

At a time when some early adopters of cryptocurrencies are looking to potentially cash in on returns and gains made from long-forgotten forays into Bitcoin, and while an increasing number of clients are considering investing in cryptocurrency businesses, tax practitioners, advisors and regulators have long been grappling with how traditional tax laws can treat cryptoassets at different stages of the token lifecycle from the point of initial offering or token generation, through to transactions and disposals. The publication by Malta's Commissioner for Revenue (CfR) in November 2018 of guidelines for crypto businesses and investors outlining how their activities and investments in cryptoassets will be treated was therefore a most welcome set of rules, bringing clarity to an industry that had grown accustomed to years of speculation and wary investigation. These documents include guidelines for the purpose of the duty on Documents and Transfers Act, on the VAT treatment of transactions or arrangements involving DLT assets, and on the income tax treatment of transactions or arrangements involving DLT assets. Alongside the bespoke financial regulatory framework for VFAs, the development of an appropriate and proportionate framework in Malta that comprehensively considers the fiscal consequences of cryptoassets across direct and indirect tax, as well as duty on documents, is proving immensely beneficial to an evolving industry, which for a long time was beset with problems arising from commonly held misconceptions and misunderstandings around the nature and function of this new asset class it had developed. As a primer, this chapter will begin by defining the key jargon that appear frequently in media surrounding blockchain and cryptoassets.

The Technology

Blockchain technologies are perhaps most famed for underpinning the digital currency Bitcoin. Cryptocurrencies of this kind are almost certainly one of the greatest blockchain technology applications, and have undoubtedly paved the way for the next evolution of money and value creation. With the financial system rapidly moving towards digitalization, the idea of a paperless economy is coming closer to reality. Blockchain technologies have however developed exponentially because they have been successfully implemented in contexts far wider than cryptocurrencies, including for example in smart contracts, intellectual property, commodities, trading exchanges, and company registries.

At its core, blockchain is a technology underpinning information-storing databases. Since there is no limit to the types of information that can be stored in any single database, blockchain technology can be applied to transform operations and service delivery in virtually any industry in which information is stored digitally. Principally, blockchain is an application of DLT. In the context of cryptoassets (or 'DLT assets', where these are recorded on a DLT), the 'distributed' nature of a DLT means that there is no one single central database, and every node within the network possesses the same authoritative cryptographic keys that power a consensus mechanism, which is used to ensure that all copies of the database are identical. As expected, the CfR guidelines adopted a 'substance over form' conclusion, and that ultimately, the tax treatment of a cryptoasset would not necessarily be determined by its prima facie categorization, but by the very purpose and context in which it is used. For this reason, an understanding of the technological mechanics underpinning a business's cryptoasset (and the DLT over which it is issued and stored) will be critical, as it can greatly influence the tax treatment of the asset and the transactions within it.

What is an ICO?

Initial coin offerings (ICOs) are perhaps the innovation that garnered greatest media attention in late 2017 and in the first half of 2018. ICOs allow businesses to raise capital through the use of fiat or cryptocurrencies in exchange for the issue of units of cryptocurrency or another form of asset, that is recorded on a DLT and verified by all participants in the ICO. Because of their capital-raising nature, ICOs have tended from time to time to be compared with crowdfunding activities and initial public offerings (IPOs).

Classifications of cryptoassets issued following an ICO are abundant. Most commonly, ICO-generated cryptoassets can be classified as digital currency tokens (such as Bitcoin), fuel tokens (such as ether, which is a necessary element to operate a distributed operation), or other tokens carrying utility and/or other rights to an underlying asset or platform, which at times can be broadly compared to rights resulting from shares. Each type of cryptoasset carries distinctive tax implications.

Classifying Cryptoassets

Digital currency tokens, also known as cryptocurrencies or coins, are based on a Distributed Ledger Technology that facilitates peer-to-peer transactions. Digital currency tokens include Bitcoin, Ethereum and Litecoin, and are designed to be used as a means of payment or mechanism for exchange. These types of assets do not have the features of securities, nor a connection with any project or equity in the issuer as they functionally constitute the cryptographic equivalent of fiat currencies.

Fuel or utility tokens on the other hand, give the holders the ability to use the DLT platform and access the services and goods to be provided by the DLT platform. The tokens are normally issued through an ICO ahead of a project launch, but token-generating events held at other times, and in different forms, such as coinswaps, are far from unheard of. Utility tokens usually do not have any connection with equity of the issuer, and do not have any of the features attributed to securities.

Equity or security tokens exhibit characteristics akin to equities, such as shares and bonds, units in collective investment schemes or derivatives. They may entitle holders to a dividend, similarly to equities or to interest payments, payments from units in collective investment schemes or performance-linked derivatives. These types of tokens can also grant incentives based on the performance, voting rights, or partial ownership of a project, or a combination of all the aforementioned.

These classifications are useful tools to frame a discussion on taxation of cryptoassets. Given the current state of unharmonized global regulation around cryptoassets and the bespoke nature of tax treatments of cryptoassets, regulators have adopted varying classifications of cryptoassets. In Malta, the CfR identified the following types of cryptoassets in its guidelines:

1. Coins and digital currency cryptoassets
2. Tokens

Cryptoassets may however include features pertaining to more than one of the categories mentioned. In an industry famed for its innovation and fast-paced development, it comes as no surprise that new cryptoassets may challenge labels and carry overlapping features. Keen to instil certainty in its regulatory framework, the Maltese tax authority recognized that some cryptoassets may be deemed 'hybrid' assets, and their tax treatment will depend, ultimately, on the exact purpose for and the context in which it is used, which may well vary from one case to another.

Malta: Tax Treatment of Cryptoassets

The CfR's guidelines on the income tax treatment of innovative technology and transactions of cryptoassets confirmed that transactions involving such assets are to be treated in the same way as any traditional transaction, and therefore be subject to the same income tax rules. A determination of a cryptoasset transaction's implications must therefore take into account the nature of a transaction party's activities, their status, and the specific facts and circumstances of the transaction.

Digital currency cryptoassets

Broadly, the Maltese tax authorities considered that cryptoassets can function as an efficient means of payment similar to any other payment. Where payments are made or received in a digital currency cryptoasset, Maltese tax authorities will treat these in the same manner as other payments made or received in fiat currency. Accordingly, when payment is made in a cryptocurrency, there is no distinction on when revenue is recognized or the way in which taxable profits are calculated when compared to fiat currency. Similarly, when receiving cryptocurrency as remuneration, including as salaries and wages, no tax should be charged on such remuneration. On the other hand, when a payment is made through a transfer of a financial token or utility token, such payment is treated as any other payment in kind.

The CfR's VAT guidelines similarly also consider transactions involving such cryptoassets as subject to VAT rules, in the same manner as any other transaction. In practice, this means that determining the VAT treatment of such assets will require reference to the EU VAT Directive. In line with the EU VAT Directive, place of supply rules must be taken into account as a general rule for supplies of services between businesses, and VAT rates applicable to a transaction depend on where a customer is located, and whether a supply is a B2B or a B2C supply. From a VAT perspective, given the generality and wide provisions of the VAT Directive, the VAT treatment of cryptoassets created debates and inconsistencies among member states in the EU: for a number of years until the ruling, in some places, Bitcoin was subject to VAT, in others it was exempt. In 2015, the CJEU ruling in Skatteverket vs David Hedqvist[1] provided guidance to EU member states on the application of the 'currency' exemption to the services of a Bitcoin exchange. It ruled that the exchange of Bitcoin for a currency that is legal tender also fell within the exemption in article 135(1)(e) of the VAT Directive (which exempts transactions 'concerning currency, bank notes and coins used as legal tender' from VAT), and that instruments whose purpose is none other than to serve as means of payment, should be treated as fiat/traditional currency used as a legal tender.

Financial Tokens

The CfR also considered the tax implications of cryptoassets that function as financial tokens. It identified that returns derived by holders of financial tokens will be considered as equivalent to payments as dividends, interest or premia, and accordingly treated as income. It also considered the tax treatment on transfers of financial tokens carried out as a trading transaction, which will be deemed as a receipt on the revenue account, resulting in the transfers made in the ordinary course of business. Accordingly, such transactions fall within the ambit of the ordinary income tax rules, and hence the profits from the sale of the tokens acquired with the intention of making profit once resold, are treated as trading profit.

If the transfer of financial tokens, however, cannot be classified as a trading transaction, an analysis as to whether it falls within the ambit of the provision dealing with capital gains has to be made. If the tokens meet the definition of 'securities' under Article 5 of the Income Tax Act, they would be treated as such for income tax purposes. Where, on the other hand, the cryptoasset being transferred does carry security-like rights, then such financial tokens might be classified as utility tokens, and would fall outside the scope of income tax on capital gains. Similarly, convertible or hybrid tokens, will likely fall outside the scope of income tax until the moment of conversion into securities.

In order to determine the VAT implications in transactions involving financial tokens, a critical analysis should firstly be made to assess whether such instrument actually falls within the scope of VAT and if so, whether it qualifies for any of the exemptions contemplated in the VAT Directive. In the event that a financial instrument is issued for the sole purpose of raising funds, such issue does not give rise to any VAT implications in the hands of the issuer. Capital raising activities are not in themselves a supply of goods or services for a consideration, and thus fall outside the scope of VAT.

Utility Tokens

The CfR notes that utility tokens are considered akin to vouchers for VAT purposes when they are issued against a consideration for the supply of goods or services and where the identity of the supplier issuing such tokens is identified. In this case, the provisions applicable to vouchers under the EU Directive dealing with the treatment of vouchers for VAT purposes likewise apply to utility tokens.

Where the underlying goods or services which the utility token represents is known, along with the place of supply and the VAT due at the time of the issue, the consideration payable for that token signifies a payment for the supply of the underlying good or service. This would establish a tax point for VAT purposes, and akin to single purpose voucher, the consideration payable for the issuance and transfer of the token is immediately subject to VAT.

On the other hand, if the place of supply and the VAT due on the underlying goods and services that the utility token represents are not known at the time of the issue of the token, akin to a multi-purpose voucher, VAT, if any, would be due at the moment of redemption of the utility token.

Maltese Tax Treatment of ICOs

Before publication of the CfR's guidelines, ICO tax treatment was uncertain. It remains so in most of the rest of the world. The CfR guidelines, acknowledged that ICOs and token generation events may concern the distribution of an asset carrying varying characteristics, in the same way as has been assessed earlier in this chapter. It noted that from a tax perspective, when an issuer initiates an ICO or a token-generated event of financial tokens, generally, a one-time capital contribution is made into the company, and thus, the proceeds arising from such issue will not be deemed as income of the issuer and thus not subject to tax in Malta.

However, where an issuer is offering utility tokens, the terms of the agreement entered into with ICO investors typically include an issuer undertaking to offer a future service or supply of goods or benefits to the token holder. To this effect, profits arising from the provision of such services or supply of goods would represent a taxable trading income, less the standard allowable expenses. The tax will however be due when the profits are realised at the level of the ICO.

The VAT guidelines, on the other hand, consider that when investors place funds at the ICO stage in exchange for cryptoassets issued for the sole purpose of raising capital for the development of a future project, 'such initial offering may not necessarily constitute a chargeable event for VAT purposes'. The reasoning adopted by the Commissioner in its guidelines for this is that at that point in time, it is likely that the future goods or services to be supplied, as well as the corresponding consideration, and the supply to the investors, cannot be identified. To this effect, the transaction would fall outside the scope of VAT, including where the money placed by the investors would serve the purpose of acquiring a security cryptoasset in the issuer.

Conversely, where the cryptoassets grant investors with rights to an established good or service, for a fixed consideration, the CfR will consider that a chargeable event subsists, and the VAT treatment of such a transaction is to be analyzed in the framework applicable to digital assets used in the transaction.

Digital Wallets

Although digital wallets used in conjunction with cryptoassets must also be considered in this discussion, they raise entirely separate issues. This is because digital wallets, or e-wallets, do not themselves hold or store cryptoassets, since cryptoassets exist only on the blockchain ledger. A digital wallet is a software service offered to cryptocurrency users to hold the private keys that allow the holder to spend the asset. This service is offered in exchange for a fee, and has therefore been considered an economic activity for VAT purposes by the CfR.

The VAT treatment of digital wallet services is thus connected to whether the wallet is considered as holding a private key used to access a cryptoasset, or whether, in a particular context, it holds the currency itself. Where a direct link exists between the consideration paid for a service and the service itself, this digital wallet service could constitute a chargeable event for VAT purposes. On the other hand, where the digital wallet service holds the virtual currency, and thus directly concerns the means of payment used to access a service, then the digital wallet service is classified as exempt without credit supply. Arguably, any uncertainty over the indirect tax treatment of digital wallet services may be less worrisome for the time being, since the vast majority of digital wallet services are provided at no charge to the user.

Mining

The CfR's VAT guidelines also considered that mining activities will generally fall outside the scope of VAT, as no direct link is established between the compensation received by the miners and the service rendered. This is because the miners receive no transaction fee in return for verification of newly minted coins. Additionally, no reciprocal performance exists between the two parties.

If, however, miners are to receive a specific transaction fee for a specific customer for other services such as the provision of services in relation to the verification of the transactions, a chargeable event for VAT purposes would be triggered, chargeable at the standard 18% rate.

Cryptoasset Exchange Platforms

The CfR's VAT guidelines also acknowledge the role played by cryptoasset exchange platforms, which facilitate peer-to-peer trading or exchanges of cryptoassets, in return for the payment of a transaction fee or commission. It viewed such services as constituting a supply of services for consideration. The VAT treatment of the trading of platform services will depend highly on the nature of the service provided, and thus it is generally to be determined on a case-by-case basis.

In cases where the services of the platform constitute a provision of an electronic facility that merely brings together buyers and sellers of cryptoassets, the supplier is considered to be providing an electronically supplied service and therefore, if provided B2C, the VAT treatment applicable to electronically supplied services would apply. The supplier would therefore have to consider the VAT treatment where the customers are located. However, where the traded DLT assets are akin to currencies or securities for VAT purposes, and if the services provided by the platform go beyond the sole provision of a trading platform, such services may potentially be exempt from VAT. This is because if the transactions concern currencies that function similar to legal tender, securities or intermediation or negotiation in relation to transactions of currency or securities, these are exempt from under the respective VAT Directive provisions.

Tax Treatment of Cryptoassets in Selected Jurisdictions

Transactions and businesses involving cryptoassets and DLTs raise interesting concerns for tax authorities. Given the piecemeal state of global regulation at the present time, it is prudent to maintain a watchful eye over positions taken by tax authorities in key jurisdictions worldwide.

Portugal

The Portuguese Tax Authority (PTA) issued a binding tax ruling in 2018 on the tax treatment of cryptocurrencies, tokens and ICOs. The request for tax ruling resulted from a particular ICO and token that had been built on the Ethereum distributed computing platform Ethereum. The PTA held that, in principle, transactions containing a token may be considered an onerous transfer of goods and thus be liable to VAT. It remarked however, that the treatment of the tokens depended highly on the characteristics and functionality of the same tokens. Accordingly, the transfer of tokens may be exempt from VAT under the exemption foreseen for transactions concerning legal tender if the transfer of tokens consists in an alternative form of payments. The view adopted by the PTA is in line with the Hedqvist case' referred to above, which held that Bitcoin, as a virtual currency that has no other purpose than to be a means of payment, is exempt from VAT, on the basis of its falling under the legal tender exemption.[2]

United Kingdom

HM Revenue and Customs (HMRC Brief 9) has issued cryptocurrency specific guidance, as far back as 2014. It considered that income received from mining activities will generally fall outside the scope of VAT, on the basis that the link between the activities and any consideration received (such as the mined reward) is insufficiently direct, with the result that the mining activity does not constitute an economic activity for VAT purposes. HMRC also stated that when Bitcoin is exchanged for sterling or traditional foreign currencies, no VAT is due on the value of the bitcoins themselves (or such other cryptocurrency). In all other instances, however, VAT is due in the normal way from suppliers of any goods or services sold in exchange for Bitcoin or other similar cryptocurrency. The value of the supply of goods or services on which VAT is due will be the sterling value of the crypto at the point when the transaction takes place.

New guidance published by HMRC on the tax treatment of cryptoassets (including cryptocurrencies) held by individuals in December 2018 set out in greater detail the HMRC's views on how activities relating to cryptoassets will be taxed. In its guidance, HMRC set out the expected view that it will not consider cryptocurrencies to be money or currency, but that it will view them as assets that are capable of being invested or traded. This means that they will be taxed in a manner similar to activities involving securities and investments, and will thus be subject to capital gains tax. Also, similarly to shares, the HMRC indicated that 'pooling' rules will also apply to gains made on cryptoasset activities. The effective essence of 'pooling' is that a 'pool' is created for each cryptocurrency held by a person, and any gains or losses are calculated within that pool on the basis that any disposal is a disposal of part of that 'pool'. The guidance also identifies that the activities carried out by some individuals may take place at a high frequency, and that where individuals are trading cryptoassets 'with such frequency, level of organisation and sophistication that the activity amounts to a financial trade in itself', their tax treatment may differ, becoming subject to income tax, where cumulative rates may rise to 45%. Further guidance from the HMRC is expected in early 2019 on the tax treatment of cryptoassets held by companies.

The United States

Regulatory guidelines published by the IRS (2014-21) have set out that virtual currency is to be considered as property. This means that virtual currency transactions must be reported on income tax returns and must be considered in the same manner as other property transactions. US general tax rules hold that the sale of property held as investment and as inventory yields capital gain or loss in the hands of the taxpayer and therefore, by investing in cryptocurrencies, investors envisage a capital gain or loss upon the subsequent exchange of the virtual currency. Consequences for non-compliance with IRS property reporting rules could be significant, and taxpayers who do not report income from virtual currency transactions can be audited and potentially liable for penalties and interest, including monetary fines of up to $250,000 or prison convictions for terms of up to three to five years.

Following the US SEC's public position on the potential classification of tokens acquired during an ICO's being treated as securities and subject to traditional securities regulation, such a classification could potentially elicit significant consequences for investors, given that the US Tax Code contains a number of regulations that deal with the sale of securities. As in many other jurisdictions however, the tax treatment of cryptoassets issued by an entity that is subject to US tax substantially depends on the characteristics and functionality of the asset. They can be deemed akin to vouchers of sorts, with the intent to be redeemed for a future supply of goods or services. However, it is also possible that like cryptocurrencies, the ICO tokens are put at par with traditional currencies.

Conclusion

Cryptoassets and the pertinent global regulatory framework are still in their infancy. Meanwhile, cryptoasset innovations have great potential to support interesting business and funding models. As recent months have shown, the publication of guidelines that assist the determination of the tax treatment of these innovations across all forms of applicable taxation in Malta will assist businesses to accurately forecast for their fiscal responsibilities and reduce the likelihood of perplexities that might arise. Finally, the key action point observed in Malta's tax guidelines is that cryptoassets' characteristics and functionality will always be considered on a case-by-case basis, rendering a careful consideration of the mechanics behind the cryptoasset to better understand its tax implications.

Endnotes

1. Skatteverket vs David Hedqvist, Case C-264/14, 2015, CJEU.
2. Rogério Ferreira, "Portuguese Tax Authority Issues Ruling on ICO and VAT", Cointelegraph, 2018.

6. Blocknomics

Jean Paul Fabri, Stephanie Fabri

Blockchain offers a new economic organizational model that possesses the Hayekian co-ordination properties of a market, the governance properties of a commons, and also the constitutional properties of a nation-state.

An economist by profession, Jean Paul Fabri leads the Digital Economy Unit at ARQ. As well as the previous Maltese PM and Central Bank Governor, he has advised 9 governments on economic development.

Dr Stephanie Fabri, has been a full-time academic at the University of Malta since 2010.

Introduction

The revolutionary technology Nakamoto presented allowed for the creation of a decentralized and distributed public ledger. Whereas the debate on the technology, especially from an economic perspective, has been on Bitcoin, and on whether it can be considered as money, not enough focus was given to the economics of the technology itself. Whereas, like any other new technology, economics can allow us to study its disruptive potential and look at the effects of its adoption and diffusion, we believe that this approach alone does not do any justice to the technology itself. The authors believe and suggest that, through the interpretation of the blockchain from a new institutional and political economy approach to the economics of the blockchain, this new technology is not only a general-purpose technology but also an institutional one. The authors believe that blockchain offers a new economic organizational model that possesses the Hayekian co-ordination properties of a market, the governance properties of a commons[1], and also the constitutional properties of a nation-state[2].

The Blockchain: A (R)evolutionary Technology

In the aftermath of the global financial crisis in 2008, Satoshi Nakamoto published the Bitcoin whitepaper that ushered in not only Bitcoin but more importantly blockchain technology. In fact, it must be remembered that blockchain is the technology underpinning Bitcoin, and whereas most attention has been devoted to Bitcoin, it is the study of blockchain, and its impact and effect that are the most intriguing. Buterin[3] argues that the worth and significance of blockchain does in fact not depend upon the value and prospect of Bitcoin. Bitcoin is merely one application of the blockchain.

A blockchain can be best defined as a public decentralized ledger platform. Ledgers record transactions, but they go way beyond the profession of accounting with which they are normally associated. Ledgers are everywhere, and in fact one can safely say that ledgers, in their different forms, record the facts underpinning the modern economy. The importance of ledgers can be distilled into a number of facts:

- Ledgers confirm ownership – when a transaction is recorded in a ledger, it also records the owner of the asset. Therefore, property registers are also ledgers, as are inventory lists.
- Ledgers confirm identity – the government register records details of its citizens and enshrines their legal identity. The companies' register records the identity of enterprises.
- Ledgers confirm status – numerous government ledgers confirm status such as the marriage register. Also, the electoral register gives details on voting eligibility.
- Ledgers confirm authority – registers are used to identify rights attached to particular people or actions.

Even from the above four qualities, it is obvious that ledgers are everywhere and everything behind today's societies. They can actually be seen as maps of economic and social relationships and interactions. Although ledgers are predominantly a technology used for accounting, they are instrumental to modern capitalism.

From the time they were first used in Mesopotamia, the function of ledgers remained unchanged until Fra Luca Pacioli, an Italian mathematician and Franciscan friar, documented the double-entry book-keeping system in a book that became the reference text for accountants in Europe. The invention of the double-entry book-keeping system allowed the recording of both debits and credits, and allowed for the reconciliation of information between ledgers. This was the true revolution that Fra Pacioli set in motion, and it was able to give birth to the banking sector as we know it today.

In fact, this system helped the Medici family, primarily Lorenzo de Medici, to establish the first merchant bank, and to sow the seeds of the global banking system simply by recognizing the importance of the ledger. In essence, Lorenzo de Medici figured out how to intermediate between savers and borrowers, all for a fee. By creating a central ledger that kept track of all debts and claims, the Medici family created a powerful centralized system of trust. With the help of their specialized intermediating services, strangers that previously had no way of trusting each other to do business could now do so safely.

By the late 20th century, ledgers had been digitized, but until the blockchain was launched in 2009, they have always remained centralized. Therefore, in essence, the proliferation of centralized ledgers held by intermediaries such as banks and state authorities meant that the power of such authorities increased, and was built around a system of centralized trust. Centralized solutions are not only expensive but also prone to problems particularly relating to trust and its abuse. Yet until Nakamoto, no effective decentralized solution to the ledger has existed.

In effect, such a distributed ledger can be applied to disrupt any centralized system that co-ordinates information. There are three main approaches to studying the economics of the blockchain:

- One way is to look at the economics of blockchain to see the disruptive impact of decentralized ledgers to centralized ledger systems. This can be seen primarily from the impact of costs and efficiency, and is therefore linked more to the microeconomic approach to economics.

- A second lens from which to approach the economics of blockchain is to actually look at the economics of decentralization as akin to a market.
- Finally, the true revolution of the blockchain is that it is trustless, meaning that it does not require a third-party and central verifier. Instead, it uses a powerful consensus mechanism with crytpoeconomic incentives to verify the authenticity of a transaction in the database. This is the area of institutions and consensus mechanisms, and this therefore brings us to the third approach to the study of the economics of blockchain, that from the perspective of institutional economics. It is perhaps this perspective that is the most thought-provoking and inspiring area of blockchain economic studies.

The Economics of Innovation

The first approach to understanding the economics of blockchain is the study of the disruption and innovation itself, its process of diffusion and adoption by firms, industries and markets. At the onset, the impact of innovative solutions or technologies is seen in the light of its impact on cost structures, particularly by adopters of the technology. As discussed earlier, centralized trust is expensive to maintain. A recent paper[4] estimated that around 35% of US employment is related to activity aimed at upholding trustful economic relationships. Therefore, the economics of blockchain can be seen as how increasingly cost-effective decentralized ledgers have become compared to centralized solutions. In particular, blockchain is seen becoming more cost-effective due to the interplay between three related digital laws, these being Moore's

Law that looks at the reduction in the cost of processing information, Kryder's Law that looks at the cost-reduction in storing digital information, and Nielsen's Law that focuses on the reduction in cost of bandwidth[5].

Therefore, one way of viewing blockchain from an economic viewpoint is that the interplay of these forces will mean that there is a general reduction in the so-called technology cost curve making decentralized ledgers more competitive when compared to centralized ledgers. This implies that the substitution of centralized with decentralized ledgers will happen. In the case of blockchain, we will see that it will adopt an evolutionary process of market and industrial dynamics. The evolutionary process will unfold just as the technology becomes more widespread and more applications that sit on it are developed and used.

The Economic of Decentralization

Economic theory and thought have focused very much on the concept of decentralization that is at best represented by the market. The qualities and benefits of the free market, which in essence is open and decentralized, were mostly expanded upon by Adam Smith who spoke about the benefits of dynamic efficiency. Hayek[6] continued to build on these arguments in his seminal work on the informational and communication efficiency of the price system and the institutions of a market order.

Over the past, we have seen systems starting out as centralized but then moving towards decentralization. Systems usually begin with centralization because it is more efficient to create, establish and enforce rules. However, those very features lead to the high costs of centralization, which are not only administrative costs, but also other negative externalities such as rent-seeking and corruption. Therefore, there has been a process of moving away from centralization to decentralization as the latter is able to make the system more robust, secure and efficient.

Although blockchains have been described in various ways, each time highlighting particular applications, they are in essence technologies of decentralization. This therefore makes them not only akin to a market structure but now also puts them at the centre of economic thought. If economics were to be defined as the study of markets, then economics can be seen as playing a central role in studying blockchains. In economics, markets are also seen as rule systems that can be designed, such as auctions, or spontaneous orders.

This decentralized property of blockchain places the technology itself as a new form of market institution, and the various application technologies that are emerging are testament to this. However, the blockchain can be seen as even more than a market. The first application of the blockchain was Bitcoin, that opened the road to the token revolution and the whole academic debate on digital money and the token economy. Therefore, the blockchain can be also seen as an economy or a catallaxy[7].

The Economics of Institutions

Buterin defines blockchains as a technology for 'building economic and social institutions' that enable co-ordination between different agents, including firms, markets and governments. Therefore, more generally put, blockchains are a new type of rule-system for economic co-ordination and can also be defined as constitutional orders. Viewing blockchains from this lens allows us to study the technology from the new institutional economics or public choice schools of thought of economics, and this will allow us to see how truly revolutionary blockchain technology really is.

As a basic introduction, the new institutional economics is focused on studying the actual transaction following an economic choice whereas neoclassical economics studies the actual choice. The seminal works of R. H. Coase focus on transaction costs and the role of institutions in bringing efficiency to markets. As a result of this work, economics started to look at the role of contracts in markets and economies, and the way interactions are actually a nexus of contracts.

In a utopic sense, we would talk about complete contracts. However, Williamson[8] said that since economies and economic agents were always dealing with uncertainty and bounded rationality, defined as not having complete information and perfect computational ability to process all the information, economic agents were faced with incomplete contracts. Such incomplete contracts will usually result in transaction costs arising from the contingencies for uncertainty, the cost of writing the contract and the cost of enforcing the contract. In addition, the possibility of opportunism, for example reneging on a contract, requires efficient governance structures. The concept of opportunism also brings back to the fore the element of trust since the cause of opportunism is the intent and ability of agents to exploit that trust.

As the authors have pointed out earlier, the essential nature of blockchain is that it is trustless. Even more so, blockchain is also revolutionary in the space of contracts and contractual relationships. Blockchain technology gave birth to the smart contract, a self-executing contract from which decentralized applications can be created. These include the Decentralized Autonomous Organisations (DAOs). Therefore, blockchains are a mechanism to control opportunism by eliminating the need for trust by using cryo-enforced execution of agreed contracts through consensus mechanisms, protocols and transparency. This greatly reduces, if not eliminates opportunism through DAOs. As a result, blockchains can usher a new era of organizations that are DAOs, and that inherently eliminate the possibility of opportunism.

Through the concept of transaction costs and the theory of the firm seen as a nexus of incomplete contracts, we have seen that the blockchain allows the emergence of firms and organizations that operate in a world of complete contracts. This is the true revolution, and in fact the question of interest no longer remains of how firms will adopt blockchain, but rather how blockchains will compete with firms and markets as we know them today. Through the Coase/Williamson perspective, we can now see and evaluate blockchains as alternative governance institutions and we can define blockchain as a new institutional technology.

The Blockchain Catallaxy

Through new institutional economics we have redefined blockchains as alternative governance institutions. However, we can start seeing whether the blockchain has the ability to also cater for other key building blocks that determine economic structures, and these include the following:

- Constitutions.
- Collective decision-making rules and procedures.
- Private money.[9]

From the above characteristics, blockchains can be perceived as a technology for making economies, specifically decentralized economies. Hayek also distinguished between an economy and a catallaxy, and this distinction has become very useful when studying blockchains from this perspective.

Hayek[10] defined an economy as 'an organization or arrangement in which someone conspicuously uses means in the service of a uniform hierarchy of ends.' On the other hand, Hayek defined a catallaxy as 'a special kind of spontaneous order produced by the market by people acting within the rules of the law of property, tort and contract'[11].

Hayek further characterized a catallaxy by a multitude of agents that are social and governed by social rules, have specialized and distributed knowledge, form their own plans, and are mutually co-ordinated through the market or price system. Given that we described blockchains as an alternative to market or price systems, then it is argued that blockchains are best described as catallaxies from the Hayekian perspective.

This perspective allows us to analyze blockchain even more specifically from the lens of political economy. Political economy is a broad branch of economics, however this introduction will be focusing on key areas such as collective choice, the role of reputation, managing the commons, rent-seeking and constitutions.

Collective Choice

One of the fundamental problems of political economy is the design of collective decision-making mechanisms. Democracy has problems that can only be solved through better institutions. Blockchains are a cryptographic consensus mechanism and an institution that can be scaled and that enhances trust. Therefore, it is believed that it can potentially enable collective choices and enhance the efficient use of democracy.

Reputation

We have seen that a blockchain can automate and execute smart contracts. However, the problem of contractual enforcement remains, especially when these voluntary contracts may not be sanctioned by a centralized government. However, public choice economics developed a focus on spontaneous private ordering rules emerging under conditions of anarchy or an underground economy.

Game theoretical approaches have shown that while agents may be in conflict within a contract, they still have a common interest in preserving the blockchain system, or their reputations within it, because of the value of future action. As a public ledger, the blockchain confirms the importance of reputation in economic systems.

Managing the Commons

A 'commons,' or more precisely, common-pool resource as Ostrom refers to it, is a resource environment or domain that is characterized by an open access problem: it is difficult to effectively bar other users from accessing and benefitting from that resource. Hardin described the 'tragedy of the commons'[12], in which humans overuse and deplete a common-pool resource even though it is not in their best interest to do so. This trend of overexploitation particularly plagues commons because the lack of individual ownership and inability to restrict usage incentivizes actors to consume as much as possible of the shared resource before others do. Hardin did not believe that a self-organized and self-governed system was attainable. He argued that the only ways to avoid the tragedy of the commons was through establishing private property or under the authority of a Leviathan-type centralized power. However, several authors pioneered by Ostrom, debunked the inevitability of Hardinian tragedy through the concept of polycentric governance. Ostrom identified eight design rules that characterized successful commons governance. blockchain is a trustless commons in which effective rules are embedded in constitutional smart contracts that are cryptographically secure and crypto-economically implemented and the authors believe that this can be a new institutional technology that facilitates polycentric governance.

Rent-Seeking

A central tenant of political economy is that, centralization of trust can lead to the abuse of such trust in exchange for rent-seeking, or corruption. To this end, decentralization can be a solution whereby trust is secured cryptographically. Therefore, blockchain technology can also reduce the risk of rent-seeking activities. However, this benefit can also prove to be a challenge for the adoption of blockchain technology. Centralized ledger institutions such as governments have rents to protect in the continuity of a monopoly over governance, and thus competitive threats from crypto-governance can be expected to be resisted in proportion to the rents at risk.

Constitutions

Political economy is typically concerned with the interface and mutual influences between the economic and political arrangements of a given society, whereas constitution commonly refers to juridical-legal norms, rules and regulations that govern the people within a given territory. In contemporary literature, the relationship between the two is generally addressed by interpreting a constitutional settlement in terms of its allocative efficiency and by constructing a political-economic system in terms of the formal rules and procedures that make its working feasible. Buchanan defines constitutional economics as the study of choice among constraints in which co-operative economic agents seek to 'live by the rules that they can also choose'. In this sense, agents make constitutional choice exchange when they mutually agree to conduct transactions on a blockchain. In addition, protocol design on the blockchain is tantamount to constitutional design.

Conclusion

The revolutionary aspect of blockchain is not Bitcoin, but the way the technology revolutionized the concept of the ledger by making it decentralized upon which any information requiring validation can be placed and exchanged. One way of looking at the economics of blockchain is from a Schumpeterian create destruction general technology perspective that will undergo phases of adoption and diffusion throughout the economy. Although this is true, the authors believe that this limits the true nature of the blockchain. Through the lens of institutional economics, the blockchain can be defined as an institutional technology that offers an alternative governance system that can compete with firms, markets and economies. It is for this reason that blockchain should not be seen solely as a technology but even more so as an economic system in its own right, or as a Hayekian catallaxy. This is the true revolution of the blockchain – the birth of a new institutional era.

Endnotes

1. Elinor Ostrom, Governing the Commons (CUP, 1990).
2. James M. Buchanan, "The Domain of Constitutional Economics", Constitutional Political Economy, 1.1 (1990), pp. 1-8.
3. Vitalik Buterin, "Visions, Part 1: The Value of Blockchain Technology", Blog.ethereum.org, 2015.
4. Sinclair Davidson, Mikayla Novak and Jason Potts, "The Cost of Trust", 2018.
5. Niki Wiles, The Radical Potential of Blockchain Technology, 2015 YouTube.com
6. F. A. Hayek, "The Use of Knowledge in Society", The American Economic Review, XXXV.4 (1945), pp. 519-30.
7. F. A. Hayek, The Constitution of Liberty (Chicago UP, 1960).
8. O. E. Williamson, The Economic Institutions of Capitalism (Free Press, 1985).
9. F. A. Hayek, The Nationalization of Money (IEA, 1978).
10. F. A Hayek, Individualism and Economic Order (Chicago UP, 1948).
11. F. A Hayek and William Warren Bartley, The Fatal Conceit (Routledge, 1988).
12. Garrett Hardin, "The Tragedy of the Commons", Science, 162.3859 (1968), pp.1243-1248.

7. From Silk Roads to Permanent Nodes

Patrick L. Young

The physical, having given way to the virtual, stands at the epicentre of the Blockchain Island concept as a half millennium of corporate practice discovered in Valletta serves as a background to our improved future networked reality.

Patrick L. Young, wrote the first bestselling fintech book Capital Market Revolution! (FT Prentice Hall) in 1999 that explored the future of electronic money – today's cryptocurrency. Patrick chairs the Blockchain Malta Association.

"We want a whole sequence of companies: digital title, digital media assets, digital stocks and bonds, digital crowdfunding, digital insurance. if you have online trust like the blockchain provides, you can reinvent field after field after field."

– Marc Andreessen

In the centre of Valletta, the heart of the Maltese archipelago, the capital city is a magnificent tribute to the process of Renaissance town-planning. Conceived after the remarkable victory against the Turks during the Great Siege of 1565, Valletta gained its name from Jean Parisot de Valette, the Grand Master of the Order of St John, the Knights Hospitaller. It was his strategic acumen that confused and thwarted the Turkish invasion despite the vast numerical advantage that the invading Ottomans had over the defending Knights of St John. As a consequence, the capital of the island was moved 10 kilometres from Mdina (perhaps nowadays best known for its many appearances in 'Game of Thrones') to the rock above Grand Harbour.

Established in the immediate aftermath of one remarkable siege, the streets of Valletta have borne witness to other conflicts. Most famously within living memory, Malta was the highly unfortunate recipient of more airborne ordnance per square metre than any other nation during the Second World War. The character of Valletta survived, although many buildings had to be rebuilt... the once magnificent opera house is nowadays an open-air theatre, having been left operative but an ostensibly derelict structure as a lasting testament to the Axis bombing.

Wander from the opera house, heading away from the remarkable 2015 Parliament House designed by Renzo Piano, along what was previously Kingsway and originally Strada San Giorgio. Around a kilometre in length, just before Republic Street descends towards the granaries outside the incredible bastions of Fort St

Elmo, is the Grandmaster's Palace – now the office of the President of Malta. Previously it was the Governor General's residence under British rule, during which time several visitors reported the presence of ghostly apparitions!

The Piazza Regina next door bustles with the patrons of local cafés, most notably the tourist hotspot, Caffe Cordina established across the Grand harbour in Bormla in 1837, and moved to its current location at the epicentre of the capital in 1944 – when war still raged across much of Europe but Malta had been relieved from its latest great siege.

The piazza is bounded by two other magnificent buildings. Above Caffe Cordina is the Casino Maltese, a historic private members' club in whose magnificent splendour this tome took shape as the editors' unofficial 'office' and contributor meeting spot. Opposite the square, behind the many piazza tables are the Doric and Ionic columns that mark a very special building indeed, a neoclassical design by the Polish-Italian architect Stefano Ittar dating from 1783. We shall return to that national landmark presently.

The Casino Maltese building is rich in history, including literary history. The author refers not to the editors of this tome, but rather serious authorial talent in the person of Samuel Taylor Coleridge, who is commemorated with a plaque on the front of the building, noting that the 'renowned English poet and writer worked here 1804-1805'. At that time the premises housed the Chief Secretary's Office and the Government Treasury. The brilliant Taylor Coleridge was Private Secretary to the then Governor of Malta, Admiral Alexander Ball.

Had more been published in Coleridge's lifetime, doubtless his works would have been ideally suited for that delightful neoclassical structure designed by Ittar that was built to house the National

Library. A magnificent standalone building, this scheduled Grade 1 national monument is an incredible treasure trove of fascinating historical works. Stepping inside the classical facade reveals a sensational sweeping marble staircase, leading to a labyrinth of shelves arranged around the elegant first floor reading room.

The origins of the National Library collection dates back to 1555, when Claude de la Sengle, the 48th Grand Master of the Order of Malta and direct predecessor of Fra' Jean Parisot de Valette, decreed that all books belonging to deceased members of the Order of St John (the Knights Hospitaller), were to be passed to the Order's treasury. Further additions to this collection included other bequests and purchases. In 1760, Louis Guérin de Tencin, the Bailiff Grand Cross of the Order, purchased for 7000 scudi a collection of 9700 books that had belonged to Grandee of Spain Cardinal Joaquín Fernández de Portocarrero who had died in Rome. One year later de Tencin opened a public library in the building known as the Forfantone (located on the corner of Republic Street and St Lucy Street). However, this location proved too cramped for the collection, leading to the commission for the new building.

Ultimately the purpose-built neoclassical library marked one of the final achievements of the Knights' reign as it was completed in 1796 just before the French interregnum. The site of the new library was formerly the Conservatoria, where gold and silver bullion of the Order's treasury were stored. The Malta Public Library would eventually be officially inaugurated on 4 June 1812 by Civil Commissioner Sir Hildebrand Oakes. So extensive is the treasure trove of data, that over 2 centuries later, discoveries are still being made among the incredible back catalogue of works.

It is perhaps fitting for money to have been actually in the foundations of the national library. However, the author is getting ahead of this chapter's narrative. Rather, let us first consider a key factor in appreciating the history of Malta: the importance of the Mediterranean in history. Malta has been a trading point since Phoenician times, if not before. Meanwhile, the Knights Hospitaller themselves, as medical pioneers amongst other pioneering pursuits (including banking, trade and finance), had been based in Jerusalem, then Rhodes before reaching Malta, not through design but rather defeat... however that is truly a separate narrative entirely. Nevertheless, from the ancient time when Phoenicia, Greece and Rome had been key epicentres of learning and culture, there was a clear linkage with Malta through trade. Thus, the tiny island may never have figured as a great power but its geographical positioning was highly significant. With the fall of Byzantium, trade had increasingly migrated back to seaborne routes that placed Malta close to the shipping lanes, which in the modern more codified era sit just to the south of the Maltese archipelago. In modern digital terminology we might call Malta a node in the Mediterranean sea routes throughout mercantile history.

Thus, having been a trading point from Phoenician times, Malta sat in the upper Mediterranean quadrant of the Chinese Silk Road. As a 'Jewel of the Mediterranean' Malta had not merely a unique aesthetic but also played a significant role in trade. As the modern energy age expanded, the islands found themselves in the vital position of being a key transhipment point for energy distribution thanks to the deep continental shelf of Europe that contrasts with the shallower depth of the coastline in north Africa directly to the south of Malta. Malta therefore remains an ideal place to aggregate or break bulk as the freeport sits barely more than a handful of kilometres from the international shipping lanes to the south. In essence Malta is the equivalent of an island truck-stop for intercontinental freighters.

Similarly, sitting only 430 miles south of Rome, Malta has long been close to the classical routes of knowledge and learning. For this reason, it was not difficult to see how the National Library in Valletta became a repository of considerable accumulated learning through volumes from the many territories and city-states of Italy, as well as the kingdoms of Sicily. In traditional Imperial style, the British chose a suitably nationalistic day, the birthday of reigning King George III, to inaugurate the National Library while it was bestowed with the additional epithet of 'Cabinet of Antiquities'.

From among the treasure trove that has rested for centuries within the said Cabinet of Antiquities, it is only recently that a reflected truism of modern corporate belief has been proven arguably false. For centuries, Luca Pacioli has been assessed as the inventor of 'modern' accounting. This position now appears to have been discredited. A Franciscan friar and close collaborator with Leonard Da Vinci, Pacioli was something of a polymath poster boy from the Renaissance era. Adept at turning his hand to understanding and explaining most anything, he was a sort of one-man learning platform – a Udemy of the age if you will, gifted in learning topics around a mathematical core, and then disbursing the information to a wider audience in an attractive format. The friar delivered near encyclopaedic summaries of the knowledge accrued in particular areas with clear aplomb. Thus, amongst his other works Pacioli surmised the mathematical knowledge of the time in his 1494 book Summa de Arithmetica, Geometrica, Proportioni et Proportionalita. This tome was also significant for discussing a summary of the method of accounts used by Venetian merchants during the Italian Renaissance. This codified practice, double-entry book-keeping, represented at the time a great leap forward in the development of business accounting. Pacioli has enjoyed a good run from history as many refer to him as the 'Father of Accounting'. Yet when Pacioli's legacy has been recently subjected to historical audit, it appears the accountants mixed up their (human) figures.

For one thing, a pedigree as an excellent polyglot chronicler of diverse topics, does lead to the probable conclusion, that perhaps Pacioli was not responsible for the actual ideas behind his work. Indeed, some decades earlier, on the eastern side of the Adriatic in the magnificent walled city of Ragusa (now Dubrovnik) Benedikt Kotruljević was born in 1416. Benedetto Cotrugli, as he is known in Italian, became an accomplished Ragusan merchant, economist, scientist, and humanist. Furthermore, as a diplomat, he spent some 15 years at the Court of Naples, where he would die in the city of Aquila in 1469, when Pacioli (born circa 1447) was still a young man.

Kotruljević wrote 'Della Mercatura e del Mercante Perfetto,' a book completed in 1458, albeit the oldest version on record dates from 1475. That said it was apparently not formally published until 1573 in Venice, in a significantly revised and abridged edition. Demonstrating a rare instance when the Anglosphere was significantly in arrears of mercantile thought, the first English edition only appeared (as 'The Book of the Art of Trade') in 2017.

It is unsurprising that so many experts weighed in to assess his masterwork. For Cotrugli's manuscript is about much more than just book-keeping. Cotrugli appears to have been a somewhat reluctant merchant, called from his studies at the University of Bologna to join the family business. This may reflect the deep consideration of his book, which is in essence the first 'how-to' business manual. 'The Book of the Art of Trade' is divided into 4 separate volumes. The first is devoted to the origin, form and essence of the merchant's profession. The second looks at the merchant's religious commitment. Herein Cotrugli espouses a lot of sound CSR that would be appreciated by ethical investors today. Similar sentiments are maintained in the third volume, which is related to moral virtues and policies. Then the fourth section is devoted to the administration of the merchant's home, family and his economic affairs. Cotrugli advises merchants to be leaders who are charitable, ethical and treat people fairly. He is keen to ensure that merchants are modest and to look for the right qualities in their wife. Gender equality was not big in 1458, hence this book is all about men working and women focused on domesticity – many Western readers may squirm when it comes to his fascinatingly archaic treatises on all aspects of dowry finance. His advice to be selective in deals has a timeless quality to it, although views may nowadays differ on Cotrguli's advice to retire at 50. Alas, the merchant from Ragusa himself only lived to be 53 albeit that was a significant improvement on the 15th century life expectancy of around 35 years.

At this juncture, you may be forgiven for thinking that this was some form of treatise in the history of accounting that had, well, immutably lost its way on the topic of blockchain but bear with the author. We are assembling several nodes on the way to our own intriguing distribution of thought through mercantile history. As mentioned previously, Malta has long been on one trade route or another for millennia. As we can see, Malta was pretty close to the seats of knowledge and learning – not just in general affairs but it transpires, in financial matters as well.

For the earliest known surviving manuscript of Cotrugli's mercantile treatise is located in that spectacular masterpiece designed by Stefano Ittar, the National Library of Malta. More interesting still in the history of double-entry book-keeping, the same library collection housed another work that further unlocked the mystery of just who was originally codifying what became the quantum leap in accounting with debits to the left and credits to the right in chronological order. Cotrugli gives a brief review of required book-keeping for merchants, but it is hardly a full course. That more expansive treatment is to be found in a manuscript that lay broadly unread for a couple of centuries. Ironically it was not merely physically proximate to Cotrugli's book, this manuscript was ultimately bound to 'The Book of the Art of Trade' by an early accounting student. That treatise turns out to be the unifying text teaching codified accounting practice. At the time these approaches were becoming standard practice across Italophone territories. It is the transitional fossil of early accounting that delivers the missing link in the arc curving through Kotruljevic, Pacioli and all the way to the 'big four' of contemporary double-entry mythology.

The breakthrough in standardized double-entry book-keeping came at the start of the 15th century. Previously only two volumes were used for accounts, a memorandum book and a ledger. Thus, control could be exerted over debtors and creditors. However, there was not much interest in calculating profit or wealth. Around 1408, the introduction of the Journal created what nowadays may be breathlessly termed a paradigm shift. The journal delivered chronology to the entries therein. In other words, time and its bedfellow duration, leapt into the consciousness in a fashion where previously they had been much vaguer. Money grew perspective in a fashion akin to the Renaissance artists' understanding of dimension. Thereafter a clear accounting narrative was created, quite contrary to the rather disparate muddle of figures in different places that had prevailed, with multiple entries scattered across many pages in a ledger. The journal also led to a form of standardization of approach. Moreover, with the journal at the epicentre of the new book-keeping methodology, the whole process of accounting became much easier to teach. Teaching (as opposed to explaining) is something that neither the volumes by Pacioli or previously Cotrugli ostensibly do. Explain: yes. Actually go through the nitty-gritty of how to create your accounts, they do not. At this juncture in search of the textbook, another Ragusan merchant enters the narrative.

Marino de Raphaeli, like Cotrugli, hailed from Dubrovnik. In 1475 he accepted a commission to teach double-entry book-keeping to Zuan de Domenego, a member of the extended family of one of the twelve original noble houses of Venice. First de Raphaeli travelled to Naples to make a copy of Benedetto Cotrugli's manuscript of 'The

Book of the Art of Trade.' Then he went to the Venetian Republic where he proceeded to teach his student by dictation.

His student would ultimately receive de Raphaeli's manuscript copy of the Cotrugli book which de Domenego bound along with his own notes as dictated by de Raphaeli. The resulting number-sequenced folio became one bound volume. This volume itself reached Malta sometime before 1747, and effectively languished in sunny obscurity in the southern Mediterranean. The significance of the De Raphaeli/de Domenego folio only became transparently apparent in July 2013 when Scottish university professor Dr Alan Sangster spent three weeks in Malta examining the historical tome. As Dr Sangster notes 'De Raphaeli is very much at the beginning of this process and it is to him and his contemporaries rather than to Pacioli that we should look for the catalyst that led to the development of accounting into the form we know it today'. Ironically the origins of double-entry book-keeping were only being threaded together by Dr Sangster just one month after the author ran the first of his 'Future of Finance' conferences, 'Young Markets', incorporating discussion of cryptocurrency and Blockchain in Torun, Poland, a city blessed with an even more ancient provenance than Valletta.

Thus, thanks to Dr Sangster's research, we now know that the history of double-entry book-keeping wended its way from De Raphaeli's rigorous course, driven by the appendix to Cotrugli's 'The Book of the Art of Trade', to eventually be popularized by the polyglot precis master Pacioli.

Great inventions in the public mind tend to be more photogenic (or at least more arresting in oils) than mere shuffling of numbers. Remarkable feats of engineering or other entirely physical objects such as Isambard Kingdom Brunel's remarkable bridges, or Karl Benz's automobile, excite vast amounts of interest. By comparison, a few notebooks scribbled full of numbers – even in chronological order – don't grab the public's attention to the same degree. Yet the invention of coherent accounting in the form of double-entry book-keeping vastly changed the world and its growth trajectory. Mill owners had to wait a few centuries for the Industrial Revolution to maximize the financial innovation enabled by Italian Renaissance book-keeping. Overall, the addition of the journal to existing accounting books created a data revolution equivalent to the development of the personal computer almost 600 years later. Accounting enabled the organization of vast quantities of financial data into these journals, in a simple, legible and coherent narrative, with the calendar at its core. From these journals, companies could produce a balance sheet as well as income statements, and thus coherently assess the success and value of their business endeavours. Balance sheets provided the clarity of assets versus debts and thus changes in owners' equity. Income statements enabling the understanding of profit and loss could demonstrate changes in profits and, of course, that affected equity. Suddenly a holistic understanding of commerce was feasible. Indeed, this rapidly led to the greater adoption of fascinating early financial instruments. The bill of exchange was a genius invention that enabled merchandise to be bought overseas using a note that could be converted into specie with a local banker. These bills effectively incorporated an interest rate component embedded in the foreign exchange rate thus avoiding the prohibition of usury by the Catholic Church. In essence, financial innovation is not a new process in a blockchain age – but it certainly gained a major foothold in society thanks to the codified accounting practice of double-entry book-keeping.

Placing together a picture at this juncture, we have a disparate cast of characters: French knights and a half-Polish architect, merchants and chroniclers from Dubrovnik, Ragusa and elsewhere, who in various cases lived in multiple states including Sicily with business flowing from the Mediterranean to the Levant and beyond. However, a clear thread of the message flowing through this chapter is not merely that great thoughts were to be found within the nation as encapsulated within the wondrous collection of the National Library of Malta, but that the archipelago itself, regardless of the type of government, was at the epicentre of trade and indeed trade routes, with multiple nationalities interacting along the way.

Now, if we take a chronological great leap forward, the merchant who had slept for half a millennium might feel comfortable awakening on the eve of 2020 to discover there is still such a thing as the Silk Road. That said, said merchant would doubtless be shocked by the nature of the diesel-electric horses pulling the carriages. At the same time, the modern merchant compared with his Renaissance forebear, is faced with a holistically different reality. In this era, what Melvin Webber referred to in 1964 as 'the elastic mile' has stretched almost exponentially. People have been able to move farther and faster in an era when distance has been compressed by everything from the automobile to the jet engine. Now, the digital world spends its life packeted at almost inconceivable speeds to the human mind. Vast data networks deploy satellite and undersea cable links to transfer all forms of digital computations. Therein lies a core reason why a small island-state like Malta has been pushing the boundaries of contemporary digital legislation to deliver the Blockchain Island strategy: In a virtual world, precise location is no longer relevant. To a node on the data Silk Road of today (and no, the author is not referring to a certain dodgy dark market busted by US authorities) distance is broadly irrelevant as is precise position. What is relevant is operating as a key node on the network that matters, not merely being perfectly aligned just off the major shipping lanes (which has served Malta well to date).

By the by, that is not to deprecate the rich reasons for visiting this delightful Mediterranean paradise. (Note to humanfolk: come visit – Malta is beauty, history and great weather combined with a wonderful, friendly population). However, the key point is that the trade routes of yesterday were defined by movements on land or across the oceans. In the digital age, bytes move through the internet networks effortlessly – commercial advantage is where you can derive a sound basis of legal and accounting practices. Hence DLT Malta and Blockchain Island – building a node with robust first-mover credibility in the newly emerging crypto-world.

Reverting to those fascinating texts by Benedikt Kotruljević/ Benedetto Cotrugli and Marino De Raphaeli, it is quite remarkable to consider their longevity. The double-entry book-keeping methodology has been the driving force of mercantilism for over half a millennium with only incremental changes around the core (undistributed) ledger concept. From the time when leeches were the common or garden medicine delivered by doctor's prescription to an era of biotechnology, we have taken accounting somewhat for granted, and certainly accountancy has not progressed in the quantum leaps that can be found in most every other area of society.

Just as progressive governments cannot afford to take technological innovation for granted, so too it is probably time to challenge the precepts of some now rather aged tools that have served us well. In DLT we trust? That is a theme recurring through this Blockchain Malta Association assembly of thinking. Indeed, it is a vital consideration. The word 'immutable' becomes as important to this era of technological revolution as 'disintermediation' was to those of us on the barricades of the original internet revolution in the 1990s. The future of accounting looks likely to be in the power of the blockchain, deploying what is being termed 'triple-entry' methods. Thus, the frauds that have blighted markets for decades, can become, if not a thing of the past, at least much more difficult to effect. Incidentally, there is a rich irony to that last sentence. As this book is going to press, the recently released from US incarceration former CEO of Enron, Jeffrey Skilling is seeking to ride the blockchain revolution with a new energy platform based upon Distributed Ledger Technology.

Certainly, looking forward, the power of networks using immutable strength delivered via blockchain technology enables a whole new means of considering the process of technology and audit. Not a moment too soon either, many might argue. A litany of historical accounting issues such as Enron, Lehman, Madoff and Olympus, not to mention Satyam in India have occurred already in this century. In the UK, major accounting scandals destroyed infrastructure giant Carillion and high street café chain Patisserie Valerie during 2018 alone.

Of course, the initial double-entry book-keeping theory has since enormously evolved through consistent increments during the past 500+ years. However, it remains in essence the same system as De Rafaeli et al. were discussing during the Renaissance. As mentioned above, some of the accounting techniques deployed by De Rafaeli have fallen into disuse in the modern era. 'Dowry Accounting' for instance fell out of favour long before the #metoo era befell Hollywood producers and many joint stock companies across the world. Nowadays it would be hard to find somebody in much of the advanced world who requires input on how much of a dowry ought to be repaid on the premature death of a bride. Likewise, the tricky question of resolving the post-dowry pass through payments for a widow who remarries has become redundant. Moreover, it is interesting to note – and a good sign of the lack of sophistication in the time before limited liability corporate status caught on in mercantile life – that merchants taught by pioneers like De Rafaeli did not separate their household accounting from their business accounts. Thus, a major source of conflict of interest was apparent in the earliest accounts. One could note that the imputed problems of mixing domestic expenses with corporate activity continues to cause issues to this day with monotonous regularity.

Thus, without the development of that central ledger to accompany the basic accounting balance sheet, it is difficult to see how any form of business, risk management and particularly financial activity could have feasibly evolved. Without the development of double-entry book-keeping, it would have left the mathematics of commerce essentially in a limbo akin to those cultures with only an oral culture and no developed habit of writing.

Leaping half a millennium or more from the deep analogue to our current vantage point on history: the early flowering of the digital world, the latest thinking in accounting has added a whole new layer to the historic double-entry method. If we take our new friend, the blockchain, double-entry book-keeping can be swiftly turbocharged to another dimension and become triple-entry book-keeping. A key facet to the blockchain is the immutable nature of the ledger. Furthermore, in addition to the impossibility of unilateral tampering with the blockchain, a distributed ledger has significance in being immediately accessible by a raft of participants/stakeholders.

Welcome to a third dimension in accounting.

History and perspective were clearly created in the original ledger that drove the double-entry revolution but it was centralized around the merchant. In other words, one merchant had a view of his accounts and the merchant next door – perhaps even the merchant on the next bench in the market – might have held a completely different view of the status of his accounts, even where it involved the neighbouring merchant. Indeed, such activity is at the root of much accounting error and indeed fraud.

There are a variety of ways in which the blockchain might help accounting and auditing in the future. For one thing of course there is always the possibility of a massive singular blockchain that might register all parties' records of every transaction. That said, a massive singularity of all things is highly unlikely. However, for auditors within a multinational company, all internal accounts could be unified on a single blockchain. This could provide huge amounts of data and be a massive boon for auditors, providing immutable evidence of transactions and their documentation instantly distributed to multiple nodes. However, the auditing profession itself might not see such vast profits in the future. Reconciling all accounting into a DLT system would enable vast amounts of automated data processing to check flows and related payments. In essence, 'bots can disintermediate the human auditors who have only ever been able to 'sample' data within large and complex companies. Nevertheless, the opportunity is there for vastly improved audit procedures to root out fraud and mismanagement – quite feasibly before the traditional quarterly accounting or annual audit periods take place.

Certainly, the use of blockchain could vastly reduce the significant number of human errors on the input side with the right kinds of DLT technology. Equally it ought to be easier to root out managers' inflating reports compared to the underlying cash flow – as after all there would be some form of immutable flow of information from the company treasury and the banks (ideally in something as close as possible to real time).

The author Alex Tapscott has noted that '35% of accounting fraud is actually due to some unintentional mistake'. He notes that 'poor Pam in the back-office fat-fingers an entry into an Excel spreadsheet and like a butterfly flapping its wings it reverberates across the whole enterprise and creates a big crisis'. He continues on to observe that 'the big issue is that modern accounting practices cannot really keep up with the velocity and the complexity of companies and businesses, and deciphering a financial statement is kind of like watching two people dancing under a strobe light. You see bits and pieces, an arm a head, someone shaking their booty but you do not actually get the whole picture because accounting is based on a principle that is actually quite ancient'[1].

It would be unfair to heap scorn on the double-entry book-keeping method. After all it has remained the epicentre of accounting essentially unchanged for 600 years precisely because it is a remarkably sound basis for managing mercantile practices. However, the world has moved on in leaps and bounds. Double entry is one of those few unique best practices, rather like the construction of a Stradivarius violin from the 17th or 18th century (deemed to have unparalleled sound quality compared even with modern instruments) that have been so brilliant as to survive for centuries as the 'best in class.' In its own unique way, the double-entry method struck a numerical chord that has given it considerable utility ever since.

However, with the blockchain, suddenly data goes multidimensional. That provides a massive opportunity to improve accounting and auditing with a series of keystrokes. The debit and credit data remains, but now it is timestamped for accuracy of input, with details of who entered data, from which point on the network, and upon what information source this is based. More significantly all that data is immutable. Of course, a subsequent update can note when Eric in accounts mistyped a billion instead of a million. However, the error will be clearly recorded. Thus, there is a transparent record of the problem that arose and the solution that was deployed (and by whom – in this case presumably a supervisor appending a consensual update). The trust in the ledger would be considerable and suddenly accounts could regain their position as something that could be credibly holistically audited. This elegantly contrasts with contemporary human audit interventions. These amount to something not awfully different to delivering a set of principles in a complex recipe while sampling the cookie mix at judicious points on the production line... to ensure it is a decent batch of credible cake headed to the oven. Indeed, accounts themselves could start to morph to some degree away from the current out-of-date by the time they are published quarterly, semi-annual or annual snapshots of the enterprise into a much more dynamic real-time environment. However, that is probably a little bit too close to the moon-shot end of the spectrum for now. The key thing to bear in mind is that where double-entry book-keeping introduced a ledger and became the explosive underpinning of the mercantile economy, ably supported by the principle of limited liability, now DLT takes the whole adventure into a three-dimensional digital age.

Whether we end up with a fully unified system of a buyer's book and a seller's book that interacts all merchants' transactions, or we still have a vast number of quasi-separate blockchains for these calculations is not the vital issue. The simple fact is that the use of this private data alongside what will be on public blockchains concerning issues such as provenance (of product, service, delivery, transport, even IP and more) will provide vast amounts of opportunity for accounts to be better reconciled, compiled faster and indeed become more readily reliable and trusted by investors and all other stakeholders. A distributed ledger, with public and private blocks confirming data can prove that there have been no manipulation, error or misrepresentation. In essence, through the judicious use of databots deploying automated approaches (and ultimately Artificial Intelligence), the art of spotting a future Bernie Ebbers could prove as easy as throwing on a toga.

Thereafter, it is not just about the accounting per se. Blockchain changes the commercial world just as profoundly as the invention of double-entry book-keeping transformed society during the Renaissance and for centuries thereafter.

Meanwhile here in Malta, we are working hard at ensuring that where Malta was a physical mercantile node from the era of Phoenician trade on, the Blockchain Island has its virtual node placing it on the immutable network of DLT power. Thus, the Blockchain Island is ideally placed to move forward from Marino de Raphaeli's genius locked away for centuries in the National Library in Valletta onto the world of the triple-entry accounting for the new digital age.

Endnotes

1. Alex Tapsoctt, Blockchain Is Eating Wall Street – Tedxsanfrancisco, 2017 singjupost.com

NB: Parts of this chapter have been extracted and adapted from Patrick L. Young's upcoming book 'Victory or Death' which discusses reflections on fintech in the blockchain era and will be published in summer 2019.

8. Is It Money?

David Zammit

Over the ten years since their inception, these cryptocurrencies have proven, in behaviour on the markets, and in their response to market forces, as well as in the latent potential for applications far beyond currency, to be far closer to assets than to currencies.

David Zammit worked in Italy and Switzerland before returning to Malta to establish Zeta Corporate and Management Limited, of which he is MD.

2018 was a rocky year for cryptocurrencies. Within the space of a few weeks, cryptocurrencies lost billions of dollars in value. These losses dramatically affected the value of the biggest contenders in the space, including Bitcoin, Ethereum and Ripple. Bitcoin, the world's oldest and most valuable cryptocurrency, hit an all-time high of $19,665.39 in the last weeks of 2017. On 11 December 2018, Bitcoin plummeted to a low of $3,373. Ethereum too has felt the heat tremendously. Ethereum reached an all-time high of $1,448.18 at the beginning of 2018, but, in December of the same year, it fell to under $100. Ripple suffered the same bloody fate, falling from an all-time high of $3.40 on 7 January 2018 to $0.32 just over a year.

Currencies or Assets?

The P2P nature of cryptocurrency on a distributed ledger provokes an ongoing debate: are cryptocurrencies an asset as opposed to a currency? Cryptocurrencies lack the stability, security and predictability enjoyed by official currencies. Klaas Knot, President of De Nederlandsche Bank NV says that 'I don't think any of these cryptos satisfy the three roles money plays in an economy'[1]. AKA Knot does not perceive cryptocurrency as a medium of exchange, a store of value or a unit of account.

Cryptocurrencies such as Bitcoin, Litecoin, Ripple and Monero, do in a sense carry out these three functions of money. Some of these specialize in one area, or another with different degrees of strength. That said many cryptocurrencies, at worst, could have the potential of performing the three functions of money.

For the likes of developing countries, cryptocurrencies may be a beneficial alternative to official currency. Africa's estimated 1.2 billion unbanked could benefit with any better means of exchange for instance. Individuals without access to banking are reliant on cash. Cryptocurrencies, offer additional opportunities to African economies, with the mobile phone providing a leap to coherent banking and payment services. Moreover, cryptocurrencies are not under the control of corrupt governments.

Bitcoin is a prime example of the advantages that cryptocurrencies offer to citizens of such states. Bitcoin is an excellent store of value since it was engineered to be deflationary. Since the supply of Bitcoin is capped at 21 million bitcoins, it cannot fall prey to the ravages and loss of value of inflation. Bitcoin's value will therefore increase over time because it has only a finite number of units, hence the term 'digital gold' since, like gold, Bitcoin is a limited resource. Bitcoin is traceable on its blockchain so it is very difficult to manipulate. On the other hand, fiat money is susceptible to manipulation, and this has led to serious financial crises, including tremendous inflation in developing countries such as Zimbabwe. In 2006, hyperinflation hit Zimbabwe and soon spun out of control. In 2007, a note for 500,000 Zimbabwean dollars (Z$) was introduced. It was valued at roughly $16 on the official exchange rate. A year later, the Z$100 billion note was introduced. It just about covered the price of three eggs. On 16 January 2009, the largest banknote ever, the Z$100 trillion appeared on the stage. Cryptocurrency will be beneficial to developing countries in the fight against inflation. The effects on the population were devastating. Unlike fiat currency, Bitcoin is immune to this problem. However, although Bitcoin's deflationary character makes it an excellent store of value, as well as immune to the problems of inflation, it is currently a poor means of exchange outside the crypto-system. This is mainly due to the fact that crypto as a means of exchange lacks scalability, and its transactions are expensive. Nonetheless, this does not mean that it cannot improve. Through the implementation of new features, cryptos like Bitcoin may very well overcome their problems to eventually become a useful medium of exchange.

While cryptocurrencies do function, for better or worse, as currencies, most of them arguably fall into the category of crypto-commodities. One such cryptocurrency is Ethereum. The digital world is now giving rise to digital commodities in the same way that nature has produced physical commodities such as oil, natural gas and gold. Digital commodities include assets such as cloud storage and bandwidth access. The crypto-revolution is creating a space that is a global 24/7 market pricing digital commodities. These new digital commodities have produced a new phenomenon in conjunction with cryptocurrencies. This new phenomenon is that of tokens, or rather as it is now being called, 'tokenomics'. This conjunction of currencies and commodities creates an economy from the combination of goods and services on a digital platform such as blockchain that monetizes these products in the form of digital tokens.

This exciting new world of digital commodities and tokenisation is the reason why the debate is moving beyond the term and concept of 'cryptocurrencies' and beginning to incline towards 'cryptoassets'. It is also the reason for the need to distinguish between the two, no longer equate one with the other, and why it is important to separate the two and not consider them as one commodity. Currently, there is little concerted effort to distinguish between the two, and this is because the space was born with the emergence of Bitcoin in early 2009. As such, the space has long been identified with Bitcoin, the creator of which called it a 'peer-to-peer system of electronic cash'. Since then, many such systems following in Bitcoin's footsteps have seen the light of day, but many of them come with vastly different functionalities, making it counterproductive to classify them with Bitcoin as 'cryptocurrencies' since they may serve radically different functions and purposes. This conflation can indeed be worse than counterproductive. Conflating Bitcoin with, for example, Ethereum is an oversight that can lead to serious consequences given that Bitcoin is a cryptocurrency while Ethereum is a platform on which the code for decentralized applications can run.

Satoshi Nakamoto originally proposed Bitcoin in 2008 as a means to enable 'online payments to be sent directly from one party to another without going through a financial institution', a radically different proposal from the centralized money that is the order of the day. Since Bitcoin's inception, awareness of virtual currencies has come along by leaps and bounds but bitcoin has yet to gain formal recognition as a medium of payment or store of value, particularly in the face of often reluctant governments and regulators. However, it is coexisting quite happily with the current financial system despite the scrutiny and debate it has attracted.

Ethereum was launched in 2015 and since grown into the largest decentralized software platform that enables smart contracts and Dapps. Although Bitcoin and Ethereum both operate on the principles of distributed ledgers and cryptography, they differ very widely in purpose. Bitcoin was created as a digital alternative to regular money, and is consequently a medium of payment transaction and store of value. Ethereum however, is a platform that enables decentralized applications to run on a peer-to-peer network using its own cryptocurrency called 'ether'. Although bitcoin and ether are digital currencies, ether is intended to serve as a digital replacement for official currencies to facilitate and monetize the Ethereum platform and the operation of decentralized applications on Ethereum's peer-to-peer network.

Valuation

In early 2018, Anshuman Mehta and Brian Koralewski, observed that the 'the central thesis running through the crypto-currency space is an unhealthy obsession with supply-side scarcity'[2] and they postulate the Quantity Theory of Money (Equation of Exchange) as an excellent tool for evaluation coins and tokens. The equation runs as follows:

M*V=P*Q

where M = Money supply; V = Circulation per year; P = Price per unit; Q = Quantity produced. Moreover, M*V=demand side, while P*Q=supply side.

Bitcoin has been through a number of boom-and-bust cycles, the enthusiasm leading into late 2013, when it first hit $1000, followed by the excruciating period that lasted into 2015 when it fell to around $200, while it soared to around $19000 in late 2017 while it is currently (March 2019) pushing around the $4000 mark.

When dealing with private equity, the J-curve refers to a portfolio's cash flows. When dealing with economics it is used to describe the effects of currency devaluation on the national deficit. Crypto is no exception and hence the J-curve has been adopted for the purpose with respect to crypto[3]. The application of the J-curve to crypto provides a potentially highly useful tool for the market's valuation of crypto over time. Chris Burniske thinks of a cryptoasset's price as composed of two forms of value:

1. Current utility value (CUV)
2. Discounted expected utility value (DEUV)

Before the commencement of trading there is a major hype around the asset, and high excitement persists for a while. During this stage, the CUV of the asset is minimal. The asset is then mainly composed of DEUV, and thus exposed to the market. This initial period of high excitement is the first peak of a crypto J-curve.

As a cryptoasset develops across time, the network inevitably meets unexpected barriers and the excitement starts to decrease. With such hindrances, market enthusiasm declines, weighing on the DEUV. Burniske goes on to observe that 'mathematically, compression of the DEUV can be thought of as any of a number of variables':

- Hiking of the discount rate, as the chances of success are deemed to be smaller and thus the asset riskier.
- Decrease in the percent penetration of the asset's target market, as it's feared the protocol will not win over as many users as initially thought.
- Slashing in the total addressable market, as components of the road map and planned functionality are deemed unrealistic.

During the tough period, sceptical investors make a quick exit, which leads to a major decrease in the DEUV, the current utility value decreases, and the price of the token suffers a drastic slump. This pattern however is part of dynamic leading to the emergence of a new market bringing the assets back to their feet as the team responsible for the asset develops the product further. During this period of depreciation, developers with faith in the product are unlikely to be deterred and are therefore likely to remain indifferent to the depressed price of the cryptoasset. Over time, and with further development, the asset's utility improves and more users start to filter in. The curve will start to rise as the market becomes aware of the growing utility of the asset, speculators will eventually drift back into the asset (or asset class), this will drive up the price, leading to the elevation of the crypto J-curve in its later stages.

Once this pattern has been concluded, the full J-curve cycle is played out to the full. The cryptoasset has gone from primary composition of DEUV, dealing with scaling and other challenges, and has plummeted to the bottom of the J-curve. The only option for developers is to demonstrate the utility of their products if these are to attract the interest of investors.

The idea of utility for an individual crypto network appears on the PQ (supply side) side of the equation of exchange. This consists of consideration of the digital good or service provided, and the price per unit of that digital service. Once this data has been collected, these costs can be applied to the decline curves. A minor case study to demonstrate the application of the equation of exchange to a cryptoasset will help to illustrate these concepts more clearly. The subject of this case study is Filecoin, a blockchain-based storage network.

Current cloud-storage vendors price their service at a dollar cost per gigabyte. Users pay a rate of a certain amount of dollars per gigabyte of storage on a cloud server on which to store their files. These factors allow us to project a reasonable dollar cost per gigabyte to store data on the Filecoin network. This dollar cost per gigabyte is the price (P) in terms of the equation of exchange.

After (P) is established, the quantity produced (Q) is then ascertained. In this case (Q) is the number of gigabytes stored, and this is determined by ascertaining total addressable market of cloud storage in terms of gigabytes with which an S-curve can then be created. The S-curve demonstrates the adoption cycle within the total addressable market, expressing the gigabytes stored by Filecoin in a particular year. Then, the price per gigabyte (P) is multiplied by the sum of the gigabytes stored by Filecoin (Q), with the product being the dollar amount of value transacted on the Filecoin network in any given year in exchange for the good being offered (cloud storage). This product of P*Q is the velocity for a given year (V). The final step in this calculation is PQV=M, by which PQ divided by V gives (M), the monetary base needed to support that economy.

Once the monetary base of the economy (M) has been calculated, the utility price per token for every year can be derived by dividing (M) by the number of tokens that are in the float. If that is projected out to the next year of a period even five years hence, that utility value can be discounted back to the current year to get the today's rational market price for the asset based on the future utility value. A percentage of the rational market price will be supported by the current utility value and the delta is the speculative value.

Taking the concepts and principles illustrated by means of this case study, it becomes possible to evaluate the assets, treat them as investments, and examine the fundamentals of these assets.

Volatility

Potential investors in cryptoassets need to consider the place for such assets in their portfolio. Before the rise of crypto, the typical portfolio included bonds or equity, however, after the financial crisis, investors turned to alternatives such as gold or real estate. Treating cryptocurrencies, such as Bitcoin, as an asset provides investors with yet another alternative for their portfolios.

It is essential to acquire a good understanding of volatility since investors react to volatility in different ways. In this context, volatility refers to market volatility, and an evaluation of volatility is necessary when looking at the relationship of a cryptoasset to the market.

This difference in reaction means that that every investor has different expectations. When talking about volatility, we are speaking about the market volatility, as opposed to other categories of volatility. We evaluate market volatility because we want to look at the relationship of a cryptoasset to the market. Volatility is commonly defined in some variation of this:

"Volatility is a statistical measure of the dispersion of returns for a given security or market index. Volatility can either be measured by using the standard deviation or variance between returns from that same security or market index. Commonly, the higher the volatility, the riskier the security."[4]

The main reason against the classification of cryptos as currency is that they are too volatile. For example, the volatility of Bitcoin against the US dollar can best be described as a rollercoaster. In the space of one week, Bitcoin leapt from about $15000 to $19000 and then fell to $10000 around a month later. Why are cryptocurrencies so volatile? Why have the prices of currencies declined so dramatically in the space of a year? The answer is complex, and many factors are involved, notably the following:

1. Hostile government regulations. Across the world, governments are in the process of regulating the crypto industry. In many cases, this has frightened investors off. In countries like China, governments have taken either hostile, or ambivalent attitudes, closing exchanges and banning Initial Coin Offering (ICO) projects.

2. Major social media platforms have banned advertising. Social media is an extremely effective platform for advertising but Facebook, Google and Twitter have all banned cryptocurrency advertisements. The stated intention is to hinder scammers, protect users from fraud, and themselves from liability.

3. Liquidation of positions and the taking of profits. Speculative

investors tend to aim for the best buck in the shortest time. The cryptospace appears to attract a disproportionate percentage of these investors, no doubt attracted by the spectacular volatility. Hence, many people are buying, but also selling at equal speed. This tendency to seek short-term reward is affecting the market tremendously.

Taxation

Tax regulations for cryptocurrency varies from country to country. In many jurisdictions, cryptocurrencies are commonly considered as capital assets. A common consideration in many jurisdictions is that for tax purposes, cryptocurrencies are held as capital assets. Nonetheless, it is also common to tax in the manner of capital gains those gains made when selling, trading, or using for profit cryptocurrencies that have appreciated since purchase. On the other hand, with equal frequency, if the cryptocurrency depreciates in value, and it is sold, traded or used at a loss, many jurisdictions permit the deduction of these losses against other capital gains for a reduction of the final tax bill.

Assets not Currencies

This chapter contends that cryptocurrencies are, in fact, assets, rather than currencies. In order to truly accept that cryptos are an asset we must first define the term asset. Although in some cases they do share the qualities of currencies, by and large, as this chapter has shown, in terms of valuation, volatility, and taxation, they appear to be closer to assets than to currencies. A general definition of the term shows significant application to this case:

"An asset is a resource with economic value that an individual, corporation or country owns or controls with the expectation that it will provide a future benefit. Assets are reported on a company's balance sheet and are bought or created to increase a firm's value or benefit the firm's operations. An asset can be thought of as something that, in the future, can generate cash flow, reduce expenses or improve sales, regardless of whether it's manufacturing equipment or a patent."[5]

This definition appears to apply with far more accuracy to cryptocurrencies, at least as they are in current use and market psychology, than the term 'currency'. In terms of crypto coins, an asset is a term that also refers to cryptocurrency. Although cryptocurrency originated with the intention of serving as an alternative to the fiat money during the financial crisis of 2007-2009, the technology has applications far beyond mere currency. Even Bitcoin, for example, which is perhaps the purest form of cryptocurrency, can be used for applications beyond that, even potentially, for smart contracts. It is therefore arguably more accurate to start calling these artefacts of technology 'cryptoassets', rather than 'cryptocurrencies'.

Cryptoassets operate entirely on a P2P network running on the internet. They are essentially strings of data recording the possession of some asset, as well as its transfer from one user to another across this P2P network. This record is maintained on a blockchain, a fully synchronized copy of which runs on every computer on this P2P network. Consensus rules across the entire network verify transactions as they occur and record them virtually immutably on the blockchain that thus contains a full and virtually immutable history of all transactions in these assets without the need of a central authority to do so. The consensus rules are powered by an algorithm that forces computers, called miners, responsible for the verification of transactions to behave honourably in verifying transactions at the expense of forfeiting the electrical cost of their participation if they cheat, but rewarding them with a certain amount of the assets issued by that blockchain if they play fair. Unlike fiat money, cryptocurrency was originally designed to be deflationary, and most use a fixed-supply model that is slowly issued transparently and outside the control of any individual entity. As such, they are generally not subject to depreciation by inflation. In this they are generally compared to gold. In fact, 'digital gold' is one of the sobriquets of Bitcoin. Essentially, therefore, cryptocurrencies are in fact cryptoassets, that is digital assets that use cryptography, a peer-to-peer network and a public ledger. The ledger regulates the generation of new units, can verify the transactions and secure transactions. A cryptoasset is a term that is not limited merely to cryptoassets intended to function as assets. It also covers digital assets whose values are derived from its blockchain but from their application to goods and services that are recorded and transferred across that blockchain. The right to acquire these goods and services is expressed in those assets that are termed 'tokens', rather than 'coins' and they include utility tokens, platform tokens, and tokenised securities, among others.

Conclusion

Cryptocurrency sprang out of deep distrust of conventional currency. It is therefore hardly surprising that this new technology was postulated as a form of P2P digital cash intended to replace the dangerous flaws of conventional currencies, most notably the intermediaries in charge of it, as Nakamoto saw them. However, over the ten years since their inception, these cryptocurrencies have proven, in behaviour on the markets, and in their response to market forces, as well as in the latent potential for applications far beyond currency, to be far closer to assets than to currencies. Thinking of them as 'cryptocurrencies' while they behave more similarly to assets is leading to confusion and doubt among regulators, investors, users, and the market and society at large. Perhaps the substitution of the term 'cryptoasset' for 'cryptocurrency' will lead to less confusion and more beneficial treatment of these new technologies for the good of the economy, and of us all.

Note: The author would like to acknowledge and thank Melanie Claire Gallacher for substantial support in the research for this chapter.

Endnotes

1. Jessica Shankleman, "When is a Bitcoin not a Bitcoin? When it's an Asset, Says G20", Livemint, 2018.
2. Anshuman Mehta and Brian Koralewski, "MV=P...Que? Love and Circularity in the Time of Crypto", Medium, 2018.
3. Chris Burniske Burniske, "The Crypto J-Curve", Medium, 2017.
4. James Chen, "Volatility", Investopedia, 2018.
5. Will Kenton, "Asset", Investopedia, 2018

PART III

LEX

Law and Regulation

9. Regulating DLT in Finance

Diane Bugeja

This comprehensive regime devised by policymakers, which is in turn supported by regulations, MFSA rules, and other ancillary guidance, has clearly placed Malta at the forefront of DLT regulation, while attracting reputable international players that are prepared to put in place the necessary systems and controls in exchange for a stamp granting them 'regulated status', and which consequently enhances their standing.

Dr Diane Bugeja is a senior associate at Camilleri Preziosi, practising primarily in financial services law, financial regulation and anti-money laundering regulation.

Background and Introduction

Malta's efforts to make a name for itself as emphatically the Blockchain Island culminated on 1 November 2018. This date was an important milestone for Malta as the VFAA and the ITASA came into force.

   The VFAA applies to issuers interested in launching an initial VFA offering (IVFAO) to the public in or from within Malta, or who are intent on admitting a VFA to trading on a DLT exchange. As a result of the VFAA, such issuers must now draw up a whitepaper compliant with the requirements prescribed by the VFAA and register this with the Malta Financial Services Authority (MFSA). Furthermore, no person shall provide, or hold itself out as providing, a VFA service in or from within Malta unless such person is in possession of a valid licence granted under the VFAA by the MFSA. The third and final role established by the VFAA is that of the VFA agent, which must be appointed by both VFA issuers and prospective VFA service providers. A VFA agent registered under Article 7 of the VFAA Act guides and advises the issuer on matters relating to the IVAFO and the white paper registration, and is also responsible for carrying out a fit and proper assessment on the issuer while being subject to ongoing obligations in connection with that issuer. On the other hand, a VFA agent registered under Article 14 of the VFAA is responsible for carrying out a fit and proper test on applicants desirous to apply as a VFA service provider, and submit the application to the MFSA on their behalf. VFA issuers, VFA service providers and VFA agents are subject persons for the purposes of Prevention of Money Laundering and Funding of Terrorism Regulations[1] and are therefore obliged to comply with the anti-money laundering and countering of the funding of terrorism (AML/CFT) obligations arising therefrom.

The ITASA complements the VFAA by creating a voluntary certification and registration regime for Innovative Technology Arrangements (TASs) and Technology Service Providers (TSPs) respectively. The present focus of the ITASA centres around DLT solutions and smart contracts, yet the flexible drafting of the ITASA allows it the necessary flexibility it requires to develop alongside emerging market innovations, such as technologies relating to AI and the IoT.

This comprehensive regime devised by policymakers, which is in turn supported by regulations, MFSA rules, and other ancillary guidance, has clearly placed Malta at the forefront of DLT regulation, while attracting reputable international players that are prepared to put in place the necessary systems and controls in exchange for a stamp granting them 'regulated status', and which consequently enhances their standing. The jurisdiction however must recognize that, while this regulatory framework is laudable and definitely a step in the right direction, it remains only a starting point for further progress. DLT, as a technology, enables the sharing and updating of records in a distributed and decentralized way, such that participants can securely propose, validate, and record updates to a synchronized ledger that is distributed across the participants. DLT therefore has the potential to deliver substantial benefits in financial services, and, to this end, the rest of this chapter will focus on other aspects around the use of DLT in financial services, which, to date, have not been sufficiently addressed by EU and domestic legislation.

The Use and Benefits of DLT in Financial Services

The disruption of traditional business models in the wake of DLT is tangible. The role of financial services institutions is evolving as trust is becoming more decentralized and customers' expectations are shifting towards faster delivery timeframes and more efficient service standards. Indeed, the consequence of the widespread use of DLT goes to the core of financial services and the assumptions on which it is founded. In the first instance, one such assumption is competitiveness in the sense that DLT is likely to lower the barriers to entry and allow non-traditional players to compete with regulated entities as we know them. This increased competition is already perceptible in the insurance, banking and payment services industries, among others, where nascent fintech firms are on the rise. Consumer products are also likely to become more standardized due to the use of smart contracts, while the level of interconnectedness may well increase since DLT is dependent on well-connected platforms and protocols .

This notwithstanding, the adoption of DLT in financial services has great potential. In the first instance, it does away with inefficient exchange of information and fragmented data sources by enabling trusted and verifiable sources of information through a shared interface with third parties across the industry. This not only saves time and resources but also minimizes the risk of fraud and identity theft while establishing a system through which AML/CFT checks can be automated (both from the perspective of client on-boarding as well as that of ongoing monitoring by screening transactions). It also automates processes through smart contracts (for example claims settlement in insurance), and improves pricing accuracy through improved risk profiling.

These considerations and apparent advantages should spur financial services players to consider the viability of their business model in the longer-term, as well as the manner in which DLT can increase competitiveness by enhancing efficiency and sustainability. This assessment is somewhat challenging, not least because a number of unknowns remain, including regulatory oversight in the wake of DLT usage, changes to conduct and prudential supervision (including cyber-security considerations and prudential requirements), and implications for data ownership and protection, among others.

The Risks of DLT Usage and How to Regulate Them

As discussed in the first part of this chapter, Maltese policymakers have recognized the benefits and the appetite in the DLT space, and have created a timely legislative framework to address them. This framework not only enables transactions in VFAs in a regulated environment, but also comprehensively addresses the associated risks, and provides mitigation for these risks by, for example, mandating clear governance structures, systems and AML/CFT audits, internal systems and controls, and so on. Still, the more traditional market players that are not interested in dealing in VFAs may still wish to adopt DLT in their day-to-day businesses due to its promising utility but may struggle to adapt the current regulatory framework with which they must comply to a situation in which they would be using DLT for their internal and customer-facing processes.

The rewards that are associated with DLT implementation are accompanied by a number of risks that must be duly considered, and which, in the heavily-regulated environment that financial services players operate in, become even more paramount. There are, therefore, regulatory limitations that must be overcome in order to facilitate a truly DLT-friendly environment across the regulated sector. In particular, these relate to governance, outsourcing, cyber-security, systemic risk, AML/KYC, and data protection.

Firstly, traditional governance structures tend to vary significantly in a DLT environment, with the system heavily reliant on automated process and smart contracts. It follows, therefore, that a glitch or failure may have wide consequences with DLT as many parties would share the same tools. In devising these processes and checking whether they are operating as intended, a new IT audit role for domain and software experts is likely to be created, and such individuals should feature prominently in the governance structure of the organization. Hence, the equivalent of the systems auditor role, and related responsibilities, for which the VFAA currently provides, may need to be extended to other financial services players that are intent on embracing DLT in their own business activities. Apart from the requirement for an annual systems audit, the role of the internal IT function can take a more prominent role such that the individual heading this project will be considered a key function holder and hence be subject to a fit and proper assessment by the MFSA. This is intrinsically linked to outsourcing rules that regulated entities are subject to, and it may be advisable for the MFSA to consider making it incumbent on supervised entities wishing to outsource processes that use DLT to make the service provider carry out an annual systems audit and report back to the regulated entity and/or the MFSA itself. The regulated entity will, as always, remain ultimately responsible for compliance with the broader outsourcing rules, including supervision of the service provider and the application of risk management practices in relation thereto. Relatedly, the MFSA ought to consider dependency risks in this respect, given that DLT-related knowledge and skills, particularly locally, tend to be concentrated in the hands of a small number of individuals.

Cyber-security has become a key priority for regulators globally, and it will certainly remain high on their agendas as DLT gathers popularity, particularly since the technology is at its early stage and remains largely untested. Indeed, EU regulatory bodies have recently introduced specific stress tests on cyber-security, which may consequently have an impact on the capital requirements of the regulated entity. Relatedly, the Joint Committee of European Supervisory Authorities has noted that the interconnectivity of market players through the use of DLT increases their exposure to cyber threats[2]. Research suggests a number of good practices that can manage the risks to cyber-security[3]. By way of example, in order to address risks associated with key management, financial services players should be encouraged to use rules that require the use of multiple signatures to authorize and/or create transactions, as well as enabling internal identification of the individual signing off the request for a transaction. With respect to cryptography and key generation, it is recommended that the keys are generated in a secure and valid way while using different keys to sign and encrypt. In terms of privacy risks, transactions should be encrypted to ensure that only the involved counterparties may access the whole information, and ledgers should be encrypted with more than one key. Code reviews should also be done periodically, supported by penetration testing on the DLT application. Even with permissioned blockchains, there remain risks associated with the loss of keys by a central authority (for example encryption keys), as well as fraudulent transactions by a single node, and it is therefore advisable to use a clear set of criteria to accept new members and remove existing ones, while enabling the use of recovery keys. The risks associated with smart contracts should be further managed by using code reviews, and standardizing regular functions into libraries, while retaining a library of approved smart contracts. This, and other similar guidance, would certainly prove very useful to financial services entities, while providing comfort to the regulator that some basic concepts are being implemented as safeguards by the industry when using this technology. In this spirit, the MFSA may wish to consider incorporating guidance of this nature as part of its conduct of business rulebook, consequently making it incumbent upon financial services entities using DLT to adopt these best practices as an intrinsic part of their systems and controls.

Insofar as systemic risk is concerned, there is a feeling that DLT may contribute to increase market volatility, and that the use of smart contracts, because of their embedded automated triggers, may exacerbate one-directional market reaction in times of stress. Shorter settlement timeframes and increased efficiency in processing transactions might have unintended consequences on liquidity. It is unlikely that the MFSA will have a say on whether this calls for more stringent prudential ratios, yet it would be important for the local regulator at least to be attuned to these risks, and to thoroughly evaluate the additional checks and balances that the regulated entity is proposing to manage these developing risks. Other aspects of system risks can also be exacerbated when DLT networks are used to hold and transfer financial assets, such as securities, money or derivatives, which can, in time, become critical infrastructures and therefore of systemic importance. The dependency of financial services entities on DLT networks once adopted, coupled by their interconnectedness, calls for the regulation of these networks in order to ensure that they are, and remain, resilient. In the absence of consensus on which party to regulate (whether it be platform provider, the nodes, the regulated entities, etc.), and to what extent, the MFSA may wish to address this on a domestic level. It may wish to do so by developing an intimate understanding of the dependency of financial services entities on these networks, and for what purposes (i.e. whether DLT is being used in connection with critical functions, customer-facing processes, etc.), the systemic risks that they may give rise to, and the controls and risk management procedures that regulated entities have established around these in order to mitigate this risk exposure.

From an AML/KYC perspective, DLT has real potential to make a transformative impact on AML/CFT compliance, both in helping to prevent money laundering and in reducing the cost of compliance. However, it is equally clear that substantial barriers to widespread adoption exist, which may well continue to limit the progress of ongoing innovation in AML/CFT compliance. In theory, DLT lends itself well to AML/CFT compliance. For example, a network of firms can come together on a DLT network and enable more effective transaction monitoring, as opposed to performing the checks themselves or outsourcing these to third parties, thereby exploiting the ability of DLT to replace paper trails with auditable, digital records that are far easier to trace. The biggest hurdles to implementing a DLT solution in this context are two-fold: (i) convincing multiple firms to adopt this technology; and (ii) the sharing of liability and AML/CFT responsibilities among the parties. In practice, apart from the limited budgets that most subject persons have, there is a common concern that the present reliance and outsourcing provisions – including the liability attached thereto – discourage the use of this technology and do not cater for a scenario in which multiple firms come together on a DLT network and share the burden of AML/CFT compliance. In fact, the current AML/CFT legislative framework assumes that reliance and outsourcing will happen among two parties in the traditional sense, and provides that the subject person placing reliance, and/or outsourcing the activity, remains ultimately responsible for its AML/CFT compliance from a regulatory perspective. In the longer term, and as more sophisticated tools of this nature become available with potential benefits to the sector, the Financial Intelligence Analysis Unit (FIAU) may wish to explore this further by reconsidering its position on the use of reliance and outsourcing in a way that secures a more proportionate balance of liability among the parties involved.

Finally, the satisfaction of data protection obligations in a DLT environment remains a highly-debated topic and one that is still a grey area. In the absence of specific regulatory guidance, regulated entities looking to adopt DLT have no option but to find solutions that comply with the general principles of the General Data Protection Regulation[4], particularly that personal data must be obtained and used only for specified lawful purposes, that personal data must only be used for the purpose for which it was collected, and that personal data must not be kept for longer than is necessary, while giving due consideration to the data subjects' right to be forgotten, and abiding with the general prohibition on the transfer of personal data from the EU to a country outside the EEA unless that country ensures an adequate level of protection for the data. To date, the most touted solutions relate to cryptographic hashing and encryption although more clarity is needed on a number of matters, including, for example, whether the erasure principle is satisfied by rendering the data permanently inaccessible. Although it is acknowledged that prescriptive guidance on the matter should come from the EU, it would be helpful if, in the interim, the Information and Data Protection Commissioner were to engage with the sector in order to set expectations on matters that are of concern to the sector, and which can lead to massive repercussions in terms of reputational damage and financial penalties.

Concluding Remarks

Simply put, 'blockchain technology has broad implications for how we transact, and the potential for innovation is hard to overstate'[5], consequently, the regulatory framework around DLT should not be underestimated. Undeniably, DLT has the potential to drive simplicity and efficiency through the establishment of new financial services infrastructure and processes, and, in fact, the use of this technology is rapidly gathering momentum within the financial services sector, and is high on the agenda of financial services market players worldwide. Unlike in other sectors, the use of DLT in the financial services sector – being a highly-regulated sector – requires a well-thought out regulatory framework that caters for the use of this technology by regulated entities. Self-regulation is hardly sufficient in this case and may effectively distort the present aims and objectives of the current regulatory framework with which financial services institutions are obliged to comply. Wise words of caution have also been sounded by the late Professor Stephen Hawking, warning us how far technology can go if it is not controlled and regulated, and stating that 'technology has advanced at such a pace that its aggression may destroy us all by nuclear or biological war. We need to control this inherited instinct by our logic and reason'[6].

The importance of regulating DLT does not only benefit regulated entities but also supervisory authorities themselves. DLT may increase complexity in financial services' processes, especially in the short term, which could effectively render risk monitoring and supervision by competent authorities more complex, at least initially. Locally, the financial services sector has been hesitant in adopting DLT as a core part of their business process and, as a result, institutions have not as yet fully considered the regulatory consequences of deploying DLT solutions in a regulated environment. This may be because institutions are still developing their own understanding of the technology, and assessing use cases for their own business activities. The situation is however changing rapidly as increasing attention is being devoted to DLT solutions by financial services market players, particularly in the wake of the

VFAA and ITASA, and the Government's commitment to develop a regulated environment that promotes the use of AI technology. This fast-changing environment makes it imperative for regulators to continuously assess how it impacts their respective regulatory approaches. It is only by observing and monitoring DLT-related market developments, engaging with stakeholders including the industry, gathering evidence on DLT usage, and collaborating with domestic and international stakeholders as well as peers, including European bodies, AML/CFT regulators, and data protection regulators among others, that regulators can position themselves at the forefront of DLT technology as well as leading authorities in DLT regulation.

It is encouraging to note that the MFSA is already doing its utmost to support the use of DLT in financial services. This notwithstanding, the volatility and speed of developments in this area is one that requires regulators to keep abreast continuously with updates, and to be in a position to react in real-time to advancements in the sector. This has a bearing on the proportionality of the regulatory response taken by competent authorities – indeed, regulatory measures taken in this space should not have the adverse effect of stifling innovation but, on the contrary, they should aim to address the risks and concerns in a pragmatic manner. Consultation with the industry is crucial, and it is strongly recommended that where the MFSA foresees gaps, risks or concerns, it should co-operate with the financial services sector to explore mechanisms that would be mutually acceptable in providing the necessary assurance and controls.

On its part, the financial services sector should seek to engage as much as possible with regulators. This engagement should however be an informed engagement that should only follow once the institution has undertaken an in-depth risk assessment in connection with the use of DLT, and appreciates that actual implementation will depend on the institution's maturity. Relatedly, the sector should recognise that there is no universal solution, and that, therefore, any proposed use of DLT should be proportionate to the nature, scale and complexity of its activities, and should be supported by targeted systems and controls that address the new risks identified following the risk assessment. Furthermore, the deployment of DLT is not a silver bullet and should therefore not be held in isolation without considering the broader ongoing digitalization of the industry.

Finally, while it is true that regulation should be 'technology-neutral', it is also to be acknowledged that the use of DLT is an exceptional development that was evidently not considered in the present regulatory framework that governs the provision of financial services. In general, the current laws are flexible enough to accommodate applications of various technologies, including the use of DLT by regulated entities. Still, as this chapter has demonstrated, some key areas do require further consideration. These challenges and risks are by no means exhaustive as regulators and financial services market players are yet to fully appreciate the risks and benefits relating to the use of DLT. This however should not be an excuse to place DLT regulation, or at least supervision of DLT adoption, on the back-burner. It is important for regulators to start by formalizing their expectations and creating some form of standardization that fosters a level playing field, while also considering whether the present rulebook deters sensible development that would benefit consumers, and hence whether changes may be needed. Unless and until regulators recognize the need for more specific guidance of this nature, barriers to the use of DLT will remain and its full potential across the financial services sector will not be maximized.

Endnotes

1. Subsidiary Legislation 373.01 of the laws of Malta.
2. Joint Committee of the ESAs, Report on Risks and Vulnerabilities in the EU Financial System, 2017, p. 15.
3. ENISA, DLT & Cybersecurity – Improving Information Security in the Financial Sector, 2016, pp. 21-23.
4. GDPR, Regulation (EU) 2016/679 27/4/2016.
5. Trevor I. Kiviat, "Beyond Bitcoin", Duke Law Journal, 65.3 (2015).
6. Tom Whipple and Oliver Moody, "Interview with Stephen Hawking", Times of London, 2017.

10. VFA Regulation

Christopher P Buttigieg, Gerd Sapiano

The concept of the VFA Agent is a novel one introduced to ensure that a first line of defence independent from the Authority is set up in order to keep persons who are not fit and proper out of the Maltese financial services industry.

Dr Christopher P Buttigieg is the Chief Officer responsible for Strategy, Policy and Innovation at MFSA and at EU level, Chair of the ESMA Standing Committee. He is a lecturer at the University of Malta.

Dr Gerd Sapiano is a policy expert in the field of crypto asset regulation at the MFSA. He formed part of the team which drafted the Virtual Financial Assets framework.

Introduction

The Maltese Government's Blockchain Island strategy has generated interest from stakeholders, with a wide range of players having announced plans to operate in or from the island. The Malta Financial Services Authority, the single regulator for financial services in Malta, identified potential risks and a number of disadvantages in having such a fast developing sector operating in a regulatory vacuum,. In this context the MFSA's Board decided that the cryptoasset sector should be regulated in Malta.

Following a positively received public consultation process, MFSA started to develop a standalone regulatory framework for the sector which treats cryptoassets as a separate investment asset class. In this respect, the regulatory framework devised by the MFSA seeks to protect investors, ensure market integrity and safeguard financial soundness, whilst at the same time proposing regulation which does not stifle innovation.

At present, there are over two thousand cryptocurrencies in existence world-wide, each having different characteristics. In this light, any attempt to regulate the cryptoasset space, will inevitably raise the question of how something, which is global and decentralized, can be controlled. The approach taken by the Maltese legislator was not to regulate cryptoassets per se, but rather the persons issuing such assets and, or providing services in relation thereto in or from within Malta. The resultant VFA Act therefore provides for the regulation of issuers of virtual financial assets, persons providing services in relation to such assets as well as a new functionary termed the VFA Agent. It is acknowledged that the classification of a particular DLT asset as a Virtual Financial Asset ('VFA') or otherwise may not always be straightforward; however the Authority has devised a financial instrument test with aim of achieving regulatory certainty in this regard.

This article seeks to complement other literature which is available vis-à-vis the cryptoasset sector, by critically examining the role of the VFA Agent as originally conceived when the framework for crypto assets was being designed in Malta and its subsequent implementation under the VFA Act. It also has the purpose of supplementing the points made in an article by Buttigieg and Efthymiopoulos[1] on the regulatory framework for crypto-assets in Malta and the international developments in this field. Prepared after research and analysis of a number of publications, the chapter also draws from the authors' professional experience, particularly in relation to the drafting and subsequent implementation of the VFA framework as well as meetings attended in local and international fora.

The central argument of this chapter is that the VFA Agent has a critical role in ensuring that Malta's cryptoassets business operates in an environment characterized by market integrity and that operators that are fit and proper get access to Malta's financial system. The chapter outlines how, through checks on an applicant for registration as a VFA Agent's governance, business model, level of competence and systems and controls, the MFSA is ensuring that registered agents are able to perform as the Authority's extended supervisory arm, thereby strengthening the level of monitoring in this field.

The Regulatory Framework for Cryptoassets – An Overview

At present there is no harmonized or common regulatory approach vis-à-vis the cryptoasset sphere – both globally and at European level. That said, the treatment of crypto-assets seems to centre on their classification into a particular asset class.

In fact, at EU level, on the 13 November 2017, The European Securities and Markets Authority (ESMA) issued a statement (ESMA 50-157-828) on ICOs highlighting that consideration must be given to whether activities undertaken in relation to cryptoassets qualify as regulated activities under the traditional financial services framework. ESMA's position may be summarised as follows – 'Where...coins or tokens qualify as financial instruments it is likely that the firms involved...conduct regulated investment activities'. More recently, ESMA appears to be advocating (ESMA 50-157-1391) an EU-wide bespoke regime for cryptoassets that fall outside traditional financial services legislation in order to address any present regulatory gaps. The European Banking Authority (EBA), on the other hand, seems to be more cautious in its approach stating that a cost/benefit analysis to assess whether action at EU level is required[2]. That being stated, both ESMA and the EBA stress the need to keep following market developments.

The Maltese initiative to regulate the cryptoasset space kicked off on the 30 November 2017 with the publication of a Discussion Paper on Initial Coin Offerings, Virtual Currencies and related Service Providers. The discussion paper proposed the establishment of a framework whereby activity conducted in relation to cryptoassets falling under traditional financial services continues being regulated thereunder and a new legislative framework would be proposed for cryptoassets not caught by existent legislation – an approach consistent with ESMA's position.

The feedback received to the consultation was positive and the MFSA proceeded to draft a new act – the VFA Act – regulating: [i] VFA Agents; [ii] Initial Virtual Financial Asset Offerings; and [iii] VFA Service Providers. The Act, which seeks to achieve consumer protection, market integrity and financial soundness in this new area of financial business, was approved by parliament on 4 July 2018, published on the 20 July 2018 and eventually came into force on the 1 November 2018. The Authority also drafted subsidiary legislation and a rulebook which underpin and complement the VFA Act – whilst the Act sets out the high level principles for the regulation of this embryonic sector, replicating the high level principles of EU legislation under the traditional financial services spectrum, the subsidiary legislation[3] and rules[4] issued thereunder provide further detail and granularity.

In line with the approach taken by ESMA, the applicability of the framework is highly dependent on the classification of the DLT Asset in question as a VFA. The VFA Act defines a DLT Asset as: [i] a virtual token; [ii] a VFA; [iii] electronic money; or [iv] a financial instrument. A VFA is then defined in the negative as a DLT Asset which is not a virtual token, electronic money or a financial instrument.

In order to ensure regulatory certainty, the MFSA designed and adopted a Financial Instrument Test[5] (the Test), which provides a number of pre-determined questions in order to help market players arrive to a determination as to the nature of the particular DLT asset and, as a result, the applicable regulatory framework.

Therefore, should a DLT asset qualify as a financial instrument or e-money, the issuance thereof and any services provided in relation thereto would be required to follow the stipulations of the applicable

EU legislation. DLT assets which qualify as virtual tokens are unregulated. Finally, the issuance of and services provided in relation to assets which do not classify as financial instruments, electronic money, or virtual tokens, and therefore are classified as VFAs are regulated under the VFA Act. Therefore, apart from ensuring consumer protection, promoting market integrity, and ensuring financial soundness, the VFA Framework seeks to provide regulatory certainty for a sector which was previously unregulated.

This contrasts with the status quo in the US where it appears that regulatory gaps still exist, with the SEC and CFTC[6] both having jurisdiction over cryptoassets but with neither having sufficient jurisdiction by themselves, or even jointly. Other jurisdictions, such as Mauritius, are taking an approach similar to that of Malta by recognising crypto assets as an asset-class for investment purposes[7]. While jurisdictions, such as Japan, have opted to integrate crypto assets into their payment services legislation[8] and are therefore taking a different approach to the regulation of this area of financial business from that taken in Malta.

Within the EU, apart from Malta, France is the only member state that has enacted legislation for the regulation of cryptoassets. On 9 October 2018, the French parliament approved the PACTE Bill at its first reading. Like the Maltese framework, it provides a legal framework for ICOs and services provided in relation to crypto assets. Whilst Article 26 sets out a voluntary regime for token issuers (Émetteurs de jetons) to apply for a visa from the AMF; Article 26a provides a requirement for digital asset service providers (Prestataires de services sur actifs numériques) to register with the AMF prior to exercising their activity. The Bill was adopted on 11 April 2019.

It is interesting to note that another member state, Italy, is also considering the possible regulation of cryptoassets in a similar way to the Maltese approach. Indeed, the Italian securities and markets regulator – CONSOB – has recently published a call for evidence on Initial Coin Offerings and Crypto-Assets Exchanges[9], inter alia seeking views on the possible introduction of a 'special regime' therefor.

Whilst it is evident that no regulatory initiative is the same, it is equally clear that regulators are striving to provide legal certainty in a field which was, until recently, unregulated. In this regard, however, one cannot but remark about the importance of having international standards on best practices in this field, which should ensure proper regulation of this field not only on a national level but also internationally.

The VFA Agent – This Functionary in the Context of the VFA Framework

The VFA Act regulates a type of functionary, termed the VFA Agent, with the aim of such functionary acting as the initial point of contact for prospective persons wishing to operate under the VFA Act, meaning issuers of VFA and VFA services providers. By conducting a fitness and properness assessment prior to on-boarding any person as its client, the VFA Agent will act as the first line of defence for the Maltese financial system against financial market misconduct by preventing persons that are not fit and proper from setting up operations in or from Malta.

The VFA Act provides for three types of VFA Agents: [i] VFA Agents appointed in terms of Article 7 – these VFA Agents can on-board Issuers of VFAs as their clients; [ii] VFA Agents appointed in terms of Article 14 – these may on-board applicants for a VFA services licence as their clients; and [iii] VFA Agents appointed in terms of Articles 7 and 14 who may on-board both Issuers of VFAs and applicants for a VFA services licence. The Act defines a VFA Agent as follows:

"VFA agent" means a person registered with the competent authority under this Act and authorised to carry on the profession of:

(a) advocate, accountant or auditor; or

(b) a firm of advocates, accountants or auditors, or corporate services providers; or

(c) a legal organisation which is wholly owned and controlled by persons referred to in paragraphs (a) or (b),

whether in Malta or in another recognised jurisdiction, or any other class of persons holding authorisations, qualifications and, or experience deemed by the competent authority as possessing suitable expertise to exercise the functions listed under articles 7 and, or 14;"[10]

Even though this definition may seem to imply that a natural person may act as VFA Agent, clarity is provided by Chapter 1 of the VFA Rulebook[11] which sets out the requirement for a VFA Agent to be a legal person.

Apart from acting as gatekeeper at authorization stage, the VFA Agent has an on-going role with regard to issuers and has the responsibility and obligation under the Act, to submit all the necessary documentation required by the MFSA, to liaise and correspond as necessary with the Authority vis-à-vis its client. Indeed, while the role of the VFA Agent appointed in terms of Article 14 stops once the process for application for authorization is exhausted, the role of the VFA Agent appointed in terms of Article 7 is ongoing and such VFA Agent is required to submit to the MFSA, on behalf of the administrators of the issuer, on an annual basis, a certificate of compliance in relation to the Issuer.

The Act also designates a VFA Agent as being a subject person for purposes of the Anti-Money Laundering Act in Malta and therefore subject to anti money laundering and counter financing of terrorism (AMLCFT) regulation. Designating these agents as subject persons for the purposes of AMLCFT was one of the policy decisions taken by the Government of Malta to ensure that Malta's financial market integrity is safeguarded, as the agent adds an additional layer of AMLCT checks in this regard.

Regulatory Requirements Applicable to VFA Agents

As stated above, the VFA Act requires persons performing the activity of a VFA Agent to be registered with the MFSA. While the Act sets out, albeit at a high level, the role and responsibilities of the VFA Agent, the detailed obligations are stipulated in Chapter 1 of the VFA Rulebook – Virtual Financial Assets Rules for VFA Agents. The chapter is divided into 4 titles as follows: [i] General Scope and High-Level Principles; [ii] Registration requirements for VFA Agents; [iii] Ongoing Obligations; and [iv] Enforcement and Sanctions. Whilst this section will highlight the salient requirements thereof, it is not intended to provide a comprehensive overview of the requirements for VFA Agents.

General Principles

The first Title of Chapter 1 sets out the high level principles that VFA Agents should abide by when providing their VFA activity in or from within Malta. In summary, VFA Agents are required to act ethically in the best interests of their clients and the integrity of Malta's financial system, honestly, fairly and professionally, and to co-operate with the

Authority in an open and honest manner and to provide it with any information it may require.

Registration Requirements

Persons wishing to act as a VFA Agent are to apply for registration with the Authority in accordance with Title 2 of Chapter 1 of the VFA Rulebook. As stated, such person must be a legal person, and at least three individuals are to be proposed to the Authority by the applicant to act as designated persons. These persons are those individuals that will be responsible for performing the activity of a VFA Agent. Furthermore, one of the three designated persons must be the VFA Agent's proposed Money Laundering Reporting Officer (MLRO) and as such also responsible for ensuring the VFA Agent's compliance with the Implementing Procedures issued by the Malta's Financial Intelligence Analysis Unit. The Rules also set out initial capital requirements applicable to VFA that which must be fully paid up and must consist of cash and cash equivalents in terms of International Accounting Standards. The Initial capital requirements are as follows[12]:

Registration Type	Initial Capital (€)
VFA Agent registering in terms of Article 7	(i) 75,000 and mandatory PII; or
	(i) 150,000
VFA Agent registering in terms of Article 14	75,000 and PII on a best effort basis
VFA registering in terms of both Articles 7 and 14	(i) 75,000 and mandatory PII; or
	(i) 150,000

Once a complete application for registration as a VFA Agent is submitted to the MFSA, as part of the vetting process, the Authority considers: [i] the protection of investors and the general public; [ii] the protection of the reputation of Malta taking into account Malta's international commitments; [iii] the promotion of innovation, competition and choice; [iv] the reputation and suitability of the Applicant and all other parties connected with the applicant. In doing so, the Authority also evaluates the fitness and properness of the applicant by assessing: [i] Integrity; [ii] Competence; and [iii] Solvency.

The registration process itself is then divided into three phases – the preparatory phase, which spans from the applicant's submission of a statement of intent to apply for registration to the submission of a complete application, the pre-registration phase, which, provided that everything is in order, leads to the granting of an in-principle registration valid for a period of three months within which the applicant is to satisfy a number of requirements set out in the principal registration. Once the requirements of the in-principle registration are satisfied, the Authority would proceed to register the applicant as a VFA Agent. Notwithstanding the registration, a VFA Agent may be required to satisfy, within set time frames a number of post-registration matters, prior to commencement of business. This phase is termed the post-registration/pre-commencement of business stage.

The Rules also contain the processes that are to be followed for: [i] the revision of a registration – where a VFA Agent wishes to amend its registration; [ii] changes in qualifying holding and beneficial ownership of VFA Agents; voluntary suspension of VFA registrations; the cessation of the business of a VFA Agent; and the approval and departure process for designated persons and appointed persons.

Ongoing Obligations

The Rules also stipulate a number of requirements that VFA Agents must abide by on an ongoing basis. Further to the general requirements applicable to all VFA Agents, the rules also set out supplementary requirements for those VFA Agents registered under Article 7 as well as those registered in terms of article 14.

- ## *General Requirements*

Section 2 of Title 3 sets out the general requirements which all VFA Agents must satisfy on an ongoing basis. VFA Agents are inter alia required to have adequate business organization, systems, experience and expertise to exercise their role, as well as to maintain sufficient records to be able to demonstrate compliance with the regulatory framework for a period of five years, which may be extended to seven years at the Authority's discretion. VFA Agents are also obliged to maintain the initial capital and to have three designated persons in place, at all times.

The title also establishes obligations related to governance, such as the requirement for the business to be effectively directed by at least two individuals in satisfaction of the dual control principle, as well as to establish and implement a number of systems (including due diligence systems), processes and procedures which should be monitored and evaluated at least every six months.

With respect to Professional Indemnity Insurance (PII) the rules stipulate that VFA Agents are to make every effort to take out and maintain full PII. While the requirement is to make every effort to obtain PII, those VFA Agents that do so may benefit from reduced capital requirements as per R1-2.1.2.6.

As stated, prior to onboarding a client, the VFA Agent must perform a fitness and properness assessment. While this is reiterated, the Rulebook also provides the procedure that VFA Agents must follow when they find a prospective client not to be fit and proper – they must inform the Authority immediately explaining why they do not consider such person to be fit and proper (R1-3.2.6.2). Apart from providing the Authority with information on persons seeking entry into the Maltese financial services sector, this will also provide the Authority with information on VFA Agents themselves, particularly the standard of the checks being performed, particularly where a person who is not on-boarded by a VFA Agent gets on-boarded by another.

The Rules also set out requirements for outsourcing, procedures for reporting of breaches, instances where more than one VFA Agent is appointed and Conduct of Business Obligations that include requirements on conflicts of interest, remuneration operational independence and personal transactions.

- *Supplementary Conditions for VFA Agents Appointed in Terms of Article 7*

A VFA Agent engaged with an issuer has a role that is ongoing and therefore there are certain obligations that the VFA Agent must satisfy following the registration of the whitepaper. First and foremost, the VFA Agent must ensure that the issuer is a fit and proper person on an ongoing basis and must also endorse determinations made by the Issuer pursuant to the financial instrument test. Where applicable, the VFA Agent must also ensure that the issuer has provided investors with a roadmap and that any necessary public disclosures are made.

The VFA Agent is also responsible to submit to the Authority, on an annual basis, a Compliance Certificate in relation to the Issuer. This certificate is to be drawn up by the Issuer, reviewed by the VFA Agent and signed by all members of the Issuer's Board of Administration. The compliance certificate is to contain: [i] a confirmation obtained from the Issuer's MLRO that all the local AML/CFT requirements have been satisfied; [ii] a confirmation from the Issuer's systems auditor that the issuer's innovative technology arrangements comply with any qualitative standards set and guidelines issued by the Malta Digital Innovation Authority; [iii] a statement, from the VFA Agent, as to whether the Issuer is a fit and proper person; and [iv] a statement from the Issuer's administrators as to whether there have been any breaches of the act.

Further to the compliance certificate, the VFA Agent is also required to submit an AML/CFT report, prepared by an independent auditor engaged by the issuer, which includes: [i] a confirmation that the AML/CFT systems and controls that the issuer purports to have in place are indeed in place; and [ii] a review of the implementation of such AML/CFT systems and controls.

- *Supplementary Conditions for VFA Agents Appointed in terms of Article 14*

The role of the VFA Agent appointed with an applicant for a VFA services licence ends once the Authority grants or refuses to grant a licence. While this is made clear by virtue of R1-3.4.1, R1-3.4.2 goes a step further and stipulates that the VFA Agent may, subject to be so proposed by a licence holder, continue his relationship with his client as Compliance Officer.

Enforcement and Sanctions

Like the Act, breaches of the rules render the VFA Agent liable to administrative penalties not exceeding €150,000. The Rules however go further and set out criteria – aggravating and mitigating factors – that are to be taken into account by the Authority when establishing the quanta of the penalties.

Conclusion

The concept of the VFA Agent is a novel one. Introduced to ensure that a first line of defence independent from the Authority is set up in order to keep persons who are not fit and proper out of the Maltese financial services industry, the VFA Agents' checks do not replace those performed by the Authority, but rather complement them by introducing yet another filter. While this is evidence of the MFSA's commitment to protect the integrity of the local financial services sector, it will also ensure effective investor protection and safeguard the soundness of operators. A proper functioning framework for VFA Agents should reduce the risk of financial market misconduct and crime, which should, in turn, serve as an additional safeguard for consumers and Malta's reputation as a financial centre.

Endnotes

1. Christopher P. Buttigieg and Christos Efthymiopoulos, "The Regulation of Crypto Assets in Malta: The Virtual Financial Assets Act and Beyond", Law and Financial Markets Review, 2018.
2. EBA, "Report with Advice for the European Commission on Crypto-Assets", 9/1/2019.

3. Subsidiary Legislation 590.01 of the laws of Malta.
4. VFA Rulebook, MFSA, Available at: <https://www.mfsa.com.mt/fintech/virtual-financial-assets/rules/>.
5. The Financial Instrument Test, MFSA, mfsa.com.mt.
6. The SEC has jurisdiction over those cryptoassets classified as securities, while the CFTC has classified certain cryptoassets as commodities.
7. Mauritius FSC, "Fintech Series, Guidance Note, Recognition of Digital Assets as an Asset-class for investment for Sophisticated and Expert Investors", 17/9/2018.
8. Ken Kawai and Takeshi Nagase, "Virtual Currency Regulation Review – Edition 1", The Law Reviews – Japan, November 2018.
9. CONSOB, "Call for Evidence: ICOs and Crypto-Assets Exchanges", 19/3/2019.
10. VFA Act, Article 2(2), definition of 'VFA Agent'.
11. VFA Rulebook, Chapter 1, VFA Rules for VFA Agents.
12. VFA Rulebook, Chapter 1 – R1-2.1.2.6.

11. Maltese Technology Foundations

Max Ganado

The ITF law will not only be an enabling and empowering law to support the new industry around ITAs but it will also impose conditions on standards and modes of operations and behaviours.

Dr Max Ganado is a senior partner at Ganado Advocates and leads the core team on the new legislation being proposed for Malta in DLT and related fields. He is a board member of BMA.

Introduction

Since the Government of Malta adopted a strategic proposal on the subject in April 2017, Malta has been pursuing an innovative path towards the regulation of blockchain. This is to be distinguished from the manner in which it has decided to regulate Initial Coin Offerings (ICOs), virtual assets and services relating to cryptocurrencies. The goal is legal certainty and support for innovation in this technology and its uses.

Blockchain – Decentralized or Distributed Ledger Technology (DLT) – has clearly challenged traditional legal concepts and rules in many areas. This is therefore a wonderful opportunity for innovation. One area identified in the Maltese Government consultation paper issued in February 2018[1] is that of legal personality for innovative technology arrangements (ITAs).

Although a lot of work and discussion had, by then, taken place on the subject of legal personality for ITAs, the Consultation Paper merely stated[2]:

"Whilst some Technology Arrangements are owned by a corporate structure, other Technology Arrangements may not have such an ownership structure. This could result in the possibility of transacting on and with the Technology Arrangement without a proper 'legal person' as counterparty. The proposed TAS Bill will try to provide a solution to such a scenario and it is being proposed that certain Technology Arrangements will be able to register with the Registrar for Legal Persons in Malta and acquire legal personality upon satisfaction of a number of requirements."

The TAS Bill is now a law called the Innovative Technology Arrangements and Services Act (ITASA)[3]. Although there are some important provisions on legal organizations, particularly how one establishes administrators and qualifying shareholders for regulatory purposes when tokens feature in the structures[4], the provisions on providing legal personality to ITAs were not included as it was considered that more detailed discussion needed to take place on the subject in view of the highly innovative nature of this proposal.

This chapter has been prepared to discuss some preliminary issues that are being studied in the path towards implementing such a proposal. The proposal relates to the design of a variant of a foundation (a universality of things[5]) as this was considered to be the most appropriate model to build on for the context for several reasons. In this chapter, the author refers to it as an Innovative Technology Foundation (ITF) that is to be distinguished from ordinary foundations existing under current Maltese law.

Definitions

ITAs are defined in Maltese law[6] as including distributed ledger arrangements as well as arrangements of decentralized computation, such as smart contracts and decentralized autonomous organisations (DAOs). The first schedule of the ITAS Act states[7] that:

"The following shall be considered to be innovative technology arrangements for the purposes of this Act:

1. software and architectures which are used in designing and delivering DLT which ordinarily, but not necessarily:

(a) uses a distributed, decentralized, shared and, or replicated ledger;
  (b) may be public or private or hybrids thereof;
  (c) is permissioned or permissionless or hybrids thereof;

(d) is secure to a high level against retrospective tampering, such that the history of transactions cannot be replaced;

(e) is protected with cryptography and

(f) is auditable;

2. smart contracts and related applications, including decentralised autonomous organisations, as well as other similar arrangements;

3. any other innovative technology arrangement which may be designated by the Minister, on the recommendation of the Authority, by notice from time to time."

The term 'arrangement' was chosen to indicate a multiple part structure or system that is designed and organized in a manner that provides facilities for use by many parties, and that may have automated operational features through computer code. It is a combination of a ledger, automated processes, and possibly other elements of open-source software coming together, possibly on other software platforms, such as Ethereum, providing yet more software to support required functionalities[8]. It has outcomes beyond the actions of its designers and users, and which may be relied upon by the same users to reach their own goals.

An earlier contribution co-authored by the author[9] of this chapter has addressed the point of whether it would be appropriate to grant legal personality to such arrangements, explaining that the software can be owned by a new form of legal person that would be designed to context. It is important to appreciate that a purpose foundation can be itself 'ownerless' or 'non-proprietary'. In such a case, the technology functionalities and the legal personality merge very smoothly into one. That is not to say that when there are ownership interests in a mixed purpose/beneficiary foundation it happens any less smoothly, but clearly with private interests[10] there is some erosion of pure purposes linked to the software functions and purposes.

Importance is given to the fact that the innovative technology arrangement has several features already supporting the argument that it could qualify as a legal entity, such as a partnership, even unintentionally. Many of these arguments focus on the active participation, as opposed to intent at establishment, of many people and related consensus mechanisms and point to 'associations of persons' like partnerships or companies[11]. This is contrasted with intent at establishment through endowment of assets subject to specific purposes.

The author also gave a presentation last April[12] explaining why, in his view, the better direction of thinking on forms of legal organizations available would be towards a purpose foundation as opposed to any form of association of persons, given the lack of associative intent of the users, the complexity of special laws like the Companies Act and the clearly identifiable purpose, which would also be public, as part of the code established by the designer in such arrangements. The software is clearly an asset dedicated to achieve a stated purpose and all that would be needed in this context is a statement of intent in English (or any other language of the developer, naturally) in the software itself or in another connected or related document, such as a white paper or a subscription document available to members of the public who wish to become users or nodes in the blockchain.

It would appear to even superficial analysis that the technology arrangement would constitute a 'universality of things' dedicated to a purpose to be achieved through some form of governance structure – automated or physical – and if the content and the necessary actions and procedures – most importantly registration

– are respected as required by law, it could qualify as a foundation having legal personality.

This is close to the definition of a foundation in current Maltese Law[13] stating:

"1. A foundation is an organisation consisting of a universality of things constituted in writing, including by means of a will, by a founder or founders whereby assets are destined either –

(a) for the fulfilment of a specified purpose; and, or

(b) for the benefit of a named person or class of persons,

and which are entrusted to the administration of a designated person or persons.

The patrimony, namely assets and liabilities, of the foundation is kept distinct from that of its founder, administrators or any beneficiaries. The fiduciary obligations in 1124A of this Code shall be binding upon the foundation and all persons administering it towards any beneficiaries for the fulfilment of the stated purposes of the foundation:

Provided that the fiduciary obligations shall be subject to such restrictions or modifications as may be stated in the statute or the terms of engagement of the administrators, as the case may be."

For this reason, it would be simple to state in a new law that:

"An innovative technology arrangement as defined in the MDIA[14] which complies with the requirements of the law shall be considered to be a universality of things destined to the fulfilment of a specified lawful purpose, which may or may not be combined with the benefit of a named person or class of persons, which when designed, endowed or acquired subject to such purpose, qualifies to be registered as an innovative technology foundation.

An innovative technology foundation may be constituted:

(i) by an instrument in writing[15] combined with an endowment or acquisition of the innovative technology arrangement;
or
(ii) by means of a software code made by a developer on his own initiative or at the request of a third party, or by another innovative technology arrangement which has been programmed to carry out such act, with the intention that such arrangement is to be an innovative technology foundation upon registration with the Registrar of Legal Persons."

From that will flow a series of logical consequences that will be the subject of legal provisions dealing with all sorts of detail, some of which reflect current law and some of which will accommodate the context to support and facilitate the innovative technology arrangement and its future sustainability[16]. The term 'arrangement' takes on a broader meaning as it now encompasses certain designed legal acts that are taken in that regard by the promoters of this type of foundation.

The split in legal theory between the two types of legal organizations – the association of persons and foundations being a universality of things – is a very long standing one and is reflected in many legal systems. We may theoretically have reached a stage of having to challenge that assumption by recognizing the potential self-sufficiency or automation of the underlying assets as a game changer: the innovative technology arrangement being a combination of DLT and smart contracts, involving virtual assets or tokens, extending into governance, compliance and other functions that make it fully self-sufficient.

This new element may justify a completely new form of legal organization, which many call a DAO, a decentralized autonomous organisation. A recent contribution the author came across put it this way:

"... tokens enable the transformational aspect of public blockchain networks, which is their ability to create and execute rule-systems that result in new organizational and institutional forms of economic governance and enable bespoke socio-economic coordination. "A blockchain is in this sense a new species of rule-system for economic coordination: so, alongside firms, markets, clubs, commons, and governments we now also have blockchains.""[17]

The author is not yet comfortable using the proposed approach, metaphorically speaking, as a noun, a new thing. So far, he has seen validity in using this term as an adjective – a description – which when appended to a foundation, an existing legal form with developed rules around it, can develop along a range of possibilities through recognition of the innovation and creativity in the right direction[18]. The author believes that starting without a model or format and launching a new form of legal entity based on a desired end-position of autonomous organizations will be a less effective process. This can happen gradually on the basis of any form and one would be inclined to choose the form, a foundation, on the basis of underlying concepts of:

· very long term or perpetuity,
· without dependence on individuals, who can come and go,
· with rules on governance that are simple,
· with rules on assets that are also simple,
· with a focus on purpose,
· with many possibilities for public and private benefit streams without too much involvement or control by the beneficiaries.

This will enable the positive to be taken up without too much change, to continue in a new direction embracing decentralization and automation. To use a term commonly referred to in this sector – we can fork the foundation into a new direction on the adoption of a new set of modified rules that will give space for the emergence of a fully automated and self-sufficient DAO.

The Fundamental Justifications

Capacity

Legal personality is the tool designed by brilliant legal minds many centuries ago to address two major issues within the context of human activities. The first is capacity to carry out the very actions that produce results in a social order dominated by a legal system. Legal personality, which is a replica of human personality, implies that the legal person can carry out the same acts as humans, subject to logical physical limitations, such as marriage, or the exercise of discretion or judgement[19], for example.

There are many arguments in theory how it happens that inanimate objects are given legal personality and quasi-human powers. Some base it on fictions and mere intent of the law, others connect to the power to exercise intent and free will in an operating context and are referred to as realist theories. In this project, we are using the reality of a complex operation with variable levels of autonomy before our eyes, and then suggesting that it be granted legal personality to enable it to achieve its purpose more effectively and with greater legal certainty. This is for the greater common good. Thus, you have a merger of both the fiction and the realist theories. That is how a state can best support innovative technology arrangements.

Indeed, the Maltese Civil Code, as do others, starts with a provision as follows[20]:

"1A. (1) Persons may either be natural persons or legal persons.

(2) When used in any law the term "person" shall include both natural persons as well as legal persons, unless the context otherwise requires.

(3) Natural persons are regulated by Title I to Title VIII of Book First of this Code.

(4) Legal persons are regulated by the Second Schedule to this Code.

(5) Legal persons enjoy all rights and powers pertaining to natural persons except those excluded by their very nature, by their constitutive act or by an express provision of law."

So, legal personality is the tool par excellence for solving the problem of legal powers and capacity[21]. In the context of blockchain technologies we have this issue staring us in the face, given the use cases we are seeing emerging with blockchain. We see a multitude of assumptions about the activities an innovative technology arrangement will be carrying out within our societies, being a combination of software artefacts – a ledger, smart contracts and other automated software processes – and human actions.

The regulatory requirements emerging in many laws and the interface between the software and users indicates many contracts that are being or will need to be entered into. So legal capacity is a critical issue. The law usually reads through the context to an individual, usually the owner of the asset, and assumes it is his capacity that is operating. But that would also imply personal liability. Lawyers have traditionally solved the problem, sometimes through trustees and sometimes through using existing legal entities, which have their own legal personality. It will clearly be more efficient if the innovative technology arrangement itself can be granted legal personality as a special universality of things achieving an intended lawful purpose. It is this new personality that displaces the personal liability of the originator of the innovative technology arrangement.

An interesting point arises with regard to the very human trait of respect for the law or fear of the law, which, of course, applies to morality as well. It is evident that technology is unlikely to develop that quality although AI is said to have the potential of developing levels of consciousness that would, theoretically, imply an awareness that can then be linked to behaviours that are law abiding. At this stage of development, however, what is very clear is that developers can design technology in any way. It can be designed to do good things (and abiding by the law is treated as good as we assume the law is enacted for good social reasons); however, it can also be designed to do bad things, including breaching the law, or to be more generous, may be designed in a manner showing lack of awareness of a mandatory law. That will imply liability, civil and sometimes criminal, as that is what happens when one breaches the law through one's actions or activity.

Any technology structure qualifying as a legal person clearly must have all the legal powers to achieve the purposes which must be ab initio lawful and a developer or coder must impliedly be bound to design software to do things that are law abiding and not the opposite. If he does the opposite, legal principles will see him as the actor, because his actions have the reasonably foreseeable consequence of breaching the law and causing harm – or allowing or enabling others to breach the law and cause harm – which is the starting point for criminal intent. This may be a complex argument even for Civil Law purposes when there is a widening distance of time and space between the design of the software by Person A and the use of it years later by Persons B and C, so arguments of duty of care, remoteness and lack of causation will undoubtedly arise and make the whole exercise very complex and uncertain.

However, there will always be the risk of personal liability for various individuals, seeing through intermediate legal entities.

Assuming lawful purposes of an organization and coding of the ITA to respect the law[22], then it will fall easily into ordinary social interactions and everyone else then relies on its many assumed powers to act within our societies. This certainty simplifies dealings and has clear economic benefits, which leads to the second point.

Distinct Patrimony

Legal personality has the effect of producing a distinct patrimony at law, just as happens when we are born. We all have a patrimony from birth to death, which is distinct from the patrimony of other persons. It is on that basis that each of us acquires assets, which are our own, and undertake or suffer liabilities that are only our own and do not burden anyone else[23]. It is also on that basis that we can go bankrupt when the patrimony is exhausted through liabilities, being more than the assets. With regard to legal persons the equivalent concept is very often referred to as insolvency.

Distinct legal personality was the tool for limited liability of persons involved in certain types of legal organizations that allowed the patrimony, of say a company[24], to be available only to the creditors of the business and not to creditors of anyone else owning or controlling the company[25]. Conversely, the rights of recourse of the creditors of the business would be limited to the company's patrimony, and all the persons involved in the ownership or control of the business operations such as the promoters or shareholders, the administrators, the employees, or others involved in the company would not be liable for any of the company's obligations.

All this happens because of distinct patrimonies that come to the rescue of the context.

The same context can be seen to apply in case of innovative technology arrangements. Under current legal principles when someone creates or designs an operating system, he is directly liable for what happens with it. We are all attributed the effects of our own actions. Until something we create takes on or is granted distinct legal personality that produces a distinct patrimony, everything we do, which can have direct causal effects to a loss suffered by another person, can be attributed to us and we are then held liable, unless legal defences[26] apply. Sometimes more than one person is liable for the same act on the basis of contribution rules, which can be based on ownership or on participation in a common activity. It is evident that the design, creation and operation of an innovative technology arrangement, and possibly participation in it or even its use, can fall within such a context. Creating legal personality out of the operational context to deal with third parties will naturally be a solution to the risk of personal liability to many persons involved in the process from design to deployment.

It is on this basis that some have already speculated that users or nodes on a blockchain may potentially be jointly liable for loss caused to other users or third parties. This is one of the biggest causes of legal uncertainty in the context and must have been the basis of attribution of substantial loss across all nodes when thefts took place in one case of a large loss as a result of hacking. Without a distinct patrimony resulting from legal personality supported by a law, this may be a logical outcome – and risk – for people involved in the design, deployment and operation of ITAs.

So legal personality will be a clear solution to this problem, particularly for users that are mostly innocent third parties participating in a very important development for our societies. A similar argument can be made in favour of designers and developers to support innovation often through open-source software development, users which are carrying on the function of oracles, or miners for the continuing operation of the systems, ancillary software developers who create DAPPS that support compliance, governance or identify management and so on.

Through clearly regulated legal personality, liability will be placed squarely onto the patrimony of the legal person with whom everyone will henceforth be dealing. That is why we then find the need, in the laws on legal organizations with legal personality, for publicity on the existence of the legal person, the requirement of accounts and audit to determine the extent of the patrimony, as well as other related behavioural requirements for it to have the intended effects and defensive mandatory rules to ensure it is not abused.

The extent of liability is limited to the patrimony, or estate, of the legal person. Technology that operates the accounting system and activities through smart contracts will undoubtedly deal with this issue. It will make immediately and generally available information about the extent of assets and liabilities as well as any limitations on the right of recourse should they exist at law. It will generally not allow liabilities to be created unless there are assets to meet them[27] except in specific scenarios that will undoubtedly have to be disclosed and be generally available to third parties. These are all the qualities one usually finds in public registers. While usually these are subject to rules applying on an annual basis and are seen in retrospect, in ITAs we have the wonderful potential of having all this information available publicly in real time.

This may justify the shift of some aspects of publicity – say the accounts and the audit reports – from the current public registers to the innovative technology arrangement itself. This is a typical example of the positive impact of technology on current law and the opportunity we have to adjust current law to respect new realities.

Other Features

Legal personality brings many other things to the solution. The subject is very extensive and applies solutions to contexts within the discussion as one moves from civil law to criminal law, for example. Within regulatory law we have yet another dynamic. See-through mechanisms are used when legal personality exists with reference to an applicant. The emergence of tokens, which operate in many contexts through smart contracts, can create challenges as to who the 'real' administrators and shareholders are, not only for establishing liability but also to determine who is subject to qualifying, fit and proper testing[28].

The use of open-source software is prevalent and poses a challenge in liability attribution that should not even arise for a party who has shared his work for the general public benefit and would not even be aware of the use of the software in an ITA. Applying a reasonable foreseeability test to an active developer launching a project would make sense; but the same test for a person who has developed and shared open-source software many years ago, which may or may not have been modified by equally publicly spirited developers over the years, may not make any sense at all[29].

Second Risk – an Achilles Heel

Another major risk for all users of a public blockchain – or even a private blockchain openly available for use to the public – is that the software underlying the ITA will be treated as part of the patrimony of the ITA, even as a legal person, and be subject to attachment and enforcement of claims by third parties suffering a loss.

Solutions based on immunity from attachment and other non-recourse mechanisms, such as making the core ITA software owned by the legal person bankruptcy remote, are critical.

In Maltese law we can also refer to the concept of segregated cells within some types of legal organizations[30], and this gives us another design tool enabling us to distinguish, to some extent[31], between assets that are subject to recourse and those which are not[32]. This is a further extension of the distinct patrimony concept, as a segregated cell is itself another distinct patrimony.

Another angle, which is very appealing, is treating the public decentralized blockchains based on open-source technology as public domain or commons[33]. This results in its not being owned by anyone at all, and hence not being available to anyone to fulfil legal liabilities[34]. Inversely, no one can attach it or enforce his rights on these kinds of assets as they are not capable of being owned, or being the subject of a contract, including for example, security or a court order attaching them or subjecting them to auction. The English law approach to this concept sees the same results emerging through such assets being held under trusts or fiduciary obligations for the benefit of the public at large as well as future generations. The end result is the same. One would not need specific law to render these kinds of assets immune from attachment or enforcement[35].

In this new context of decentralized technology arrangements, the software needs to be protected from withdrawal, freezing, attachment, and like acts that will affect all users more dramatically than the designers, developers or operators of the systems.

For now, this chapter has highlighted the two main features of legal personality. Others will be addressed in future contributions. Much has been written on the above topics though sources[36] are fairly difficult to find and it is heartening to note the development of law-focused communities in many countries dedicating time to solutions in the contexts discussed in this article. This is happening in Malta too and we all look forward to global solutions for what is evidently a cross border challenge. Until these happen, we need to address challenges within our own legal systems.

Some Theoretical Challenges

There are some issues that commentators throw up against the concept of legal personality for innovative technology arrangements. Others support the idea as inevitable. There are of course issues that, upon analysis present themselves as challenges. It would be good to address some of these issues at the start as they tend to return in other discussions[37].

Is Legal Personality Good or Bad in the Context?

In Malta we have been focusing on legal personality for innovative technology arrangements, which to date does not extend to robots operating with AI. Malta may well do so in the future[38]. Innovative technology arrangements, not amounting to robots with AI, are an easier challenge, and one that draws less emotions into the debate. At this stage, the object of the Maltese laws is partially or fully autonomous arrangements that support use cases, which many see as public benefit, such as commercial enterprises, charities and education or health records and so on. Robots are seen as a threat, or at least that is how some perceive them. Discussing legal personality for robots is therefore much more complex as some of them look like humans when they are clearly not human at all. Why they have been given anthropomorphic form is naturally out of scope of this chapter, but it is fair to say that, like many other things in this new technology language, this is a cause of great confusion[39]. The 'personality' debate, which should be based on completely different premises (such as the utility of achieving designated purposes, or to ensure perpetual existence of functions, or to ensure independence from the individuals involved in its activities at a particular time), often veers into discussing anthropomorphic features, like the ability to think or to solve problems, or to remember and learn, which have nothing to do with the reasons for which legal personality is granted to objects, such as a company, a church, a municipality or a state, or to universalities of things or people.

Already there is resistance building up against legal personality for robots, just as we have seen some resistance to a far less impactful legal personality for an innovative technology arrangement. It is important that, while we do make the distinction between one factual context and the other, we do appreciate that the same argument may arise in both contexts and that is why it is being highlighted briefly here.

In a recent article by Janosch Delcker[40] entitled "Europe Divided over Robot 'Personhood'", reference is made to a European Parliament Report[41] proposing that self-learning robots be granted a 'form of electronic personality' as part of what is referred to as 'a high-stakes debate'. We have also read reports that a robot was given citizenship by Saudi Arabia[42], and Malta is said to be exploring the idea.

One reason for such a proposal is described: 'Such a status could allow robots to be insured individually and be held liable for damages if they go rogue and start hurting people or damaging property'[43], which is seen as common sense by many, but '156 AI experts hailing from 14 European countries, including computer scientists, law professors and CEOs, warn that granting robots legal personhood would be 'inappropriate' from a 'legal and ethical perspective'[44].

The central issue highlighted in the chapter poses the need for legal certainty on liability issues. It was written in reaction to statements such as 'manufacturers were merely trying to absolve themselves of responsibility for the actions of their machines'[45]. and the doubts expressed in the following question: 'In a scenario where an algorithm can take autonomous decisions, then who should be responsible for these decisions?[46]' These are important issues for all software, whether involving AI or not.

In a comment attributed to a Milan based lawyer Stefania Lucchetti[47]:

"Today, virtually every country of the world applies the model to companies, which means that corporations have some of the legal rights and responsibilities of a human being, including being able to sign a contract or being sued. A similar legal model for robots, its advocates argue, would be less about giving rights to robots and rather about holding them responsible when things go wrong, for example by setting up a compulsory insurance scheme that could be fed by the wealth a robot is accumulating over the time of its "existence.""

The author agrees. The problem we all have is whether the existing approach of using agency principles in relation to actions of things, as in vicarious liability, which we use for animals for example, can continue to apply with some certainty to this context or not, given the increasing remoteness between a human individual – whether he or she is an owner, an operator or a developer – and the software operation. The difficulty on which there is an evident design choice for legislators, is whether to apply liability to the thing that caused the loss or whether you need to keep going up until you find a human or legal 'person' who can at law be liable. This is what current legal process in most legal systems does. However, the innovative developments we have been seeing in recent years have posed serious challenges to processes based on existing legal logic and, in the author's view, it is therefore time to redesign legal solutions to context.

The author is favourable to granting legal personality in contexts as is explained below, even if he does not yet see the basis for granting citizenship, and disagrees with the objections above summarized. Of course, one needs to see the arguments raised in more detail as deep legal analysis is surely available for such positions, just as it is available for the contrary view. One needs to see what is motivating negative reactions, and one needs to see if this is focused on the context of AI and robots, which the author suspects is the case, or whether the objections go wider to any technology arrangement that can act independently and is self-sufficient and automated, whether involving AI and robots or not.

In the next part of this contribution the author argues in favour of legal personality for innovative technology contexts. He bases himself on the need for legal certainty on two main aspects: capacity, which is critical to the stability of legal relationships that are inevitable in the context, and liability, which needs to be, at least, predictable, whoever or whatever may be exposed to it.

The author does agree that insurance will help in the context and we are currently debating solutions in that sense even in the Malta project on DLT and smart contracts that does not involve AI or robots.

The author does not agree that by making technology arrangements 'persons, who will be liable for their actions', one is necessarily excluding liability from other persons whose actions cause loss, breach of law or other damage. That is a policy choice open to design and many options exist. We see this in commercial partnerships and other structures that have legal personality, but where the partners remain jointly and severally liable among themselves and with the partnership. Equally we see managers and executives in legal entities with legal personality liable for their own wrong doing. The principle that legal personality cannot be used to carry out fraud[48] ,and catering for piercing of the corporate veil is also a tool used by the law and the courts in many countries to avoid abuse and injustice. On the other end of the spectrum we may easily make the argument that applying liability to persons who are not the cause of the loss just because they may have developed some part of the software many years ago, unaware of the contexts in which it could be freely used, possibly even after partial modification, by third parties, could equally lead to gross injustices that we must of course seek to avoid by any means, be they insurance, legal personality or redesign of law.

No doubt this discussion will gain greater relevance in the near future.

Decentralized Organizations and Centralised Features

The principle argument made is that legal organizations are by definition centralized while in the context of DLT and DAOs we have decentralized structures. So the argument goes that we cannot have concepts of legal personality from the centralized world applying at all. Various responses have been suggested to this argument, the main one being that the single ownership of a decentralized software does not make it any less decentralized, as the issue of ownership can easily be distinguished from control and operation of the automated asset. Indeed, the single ownership of an ITA by a purpose foundation that could be, by design, an ownerless or non-proprietary structure[49], admirably eliminates much of that argument[50]. One can also have proprietary – owned – legal organizations that are not granted powers of control in a centralized manner, or which do not have owners who can control, as their tokens do not give them such powers in view of the context, being equally caught by the same argument[51].

Maltese law caters for purpose foundations[52] based on very long-standing Roman law concepts[53], reflected in Canon law and hundreds of years of court judgments. These were reflected in a specific part of the Maltese Civil Code in 2007[54]. In 2007, the law also catered for some enhancements to the traditional concept, such as segregated cells and rules on fiduciary obligations focused on purposes. Since 2007, purpose foundations have been used as non-proprietary structures for charities, securitizations[55] and other commercial transactions.

Apart from the requirements based on a paper-based world that are easily eliminated and the publicity requirements that can find substitutes in appropriately designed ITAs, the main challenge to the use of the current model of purpose foundations is the imposition of a defined form of a Board of Administration, usually made up of three individuals[56]. Another challenge is the lack of legal certainty created around the potential automation of compliance and related functionalities by an innovative technology arrangement addressing mandatory legal obligations, like AML and GDPR: is it compliant, and who is responsible for non-compliance?

Laws deal with persons as subjects. When a legal organization fails in carrying out a statutory duty, the responsibility falls on individuals, usually the administrators. Could the law cater for non-compliance, being a breach of contract, a tort or a breach of criminal law, by an automated arrangement without seeing through to designated individuals not because people are being exculpated but because there are none to see-through to?

The reason for this see-through feature is common to all legal organizations, which are an artificiality or a creation of the law. It has always been presumed that the purpose can only be practically achieved through people who could think and act under a presumed mandate from the legal organization – the foundation – to achieve the stated purpose with the patrimony of the legal organization. Likewise, only a physical person could breach the law, although after many years we now see that this has changed in many legal systems and a legal organization is now capable of being charged with and penalized for crimes. Indeed, one of the suggestions being discussed in Malta, in the DLT/smart contracts context, is the development of corporate responsibility law also addressing the criminal law aspects, given that current law is insufficient to cater for the issues that may arise.

The artificial legal organization could not do anything itself, nor could the physical assets that are, by nature, passive. So the Romans envisaged that a collection of inanimate objects destined to a purpose would be supported by the law[57] so that the purpose might be achieved in a more effective manner. That influenced the development of corporate law for the next two millennia, but it also influenced the way criminal law reacted as the system wanted its pint of blood and no one was going to be happy with what a legal organization could provide[58]. Could this be an opportunity to introduce a clear rule on non-conviction based liability for an ITA organized as an ITF?

Furthermore, as the purpose of a foundation may be one that is long-term, or even perpetual, and would be reasonably expected to extend beyond the life of one person, a Board of Administrators, the membership of which is regularly renewed as the need arises, a foundation has traditionally been seen as the best solution. Foundations can act, communicate, contract as agents, they can be sued and be held liable directly or subordinately. This is clearly a centralized feature. Let us assume a Board of Administrators is appointed, and is not substituted fully by automated governance, is that a problem in this debate on innovative technology arrangements being provided with legal personality? It clearly is not a problem for centralized ones, but is it a problem for decentralized permissionless blockchain arrangements?

It can be a problem to some, particularly on the philosophical level, as it may undermine one of the central conceptual qualities of DLT, which allows for peer-to-peer transactions without the need of any intervention by anyone else, supported by multiple nodes without the need of any central organ or body. But that depends on what the Board of Administrators can and cannot do or rather what they historically and theoretically have done so far. Let us look at the functions of this centralized organ.

The first is administration of the relevant assets belonging to the organization to ensure that it achieves the designated purpose. In this case, the administrators would be administering the blockchain software and smart contracts to the extent that they need administration. What if they do not need any? Is a centralized Board of Administrators still a threat?

The second is to administer non-relevant assets – generated through investment – to support the principal purpose and to hold a patrimonial pool to cover any obligations it may enter into, including potential liabilities. This is the main fiduciary function of the board consisting of the administration of assets belonging to another to achieve the designated purpose established for the legal organization. Same question as above. What if the direction of cash flows to liability pools to cover obligations (costs, distributions, debts and others) is automated, rendering the administrators unnecessary? What if the law allows that the Board of Administrators is effectively disintermediated on many key functionalities, so typical of what blockchain does? Would the central administrator or administrators still be a threat? It seems to the author that not being able to pay one's bills, when these are not contemplated in advance, is a greater existential threat than having a centralized functionary who can intervene when the automation stops.

The Functions of Administrators

The relevant asset here is the software that is now capable of automation, and this can be further enhanced through smart contracts. Once designed to operate in a certain way to achieve a defined purpose – which can be as simple as to host user wallets and allow for peer-to-peer transactions with their assets – the bigger debate taking place is whether the software can be changed more than whether it will do what it has been programmed to do.

What Maltese law has proposed in the law enacted to address ITAs is that the Malta Digital Innovation Authority – the new regulator for this sector – will certify the arrangement if positively assessed by a systems auditor[59] to do what it says it is programmed to do. So if it is programmed to administer its assets, to receive and accept additions, to apply its assets to the purpose, to generate and apply assets from transactions and so on, we do not need general administrators[60] to do so. In Maltese law we have designed a role for a human functionary – called a technical administrator[61] – but that relates only to what he is engaged to do, apart from some very limited functions required for certification under the law, and anything beyond that is up to the software. This should not contradict the proposition.

Then there is the administration of assets other than the distributed ledger, being mostly the initial capital, cash flow that is paid out of some wallets to others pursuant to smart contracts that automate a series of payments from transactions or other sources, which could be an ICO, so as to implement the capital fund that is available to promote and achieve the purpose of the arrangement.

There are payments for the ITF to meet, such as annual registration fees, annual returns, taxation, accountants and auditors, including systems auditors, the technical administrator's fees, lawyers, rents, if premises are required, websites, and communication strategies, and the like. These can all be automated to happen when due but clearly the movement of money into an administrative pool must happen to allow for contingencies, and variations can even be predicted and programmed to happen based on formulae.

At some point, however, as not everything can be predicted, one will need a physical person to act, and this could be the technical administrator, though this was not envisaged in the minimum requirements in the ITASA. This is a task that could reasonably be carried out by the local agents in Malta. Our laws contemplate a VFA Agent[62] and a local representative[63] for different contexts. If they are willing to so act and the promoters have sufficient confidence in their abilities and consider their fees reasonable, then there is a ready solution as these are clearly physical persons. We must however ask: is there a problem on the point of 'decentralization' to appoint an administrator with defined and limited powers to carry out these functions?

Will this make the arrangement inconsistent with the decentralized technology? Will this upset theory to such an extent that the ITF being proposed in Malta will not be a potential solution to many of the problems for decentralized organizations out there? Will the quality of the proposed solutions re-dimension the theoretical arguments?

Then administrators act in a representative capacity and bind the foundation through contracts with third parties, some of which could be very important for the security and credibility of the operations on the DLT platform.

Every achievement of a purpose requires the interaction with third parties. The engagement of the administrators themselves is a contract, as is the acquisition, donation or endowment of the assets dedicated to the purpose, in this case all the software of which is owned by the ITF. With regard to the software not owned by the ITF, there are contracts often caught under the term 'licence agreements'.

For these to be valid someone has to accept them on behalf of the organization – every donor needs a done, every seller needs a buyer – and the members of the Board of Administrators usually do this on behalf of the organization. The engagement of staff, the investment of assets, the purchase and sale of assets, the distribution of assets by way of support of the purpose and hundreds of other actions are all contracts that need to be binding on the parties, including the organization, as these are bilateral or multilateral agreements.

It is not possible to contemplate everything one needs for the future operation on inception, and things happen from time to time and need intervention. Is it a problem to have a solution of an available administrator, or merely a representative, for where it is needed that is set within parameters of a vision – the decentralization of an automated DLT?

Some still insist that the centralized nature of a Board of Administrators must be a problem. That is only correct if one disregards the context of innovative technology arrangements that can provide a completely different approach to the above issue through its power of automation, especially through smart contracts[64].

This realization allows us to think outside the box and cater for effective alternatives to the long-held tradition of requiring a Board of Administrators with full powers vested in them to do everything, in all legal organizations. We can challenge the premise that a legal organization cannot exist or act without an administrator, though this does pose problems at the extremes.

One function of administrators is to act as a representative that in practice may be dramatically reduced in relevance, but at some point it may still be required so even if we reduce it to very small relevance, and vest that power in a very limited designated functionary, we have to address the issue at some point.

When smart contracts operate in situ there will be little need for legal representation or legal capacity as the context may not even be contractual, being limited to pure process. When smart contracts are actually contracts, then they will operate in relation to users who voluntarily subscribe to the arrangement, and, who one can presume, agree to the terms of the smart contracts on joining the platform, so the question relating to the power of the platform to bind its legal owner – the ITF – does not really arise as we are past that stage. Of course, one has to overcome the problem of 'consent' as in some cases, such as those relating to consumers or submission to arbitration or jurisdiction agreements, the demands of the law may be more onerous.

Designs for the Future

We can now design solutions based on context – the features of blockchains and smart contracts – which allow us to actually either eliminate or possibly decentralize and disintermediate the Board of Administrators or its responsibilities and many, if not most, of its functions.

If we eliminate the Board then the issue goes away. If we decentralize the functions carried out by the Board then we no longer have a problem of the same impact on the core features of the innovative technology arrangements. This will depend on context and maybe we can do a bit of one thing and a bit of another and give the developers choices that will enable them to maintain the integrity of ideas.

The best solution appears to cater for a range of possibilities from 100% automation to very little automation and allow for different calibration on different topics or matters. The argument the author would make is that once you open the door to automation of governance structures, even if limitedly, and you recognise the combined dynamic of automated operation, and participation of human action in the innovative technology arrangement, you have done enough to permit a quantum leap to a new set of rules on legal personality.

In Malta we are working on a variant based on the impacts of innovative technology. It may not go so far as to meet the imagination or ambition of some through the imposition – leave no choice or flexibility to developers – of a completely human-less distributed autonomous organization that is fully self-automated. Leaving a choice in design still appears necessary and useful, and, in some contexts, important[65]. One can imagine a time when technology will develop to make this unnecessary as all will be automatable and flexibility today will not hinder development in that direction.

One should remember that the central asset of the foundation will be the innovative technology arrangement – the software – and everything will be taking place within its confines. Much less will be done outside and these 'external' actions can be identified and placed within the responsibility of a physical person or more than one. This has to do with governance of blockchains and smart contracts on which much has been written already with different focuses. Of course, a time might come when this challenge will be met, maybe by AI, and human actions may no longer be required in any context.

It can be noted that some of the external actions could themselves also be other ITAs that have functionalities the relevant ITA itself does not have. Oracles can also be used to verify information that can be the basis of action by the ITA and that can itself raise very difficult questions on liability that are usually addressed in the contract between the ITA and the Oracle. Having a Board of Administrators made up of people who will not even know these things are happening through the technology means there is ample justification to adjust our long-held views on who should be liable, to the point we are now discussing, and ask again: where does that cause a problem to decentralization?

Will Different, Unregistered and Non-Compliant Structures Be Recognized as Equivalent to ITFs?

Another doorstop issue that also needs to be addressed is the issue of whether an innovative technology arrangement could be considered to be a legal organization if in a different form from an ITF, if not within an ITF, or if not in compliance with the requirements of the proposed ITF law. Another way of asking this question: can one have an Innovative Technology Company, or Partnership, or an irregular ITF?

The ITF law will not only be an enabling and empowering law to support the new industry around ITAs but it will also impose conditions on standards and modes of operations and behaviours. In the ITASA, Maltese law already requires a systems audit for an ITA to be certified by the MDIA. It is therefore evident that with the benefits must come burdens. That would imply some clear strategy on what happens when existing and traditional laws on legal organizations, catering for existing forms, are used by promoters as well as when promoters either intentionally avoid them or adopt them irregularly.

In practical terms the questions are:

- Would the benefits of this innovative thinking around ITAs apply if:
- A limited liability company under the Companies Act – which is a registered legal organization in the form of an association and having legal personality;

or

- A foundation under Sub-Title II of Title III of the Second Schedule to the Civil Code, as opposed to the newly designed Sub-Title IIA on ITFs – which is a registered legal organization in the form of a universality of assets and having legal personality;

were to be set up to own and operate the innovative technology arrangement?

- Would the proposed regime apply if the promoters set up a partnership or an unregistered association, both of which are recognized legal organizations but which do not have legal personality?
- Would the regime apply if a promoter does a lot of what the new rules require but then fails to comply with the proposed law and fails to register the ITF under it?

Under standard legal thinking in this area, it is the intention of the persons who promote a legal organization that leads to its creation, as it is they who state its purpose and then choose its legal form by pursuing the formal and procedural rules for the creation of the organization they intend to create. Registration in a public registry may or may not be a key requirement and what is clearly evidence of intent to create a legal organization is a statute in writing according to a stated formula with a mandatory minimum content.

Some legal systems require different forms of publicity and others grant legal personality on the basis of registration with a public registry or a court or other state entity. Malta follows this latter rule and provides for a Registrar for Legal Persons forming part of the Public Registry so that only registered organizations may obtain legal personality.

However, many legal systems still recognise legal organizations even if they do not have legal personality, as does Maltese law. These are called 'unregistered organizations' that do not have legal personality and the legal effects are usually more limited, with liability burdening the persons involved, unlimitedly but possibly in a subordinated manner.

So it is clear that once it is agreed that a technology arrangement involving an ITA, smart contracts. and participants has all the elements needed to establish a legal organization, it is easy to see that the very fact situation can result in an interpretation that the parties involved have impliedly created one or more forms of legal organizations – those that do not need a written statute or registration. Likewise, it is easy to see that if a statute is written and signed, or subscribed to by additional participants, then that fact situation will lead to the emergence of yet other forms of legal organizations, which are now formally existing rather than merely implied.

It is therefore quite possible for the ITA context to create a lot of confusion in the market from this angle alone. This has created a lot of uncertainty already and the policy approach being proposed on this score is to eliminate the uncertainty by some legislative provisions: stating that any actions, including written statutes, which seek to create a legal organization around the factual context of innovative technology arrangements[66] shall have no effect and will neither create a legal organization nor will it create a legal person under the law, impliedly or constructively.

It is recognized however, that these actions may reflect valid actions of individuals that have capacity. If the purpose (causa) is lawful, they will produce some legal effects, which can obviously impact on consumers that engage in or with such arrangements. This can be very dangerous and damaging, and so it is suggested that the law should declare expressly that such actions will be deemed to produce only a personal right or obligation or, if multilateral, a contract, or a series of contracts, between the parties for which the actor will be personally and unlimitedly liable[67], both civilly towards third parties should they suffer loss or under statute or criminally should a breach of a mandatory statute or of a criminal law take place[68].

It is also recognised that the ITA can be owned by a registered limited liability company, a traditional foundation or other recognised legal form of organization and in that case then such organizations will be the 'actors' with the above consequences until such time as they convert to the new form of foundation being proposed, which will then of course extend all the legal regime to the context[69].

Stating that notwithstanding the establishment of a legal organization through all relevant procedures and forms (including for it to acquire legal personality, as would be the case with a registered company, for example) unless the organization is a properly registered ITF, the legal effects in the new regime will not arise and the liability of all persons involved will be governed by the laws applicable to the selected legal form. This will be choosing to adopt the uncertainties of current laws and foregoing the new facilities that can enhance the protection to users and promoters and allow for new ideas to be implemented reflecting the new decentralized and automated contexts. The existing legal debates will continue for some but not for others.

It is not considered appropriate to prohibit this freedom in view of other provisions of Maltese law that recognize the freedom of individuals to set up legal organizations as they see fit[70]. One might have to consider some other forms of consumer or investor protection rules, as users may not be aware of the strategic options the promoters have when establishing an ITA in so far as the legal form and structure are concerned.

It is true that this can also create some confusion in the market but we have been used to multiple forms of legal organizations with different legal effects for centuries and this should be tolerable.

Will ITAs Need to Be Certified by the MDIA for Legal Personality to Be Extended to Them?

Some questions arise as to how the existing regulatory laws on innovative technology arrangements will combine with the new law on legal personality. In particular will it be mandatory for an ITA to be certified by the MDIA for legal personality to be extended to them? There are valid arguments on both sides of the coin. If we do not impose pre-certification of the ITA for the ITF to be formed then it would mean that the ITF would be more popular as anyone setting up an ITF can use it just like anyone setting up any other business may set up a company. There is no need to show that the business meets any standards before one sets up a company. On the other hand, this is a very bold move forward, and Malta will be offering a privilege of legal personality to support outcomes from this new technology. It stands to reason that the ITA asking for such privilege should (a) be of appropriate type and design; and (b) meet certification standards through appropriate systems audits.

The first point implies that the ITA needs to be of a level of complexity and social impact to justify the grant of legal personality based on the value of legal certainty towards the achievement of its purposes. That it will have a level of self-sufficiency or automation seems to be clearly required as, if nothing in an arrangement is automated, then you do not need new approaches. Likewise, if a simple smart contract automates only a payment on a date it is certainly not one that would justify – nor will be need – granting it legal personality. So the law will need to limit the type of ITA that will be eligible by clear definitions based on types and qualities, and one will need a regulatory body like the MDIA to assess if an applicant ITA does meet these technology requirements as a support service to the Registrar for Legal Persons who accepts a registration of an ITF. Do we need a full certification for this kind of support? No, but it would be catered for in a certification if this were done in advance.

The second point goes to deeper quality assessment given the special features in the ITF law. Is the purpose legal? Is the code properly reflecting the legal purpose, is the accounting system respecting the non-recourse software cell division from all other assets and liabilities, and so on. In other words, there will need to be a systems audit catering for the ITF features apart from the standard blueprint for an ordinary ITA that does not wish to use the ITF legal personality facility. Otherwise we risk having an ITA that is inconsistent with the rules set out in the legal personality law. Again, could not a specifically designed systems audit confirm the same to the MDIA or the Registrar for Legal Persons without requiring an MDIA certification under the ITASA? That may well be the case.

In the author's view, since a systems audit for an ITA to be certified will be necessary, and since an ITAS registered system auditor, and an ITAS registered technical administrator will need to feature heavily before we can be sure that an ITA qualifies for legal personality, and that the MDIA will be the natural authority to confirm the eligibility to certification of any ITA, it is a short step to encompassing all that into a specific category of certification. So the author would simplify things by just demanding that any ITA must be certified to the ITF standards before it can obtain legal personality through the registration of an ITF. Even already certified ITAs will need to obtain this additional certification if they want to take the next step and obtain personality. So this is one of the issues on which debate is still very open.

Going back to the question of non-ITF legal structures like

companies or partnerships, which choose NOT to use what Maltese law offers or fail to meet the requirements of the new regime, the big question will be whether the MDIA will certify an ITA in that context, i.e., where the promoters advise the MDIA that they will vest the ITA in a legal organization but will NOT be using the legal form of an ITF for their project.

This is a policy decision that the MDIA still needs to consider. To date the law does not state that for an ITA to be certified it must be embedded within an ITF for the simple reason that ITAs are the subject of a legislative project that has not yet been completed and is still a work in progress.

In the author's view, when the law on ITFs is enacted and the option is granted in a way that will protect consumers, investors and the national interest in a better way than other existing legal structures, then one should seriously consider imposing the ITF model for certain complex ITAs, such as public and permissionless ITAs with multiple smart contracts. That is the only way, for example, that users will benefit from the bankruptcy remoteness proposal for the non recourse software cell or the mandatory insurance cover proposal for risks to user assets, apart from the declared fiduciary status of the user assets on the ITA, which has important implications for the protection against third party attachments and bankruptcy in any case.

This approach would be one step short of prohibiting complex ITAs to be structured as anything else other than Maltese ITFs, if they are to operate in or from Malta, which is of course the final option in this debate. Controversial and in need of more debate, especially from the angle of the need to be technologically neutral in approach, this appears to be the dominant view supported even in legislation; however, the context of technology having self-automation features may need to be given some legal effect. While this may raise a new risk of uncertainty, as with new technologies, the law may find itself stuck in a time warp, as automated technology may no longer be neutral in an absolute manner. Unless, of course, we invent self-automating laws that can automatically adjust to context as innovation occurs.

Non-Compliant Structures

Under the above scenarios, an ITA will therefore have the benefit of an ITF only if there is full compliance with all matters of form and substance as required in the new law and it is properly registered with the Registrar for Legal Persons as required by the new provisions. No other configuration will produce the full effects of an ITF, directly or indirectly. This may be seen as overly restrictive.

Maybe what can be done, in line with the pace of development of the technology in this field and consistent with Malta's strategic direction, is to provide the non-compliant structures with (or make available, or just impose) a mandatory suite of smart contracts that will ensure that the non-compliant legal organization – or simple ITA – will act in a manner that is of sufficient quality on critical issues, and tolerate that what is not within the critical list of behaviours is left free of imposition.

If that happens, we shall be applying the excellent approach of substance over form through technology, not bothering about legal shapes or forms but ensuring that compliance on critical issues is also respected outside the realm of an ITF. This may be necessary because there is no law of Malta that makes it mandatory to certify an ITA – the ITASA is a voluntary regime. Of course, the benefits of an ITF cannot be extended outside the design if they do not already exist in the context of a simple ITA or in other non-compliant forms.

Conclusion

The new regime will be an extraordinary grant of legal status in a very innovative context. It will bring high levels of legal certainty to various aspects of the discussion about ITAs, including that on capacity, liability and recourse.

It will extend clear protections to users of the technology through the use of segregated cells that can even extend to immunity of the technology from attachment and bankruptcy, as that is the only way to protect users from actions of third parties, who should be adequately covered by insurance or other liability funds.

That needs legal personality to be properly in place. It will give clear rights of action on specific assets and cash flows to creditors without endangering the common public platform that can be treated as public domain, or the new commons, in decentralized permissionless arrangements. It will start setting out the limits of liability resulting from autonomous actions and avoid unpredictable liability to undefined and unlimited classes of persons and will address fiduciary duties more clearly by defining contexts, such as loss and breach of mandatory law, which provoke the need for intervention to avoid such loss and breach of law.

Note: This is a revised version of the original article published in August 2018[71]. The author would also like to thank Dr Christine Borg, Steve Tendon and Joe Ianelli for their helpful comments on earlier drafts of this article. Thanks are also due to my colleague Dr Ian Gauci who has contributed to the debate with detailed analysis and suggestions in the context, particularly around the idea of DAOs.

Endnotes

1. "Malta: A Leader in DLT Regulation", The Parliamentary Secretariat for Financial Services, Digital Economy and Innovation, 2018, meae.gov.mt.
2. Ibid, p. 18.
3. ITAS Act, Chapter 592 of the laws of Malta. This Act came into force on 1 November 2018.
4. Ibid, art 8. Also: Fourth Schedule.
5. Most are called 'foundations', but these come by many different categories linked to form or purpose such as institutes, schools, funds, churches and the like.
6. MDIA Act, Chapter 591 of the laws of Malta, art 2(1). Also: ITAS Act, First Schedule.
7. ITAS Act, First Schedule.
8. To be distinguished from 'organization', as happened with Decentralized Autonomous Organizations, which can also be contextually appropriate but would create confusion with a well-defined legal concept being an entity. Indeed, the challenge is now linking or bridging the two concepts.
9. Steve Tendon and Max Ganado, "Legal Personality for Blockchains, DAOs and Smart Contracts", Revue Trimestrielle De Droit Financier, 1 (2018), pp. 1-9.
10. Such as rights to capital or income from the underlying technology functionalities, or that in development, which could, when completed have a market value. Excluded should be user rights to their own property recorded through tokens in wallets as these are not 'private interests' in the decentralized platform.
11. Philipp Hacker (SSRN: 2998830) argues for the adoption of a corporate governance framework to blockchain-based

organizations as a means of reducing uncertainty. He compares a blockchain with voting and profit participating tokens to traditional companies and other forms of legal organisations,and says: '....it has even been suggested that blockchain-based networks might, in themselves, be partnerships in a legal sense, particularly if users follow a joint purpose and share profits;'.

12.   Max Ganado, Legal Organisations and Technology Arrangements, (Ganado Advocates, 2018),

13.   Maltese Civil Code, Chapter 16 of the laws of Malta, Second Schedule, art 26(1).

14.   MDIA Act, which is in force.

15.   Defined to include electronically.

16.   Reference is made to some important proposals on the general subject of this article by the author's colleague Dr Ian Gauci as follows: "Demystifying Smart Contracts", "The DAO as a Step Forward for the Digital Economy", "Blockchain & Smart Contracts. The Possible Manifesto for Legal Personality and Certainty".

17.   Sinclair Davidson, Primavera De Filippi and Jason Potts, "Economics of Blockchain", 2016. Quoted in Rodrigo Seira, "Blockchain Protocol Developers are not Fiduciaries: An Analysis of the Cryptoeconomics of Open Source Networks and the Role of Protocol Developers in Public Blockchain Network Governance", Good Audience, 2018.

18.   It is not very clear why this should apply only in decentralized contexts as decentralization is distinct from automation that seems to be the real game changer.

19.   This is one of the more sensitive challenges that also raises the potential of AI playing a role, to the extent it is at all possible.

20.   Maltese Civil Code, art 1A.

21.   It should be acknowledged that legal systems also give some legal powers to unregistered organizations based on the factual reality of their existence and activities they carry out without

attaching or extending to them a legal personality. This is complex and uncertain in this context as will be discussed below. Yet other legal systems provide for trusts, being segregated legal patrimonies, relying on the existing legal personality of the trustee to provide for legal capacity.

22. Naturally as it stands at the time the code is developed. However, there is possibly an implied duty – on whom it is not clear – to keep the code compliant with the law as it changes. Indeed, in the Maltese law reflected in article 8 of ITAS Act, there is a direct legal obligation for the technology to be designed in such a manner that it can be modified when it is reasonably foreseeable that the applicable law is subject to change over time. That is coupled with the duty of a functionary referred to as a 'technical administrator' to intervene when there is a cause of loss or a breach of mandatory law. The technology must therefore also have code allowing intervention by such a person in such circumstances. Pure technology can have no powers to do these things and it is almost assumed that there will always be an owner or operator who can be called upon to exercise these powers of variation and intervention. However, in a fully autonomous and decentralized organisation the challenges multiply tremendously and so a solution involving a type of legal entity that can fill in the gaps without undermining the decentralization and the autonomy, while at the same time giving the technology legal personality with powers to act in a lawful and binding manner, is a critical step forward.

23. There are of course some exceptions as with children or animals, which come under the concept of 'vicarious liability'.

24. The legal form of 'company' is being referred to as it is easy to visualize. Historically, companies were established to limit the risk of people involved in a business venture, and many are aware of this context too. The same principles, if not the reasons, apply to any legal organization that is given distinct

personality. There are, however, variations, and we see, for example, partnerships that have legal personality, if registered, but where partners are still jointly and unlimitedly liable for obligations. On the other hand, we have foundations that have legal personality and no one else is liable with them in the normal course of operations, barring fraud and some other specific abuse contexts.

25. Again, subject to specific exceptions where we see piercing of the corporate veil.

26. These could be in the law itself, like force majeure, in contracts, or exclusion clauses.

27. Using the vending machine comparative, we can imagine a question: should the vending machine run out of drinks, will not the software refuse to accept payments, or if coins are taken will not the software ensure that the machine would immediately and automatically return them back to the payor?

28. See ITAS Act, Fourth Schedule on this very issue. Rules are there set out on who qualifies as a shareholder and an administrator for regulatory assessment and compliance purposes.

29. In these contexts, the argument that has been made is that of caveat emptor, which is the legal principle making the buyer – in this case the user – bear the risk of his voluntary action in making use of the open-source software, well knowing the risks that he is considered as happily assuming.

30. These are available in investment funds, certain insurance companies, securitisation vehicles and foundations.

31. This is clearly possible in contract through waiver of rights but, unless supported by a statutory provision, may not bind a third party unaware and not consenting to the immunity.

32. The author has been long promoting the argument that when an innovative technology arrangement is opened to and made available to the public to use, to store, and to transact with their assets, it is unacceptable and disproportionate to allow the very public technology or infrastructure to be seized and enforced

upon by a creditor of the owner of the infrastructure. Can anyone imagine that happening with a public land registry? Such publicly available infrastructure should have the status of public domain and be held by the owner – if there is one – on a fiduciary basis for all users. Creditors should know this in advance and while they too can be protected through income generated on the platform, they should not be able to freeze or attach it – stop it from working for the community using it – affecting all the public member users and their assets. Of course, there are many detailed implications emerging from this argument that will be the subject of another study.

33.   The author was the main legal drafter of a part of the Maltese Civil Code dealing with things in the public domain. See Maltese Civil Code, Fourth Schedule. Also: Patrick Kershaw, "Decentralised Autonomous Co-operative's (DAC) and the Rise of the New 'Commons'", Medium, 2018.

34.   In civil law systems based on Roman law, these assets are referred to as res nullius, or possibly as things extra commercium, either not owned by anyone (like the sea or the air) or not capable of being the object of legal transactions (like the seashore or the cliffs). Modern Maltese law (Maltese Civil Code, Fourth Schedule on the Public Domain) merges Roman law and English law concepts and applies to both land and designated movable things. It does not however go so far as referring to technology arrangements. This may be something to consider.

35.   In this regard there are some laws that render certain services 'essential supplies' imposing an outcome that forces suppliers to continue supplying services, such as gas or water, even in the case of bankruptcy of the debtor client. This has been extended to IT services as follows in the English Insolvency (Protection of Essential Supplies) Order 2015 amending section 233 of the Insolvency Act 1986 in so far as relates to: point of sale terminals, computer hardware and software, information, advice and

technical assistance in connection with the use of information technology, data storage and processing and website hosting.

36. Legislative work appears to be taking place in this context in only a few other legal systems, and reference can be made to Wyoming and some other US States that appear to be dealing with corporate law impacts of the use of this technology.

37. A wonderful discussion on this subject takes place in many writings of Primavera De Filippi and Aaron Wright reaching seriously inspirational levels in their recently published book Blockchain and the Law – The Rule of Code. Reference is made to Chapter 8 on 'The Future of Organizations' where many relevant issues are discussed in some detail.

38. The Government of Malta is on record to the effect that it intends to extend the innovative technology laws to AI and it is an easy step to carry out given the modular nature of the legislation on innovative technology arrangements already in place.

39. 'Cryptocurrencies', which mostly refer to non-currencies, and 'smart contracts', which are mostly not contracts, are typical examples.

40. Janosch Delcker, "Europe Divided over Robot 'Personhood'", POLITICO, 2018.

41. EuroParl. Report with recommendations to the Commission on Civil Law Rules on Robotics (2015/2103(INL))- Committee on Legal Affairs, 2017.

42. Andrew Griffin, "Saudi Arabia Becomes First Country to Make a Robot into a Citizen", The Independent, 2017.

43. Janosch Delcker, "Europe Divided over Robot 'Personhood'".

44. Ibid.

45. Ibid.

46. Ibid.

47. Stefania Lucchetti quoted in Janosch Delcker. Also: Stefania Lucchetti, "Why Artificial Intelligence Will Need a Legal Personality – Law Cross Border", Law Cross Border, 2017. This

article very helpfully outlines the issues on which innovative legal design will be critical for AI robots going forward.

48. The Maltese Civil Code states that 'Legal personality may not be set up against a person in good faith in order to perpetrate fraud'. Maltese Civil Code, Second Schedule, art 4(11).

49. Reference is made to a purely lawful purpose foundation that can be distinguished from a beneficiary foundation. Both can be private or public benefit.

50. In the case of a private blockchain where there is a private owner or owners, that would be achieved through a beneficial interest/s in the foundation and there it is of course centralized by intent in terms of control, not ownership alone. Even there, however, the operation of the blockchain may still be operationally decentralized as the structure can cater for limitations on what ownership and control actually can do in terms of powers that impact the decentralized operational design.

51. See Ori Brafman and Rod A. Beckstrom, The Starfish and the Spider(London: Portfolio, 2006) which explores decentralized organizations and shows the range of possibilities that exist, and where the focus of the analysis should be. It shows that it is possible to have decentralization at different levels of an organization.

52. Purpose foundations can be contrasted to beneficiary foundations, which naturally also have a purpose, but when the duty of administrators is to protect and give benefit to beneficiaries, the focus on purpose is reduced and rather than non-proprietary in nature – meaning no one indirectly owns the assets – the structure becomes proprietary, which means that the beneficiaries have indirect ownership of the assets.

53. H. F. Jolovicz, Roman Foundations of Modern Law (Greenwood Publishing Group, 1978), p. 107.

54. Maltese Civil Code, Second Schedule, Title III.

55. A. Cremona, "Malta: Building Your SPV on Solid

Foundations", Trusts & Trustees, 17.6 (2011), pp. 563-568.
56.   Maltese Civil Code, Second Schedule, art 35 by which it is also possible to have one corporate administrator with three directors.
57.   Not necessarily by granting legal personality from the start. They used segregation of patrimonies and granting of legal powers through limited forms of capacity to contract. This concept appears to have developed later on and we now have a range of possibilities where some organizations are recognized without having legal personality and they can still achieve their purposes through limited powers.
58.   See the Maltese Criminal Code, Chapter 9 of the laws of Malta, art 121D on corporate liability for certain offences. A legal organization cannot, however, be sent to jail, and on that score the issue still passes to the real actor who needs to form a criminal intent (mens rea) to be guilty, and so is always assumed to be a physical person. However, the in-roads in various countries towards allowing pecuniary and other remedies, like ones of an injunctive or confiscatory type (non-conviction), to be applied to legal persons shows that the law can adopt effective alternatives when on a policy basis there is good reason to do so. Also: Stefano Filletti, Towards a European Criminal Law System (Kite Group, 2017), p. 60 et seq., where the author discusses non-conviction based confiscation where assets in the hands of third parties can be seized, thus suggesting that if a legal entity has assets, they can be confiscated even if only the directors, and not the legal entity, have been convicted of say, money laundering. The question we face now is that it is apparently time for the next step in legal development, where the subject person is fully automated and no physical person acts in a manner that there is cause attributable to him or her relative to the harm.
59.   ITAS Act, art 8.
60.   The term 'general administrators' is being proposed to cater for

the default and general powers of the members of a Board of Administration as opposed to 'designated administrators' whose function is defined and very limited to a process, function or context and who will clearly not be liable for anything other than carrying out their designated duties. The technical administrators are an example of designated administrators.

61. ITAS Act, art 8.
62. VFA Act, Chapter 590 of the laws of Malta.
63. This is a requirement under the ITASA when the key persons involved in an ITA are not present in Malta.
64. It is evident that not all smart contracts are 'contracts' in the legal sense, and so, when reference is made to smart contracts in this discussion on contractual powers and signing of contracts, the author is referring only to those smart contracts that meet the definition of a contract under the legal system.
65. In particular the actions around compliance with mandatory laws that can change from time to time. Indeed in the ITASA the law imposes a requirement as follows: 'The innovative technology arrangement has a registered technical administrator in office at all times, and who is able to demonstrate to the Authority the ability of the innovative technology arrangement to satisfy – (i) all pre-requisites for the certification which may be granted to it under this Act; (ii) its ability to meet standards on a continuing basis and to address critical matters, and how to address them, as are stated in guidelines, if any, by the Authority in the event they occur; (iii) its ability to vary parameters or functionalities where the objective of the system is to address mandatory legal requirements which may reasonably be predicted to change over time; and (iv) with reference to matters, if any, upon which – (A) the technical administrator; (B) the Authority or other national competent authorities; or (C) any other designated person, may be given the discretion or may be required to

intervene and which are addressed by the software, all authorisations or powers required to carry out such interventions exist and operate as intended'. Innovative Technology Arrangements and Services Act, art 8(4)(c).

66.   It is not yet clear whether the focus should be on ownership or control or both.

67.   The problem here is that blockchains, although an operational reality, are only extensions of their developer and he should act in his own name, and not in the name of an arrangement unless the arrangement is a legal organization, whether with personality or not. If anyone acts on behalf of an inexistent organization, whether registered or not, the law in Malta would see through the action and read it as the personal action of the actor.

68.   This is a technique already used in the Trusts and Trustees Act, Chapter 331 of the laws of Malta in relation to ambiguous fiduciary arrangements.

69.   It is proposed that this will apply to both Maltese organizations (which may convert into an ITF) as well as foreign organisations (which will be able to redomicile into Malta and continue as a Maltese ITF).

70.   Maltese Civil Code, Second Schedule, art 1(9).

71.   Max Ganado, "Maltese Technology Foundations – Initial Thoughts on an Important Proposal", Ganado Advocates, 2018.

12. Regulating Smart Contracts

Lara Tanti, Max Ganado

Those who wish to deploy smart contracts in the belief that they can never give rise to contractual relations or tortuous liability between the parties should be wary of accepting that conclusion uncritically.

Dr Lara Tanti has over 18 years of professional experience as a practising legal counsel for several prestigious large cap tech firms in Europe, Asia and the US.

A leading light in Malta's Blockchain revolution Dr Max Ganado, has been responsible for the drafting of several pieces of legislation at the request of the Government of Malta and its agencies.

Introduction

Before 2016, blockchain was known, if at all, as the technological backbone of Bitcoin. Since then, blockchain has come into its own as a technology with huge disruptive potential. Likewise, the smart contracts that can be hosted on it, and other emerging technologies. Some are predicting the end of the State, the end of banks, and the radical transformation of every human institution, process, and organization that involves trusted middlemen[1]. Such an extent of disruption may be unlikely, but the possible uses of Distributed Ledger Technology (DLT) seem endless. As governments and corporations roll out test cases in financial services, digital identity and everything in between , the question does not seem to be so much whether DLT will proliferate, but rather when.

So far, blockchain, DLT and smart contracts are still in their developmental stages. The technology is displaying a wide range of fundamental design differences: some rely on open-source software, others use proprietary code. Some, such as Bitcoin and Ethereum, use un-permissioned blockchains, which are open for anyone to interact with, others limit access to select parties. As with any new technology, there are practical, commercial, and regulatory issues to overcome before the technology can be more widely adopted. For example, due to their design, smart contracts on a blockchain, particularly the permissionless variant, can pose major regulatory challenges. Are they actually contracts? Are they binding? In fact, a lot of the innovation in this space was initially born out of a libertarian desire to skirt the law or to exploit a lack of regulation in certain areas. A case in point is the infamous and now defunct Silk Road that allowed users to trade drugs anonymously against payment in Bitcoin over the blockchain.

Blockchain is not the first digital technology promoted by some as being immune to regulatory interference[2]. Yet, even the most advanced, decentralized protocols, which were specifically designed to reduce control to a minimum, such as peer-to-peer file sharing technologies, have struggled to cope with ongoing (albeit imperfect) efforts by third parties and regulators to curb illicit activity. Therefore, whether DLT is immune to regulation is probably more of a rhetorical question. The more pressing one is what are the regulatory challenges posed by this technology, and what are the best ways to address them.

With this backdrop, the aim of this chapter is to determine whether existing regulation in Malta, including the recent enactments of the MDIA Act, the ITAS Act, and VFA Act, successfully address the challenges that will be presented if blockchain technology and smart contracts were to become widely adopted.

Policy Objectives

Regulators across the globe are still exploring blockchain and how its uses fit within existing regulatory regimes.

Some have already taken action. In the run-up of the G20 Summit last December, France and Germany requested the inclusion of cryptocurrency and blockchain regulations in the G20 meeting agenda[3]. This was seen by many as a clear sign that Europe wants to position itself as a tech and innovation pole for the future.

Delaware,[4] Vermont, Nevada, Arizona,[5] Wyoming, Hawaii, amongst other US states have adopted, or are seeking to pass, legislation to recognize and capitalize upon the use of smart contracts and blockchain technology in various commercial contexts. By way of example, Arizona led the way in 2017 by passing legislation allowing the use of smart contracts in commerce and preventing a contract from being denied legal effect solely because the contract contains a smart contract term. The bill also recognizes signatures and records secured using blockchain technology as valid electronic signatures and records under state law.

In Vermont, a bill was signed into law in May 2018 allowing limited liability companies organized for the 'purpose of operating a business that utilizes blockchain technology for a material portion of its business activities'[6] to elect to be a blockchain-based limited liability company. The bill allows such companies to use blockchain technology for various aspects of corporate governance, including the use of smart contracts to administer voting procedures.

In Malta, the government launched its own national strategy in April 2017, with the distinct purpose of making Malta one of the first countries in the world to embrace blockchain and blockchain-inspired technologies. This was followed by a trio of enactments that established the first regulatory framework for cryptocurrencies and ICOs and DLT/smart contract arrangements. As a result, DLT platforms can now achieve a level of credibility and certainty through certification by the MDIA. The use of ICOs as a means for raising project funds is now covered by a specific regulatory regime as is the setting up of exchanges and other intermediaries operating in the cryptocurrency market. As will be seen later on, these enactments also provide much-needed definitions for some of the key jargon used in the industry.

The key debate surrounding regulation of technology has always been on how to strike a balance between stimulating innovation, protecting innocent participation, and preventing crime and illicit activity. It is widely accepted that high-stakes technologies introduce a myriad of new risks, as well as transfer old risks to new places, both from the perspective of investors, as well as businesses and participants at large. As the emergence of peer-to-peer file sharing has shown, without the early engagement of scientific and policy research, the unexpected, often undesirable consequences of rapid technological developments cannot be addressed, let alone mitigated. However, predicting how an emerging technology will be used, and what impact it will have on society, culture, institutions, and practices is not an easy task either, and could result in the enactment of 'blind' legislation that not only hinders the evolution of technology but, worse still, pushes innovation towards regulatory avoidance[7].

The chapter seeks to analyse aspects of the existing regulatory regime in Malta with a view of identifying areas for forward-looking regulatory consideration. For this industry to take off, legal, commercial, technological and regulatory demands need to be reconciled before smart contracts can become ubiquitous.

Terminology – What are Smart Contracts

The term 'smart contracts' was coined in 1996 by computer scientist Nick Szabo[8]. Since then, various definitions of this phrase have been suggested, however none are yet universally accepted.

In essence, a smart contract is an algorithm that performs the terms of a contract automatically. This definition is attractive for its simplicity, but it does not explain the difference between smart contracts and other already well-known contractual constructs involving automated performance, such as, for instance, the humble vending machine. Vending machines are programmed with certain rules (that could be defined in a contract) so that the machine automatically dispenses goods when some form of payment is made. Could the vending machine be a primitive smart contract? If there is no difference in principle between the two, then we would have to admit that smart contracts are not half as innovative as they are made out to be.

Identifying the innovative step in smart contracts is particularly relevant when we consider other automated computer systems such as those used in exchange markets. For instance, FX trades are frequently executed not by human traders, but by computer systems that are designed to buy or sell in accordance with pre-progammed trading strategies. As of 2014, more than 75% of the stock shares traded on United States exchanges originated from automated trading system orders in this way[9]. Automated contracts per se are not something new: they have been widely used in many spheres for a long period of time already, so what is so special about smart contracts?

For this, it is useful to refer to another definition of smart contracts provided by Gideon Greenspan: 'A smart contract is a piece of code which is stored on a blockchain, triggered by blockchain transactions, and which reads and writes data in that blockchain's database'[10].

This definition is more concrete, as it places emphasis on the blockchain technology and identifies that technology as one of the core features of smart contracts. This same approach was adopted by the MDIA, also putting the concept of the blockchain (referred to in the Act as an 'innovative technology arrangement') at the heart of the definition of a smart contract. According to the MDIA[11], a smart contract is:

"a form of innovative technology arrangement consisting of:

(a) a computer protocol; and, or

(b) an agreement concluded wholly or partly in an electronic form which is automatable and enforceable by execution of computer code, although some parts may require human input and control and which may be also enforceable by ordinary legal methods or by a mixture of both;"

A key feature of this description is that a smart contract (1) can be an 'agreement' and (2) it requires automation capability ('automatable') meaning there must be some degree of self-sufficiency, self-performance or self-enforcement by the software itself without third party intervention. In other words, a set of instructions that can result in some (but perhaps not all) decisions', whether simple or complex, being taken automatically without recourse to human control.

Using this interpretation, the definition of smart contracts under the MDIA can encompass a whole spectrum of smart contract possibilities. On one end, the smart contract may operate as a simple gift or some other non-binding transfer that happens automatically through mechanisms embedded in software code. It could operate as an arrangement of rights and powers within the context of a distributed autonomous organization as was the case with the DAO[12] (albeit with disastrous consequences)[13]. Or it could be an agreement that is either expressed entirely in code (smart contract code) or which is expressed in natural language but implemented wholly or partly in code (smart legal contract)[14]. Other permutations are, of course, possible and likely to emerge as the number of smart contract applications increases. This definition in the MDIA is welcomed for providing a much-needed baseline point of discussion in an ecosystem that is developing without a standard set of definitions. The broad approach that was adopted is also commendable, not least because the industry is still in its infancy and the flexibility built into the definition makes it more likely that the law will remain relevant as the technology evolves and gains more traction.

The Validity of Smart Contracts Under Maltese Law

Every legal system has its own applicable rules on what makes a contract valid and binding, and in each jurisdiction this question will need to be assessed in the context of its applicable rules. This part of the discussion will not consider the private international law issue of how to identify which domestic law applies. Instead our analysis will focus specifically on the requirements applicable under Maltese law, in particular Chapter 16 of the Maltese Civil Code that defines a contract as 'an agreement or an accord between two or more persons by which an obligation is created, regulated, or dissolved'[15].

It should be noted that in principle, the Civil Code does not require a contract to be executed in a particular form in order to achieve legal effect, and consequently a contract can be both verbal and electronic, except for a few designated types of agreements that require particular form like a public deed or a private writing[16]. As long as the basic elements identified below are met, a contract can be made even implicitly by behaving in a particular way.

In a court's assessment of whether a legally binding contract has been formed, there is often no clean separation of each of foundational elements. For the purposes of our analysis, however, it is expedient to deal with each of them in turn:

- there must be multiple parties each of whom has the capacity to contract,
- there must be a mutual manifestation of consent,
- the object which constitutes the subject-matter of the contract must be certain, and

- the consideration (causa) must be lawful.

Capacity

For a contract to be enforceable, the parties to it need to have legal capacity. In practice, this means that only natural and legal persons of certain age can enter into contractual arrangements. Within these categories, the law creates a presumption in favour of capacity: Incapacity is the exception that must be proved case by case[17].

A distinction exists between personality and capacity. Capacity is usually linked to a person and therefore presumes personality, though the law can, in specific cases, attribute contractual capacity to certain legal organizations even in the absence of legal personality. An entity or an individual to whom the legislator has not conferred personality does not have juridical life and is therefore not a person in the eyes of the law. Capacity in the absence of personality is not possible.

Looking into the (near) future, as we see the emerging developments around the IoT, we can easily envisage a situation in which one or perhaps more parties to a contract will be inanimate and therefore devoid of personality in the legal sense, such as a contract taking place between two things: our fridge and the supermarkets' supply depot. This points to the potential dual functionality of a smart contract namely that through the engagement of smart code (also known as 'software agent'), it is not only possible to achieve automation of contractual performance[18] but also possible to automate the process of conclusion of the contract itself[19]. This latter point, namely the automatic conclusion of a contract is very challenging from a legal perspective not least because the counterparty is inanimate and lacking in contractual personality and hence capacity. In fact, this raises the question of whether the computer system generating the contract might be seen as a party to a smart contract and, if so, whether the contract it creates can ever be binding.

Under Maltese law, a programmed computer, no matter how animated, is not endowed with legal personality, nor is it given any statutory capacity to contract in any context, and it is therefore not capable of entering into binding agreements with third parties. Within Europe, this issue was touched upon in the initial proposal of the E-Commerce Directive that stated that member states should 'not prevent the use of certain electronic systems as intelligent electronic agents' for making a contract[20]. Unfortunately, this reference to electronic agents was eventually dropped even though, it is most likely that the term 'agents' was not intended to suggest that such machines are endowed with personality in the same way as perhaps delegates and brokers.

Several years down the line, the legal and moral questions that surround the use of robotics and M2M transactions are still not solved. In the meantime, the conclusion of contracts by electronic agents is not regulated at all within the Directive or the Electronic Commerce Act which brought it into Maltese law with the result that contracts concluded in this way will fail to produce binding obligations for lack of capacity of one of more of the contracting parties.

An alternative perspective on the issue would be to apply the doctrine of agency, meaning to regard the software as an 'agent' (lunga manus?) for a third-party principle entering the contract. As such there is no Maltese authority on this specific point that we have come across, but the UK court considered a similar question in relation to a software programme in Software Solutions Partners Ltd, R (on the application of) v HM Customs & Excise, and found that an automated system could not be regarded as an agent, because only a person with a mind could be an agent in law. Indeed, if an intelligent agent has no juridical standing in the eyes of the law, how can one speak of an agent contractually binding a human being?

In reality, automated computer systems are considered by many to be merely tools in the hands of people who operate them. On this basis, an alternative interpretation, and the one that is most likely to be adopted in the absence of an amendment to existing legislation, is to characterize[21] the actions of a programmed computer in concluding a smart contract as a communication on behalf of a contracting party[22]. According to this view, a legal fiction is created so that an act ensuing from the electronic agent becomes an act ensuing directly from its human controller as a result of his programming the computer (or engaging someone to do that) in the first place. The electronic agent is therefore put at par with a machine such as the telephone or fax machine. In such a case, one would no longer be able to say that the electronic agent has automatically concluded a contract on behalf of the person in whose interest it has acted. On the contrary, it is the human controller who has concluded the contract through a means of communication in the form of a programmed computer that he has deployed to transmit his will[23]. The problem with this approach is that when factual contexts become complex the relationship between a person and the programming of the computer can become very tenuous. In such circumstances, it remains to be seen whether the above arguments will in fact stand up to scrutiny.

Some commentators have argued that for the time being it is perfectly acceptable for the law to adopt a 'wait and see' approach. There is no pressing practical need, they argue, for software to contract on behalf of, or legally bind, a contracting party (for example, as agent), or to enter into an agreement as contracting party itself (as principal)[24].

However, it is conceivable that in the longer term and as smart contracts become more sophisticated, it may be beneficial or even necessary to provide for a fictional construct around the software itself[25] to be a 'party' to a contract. For example, in cases where a computer program is used for the conclusion of a contract (as opposed to merely as a means to automate performance) it may become more difficult to characterize software as a mere messenger where the software uses AI or machine learning (rather than conditions that are expressly pre-programmed by the parties) to determine whether, when and on what terms to issue offers, provide consent and so on. We can look through things to identify persons in the background but soon enough we will see cases where this too will be impossible due to barriers to identification.

Linked with the question of capacity is the question of identity and authority. If the parties cannot be identified, legal capacity and adequate authority cannot be determined. Knowing the identity of the counterparty may also be important, apart from establishing basic issues such as age, for example, in order to satisfy applicable compliance requirements such as those concerning anti-money laundering or for a party's own internal risk assessment purposes.

In an offline world, parties to a contract typically know of each other's identity and, often through a combination of market reputation, prior dealings, and due diligence, the relevant characteristics associated with a counterparty's personality and capacity will become known. This is not the case within the blockchain context: Ethereum, and in fact most of the other existing (permissionless) blockchain platforms, do not carry out any meaningful checks as to a party's identity, meaning that anyone who has access to the internet can open an account and start transacting on a blockchain, either anonymously or pseudonymously by reference to an IP or wallet address. This is therefore one area for consideration by regulators, namely how to solve the identification issue in smart contracts, in particular, what evidence should be permissible in cases where capacity is called into question. Should it be sufficient for a contracting party to be identified through cryptographic keys or should real world identity be required? If not, existing laws may need to be amended to expressly permit such evidence to be considered by the courts when assessing contract formation.

Consent

Following on from the requirement of capacity is the question of consent. Both civil and common law systems consider consent to be an essential element in the formation of a contract. Under Maltese law, the general rule is that the parties are free to choose the method for manifesting consent such as by signature or by performance, except in a few specific cases where form is imposed in the Civil Code for publicity or evidentiary purposes. In the case of smart contracts, it can be argued that consent manifests itself from the actions of a contracting party for instance, by initiating actions to execute an agreement or ceding control of a private encryption key over a specified number of digital tokens.

In a more traditional digital context such an in the electronic procurement of goods and services, consent has typically taken place by the contracting party clicking on an 'I Accept' button as part of the transaction process. This method of providing consent is regulated in Malta by the Electronic Commerce Act and the EU eIDAS Regulation (eIDAS) which has direct effect. The eIDAS was enacted to bring uniformity inter alia, in the area of electronic records and signatures, and in some cases also to bring equivalence to handwritten signatures. The eIDAS defines three tiers of electronic signatures, each tier meeting a higher level of ID verification, security, and non-repudiation:

- Simple Electronic signature: This category covers all forms of digitized signatures including an attached image of a signature or the click on an 'I Accept' button.
- Advanced electronic signature: This form of signature requires that only the signing party could have created the signature. In addition, the signature is linked to the data it is seeking to sign off on so that if the data changes afterwards the signature is invalidated.
- Qualified electronic signature: This is the most advanced form of electronic signature created using a qualified certificate and backed by a Trust Service Provider (TSP). This is the only type of signature universally recognized by all EU states and the only one that is given the equivalent legal effect of a handwritten signature.

In the case of smart contracts, it is interesting to remember that blockchain technology provides a 'paper' trail of timestamped data records that are identifiable using cryptographic keys. Due to the unique nature of such keys, it can be argued that they provide a function equivalent to a digital signature of the contracting party and in principle should be accepted as evidence of identification and consent by electronic means, at least with reference to the electronic wallet or tokens to which it refers. So even if X owns a wallet, and its contents and the private key are given to a trustee/nominee/custodian, or are stolen, and with the private key a contract of sale takes place of the tokens in the wallet, the 'signature' is correctly connected to the assets and can affect that transfer validly towards a third party, even though the real owner did not consent as required by law. Here is a case of presumed consent by the owner because of the apparent demonstration of a link of a power of disposition to specified assets that will result in the buyer for value receiving title on the basis of his good faith.

At the very least, cryptographic keys seem to fulfil the definition of advanced electronic signature in that they validate that a person with access to the relevant private key 'signed' the transaction with reference to the connected assets. The advanced electronic signature does not, however, guarantee legally binding status under the law as there is no identification that takes place when a private key is used. For this level of security, the transaction would need to be signed with qualified signatures.

As such, there is a fundamental mismatch between signatures on public blockchains and qualified signatures. Public blockchains provide a way for anyone to approve a transaction without any formality based on a private key – which is a physical bit of information – empowerment. The author of a qualified signature needs approval from a TSP, meaning to be identified, audited, and to implement a number of strict policies. For blockchain signatures to be qualified signatures, every signatory would need to undergo a costly and time-consuming process required for obtaining a certificate and that will still not immobilize the private key that can easily be given to another person by the identified party. They will be under constant scrutiny from the TSP, which will have to manage millions of certificates. It would seem that requiring qualified signatures as a means of providing valid consent on the blockchain may defeat one of the efficiencies of a permissionless decentralized ledger.

To date there is no rule (local or at EU level) requiring the use of a particular level of signature for specific actions. Therefore, the first step would be for lawmakers to determine what sort of evidence (if any) courts would accept in support of a claim that a smart contract has been properly entered into. In addition, they will need to determine the weight that should be given to such evidence by the court and consider how such evidence may be presented in practice. For example, whether cryptographic keys should be treated as equivalent to the use of a wet-ink handwritten signature, and in what circumstances such evidence might be challenged or overridden. Unless we treat private keys as bearer instruments that are proof of ownership and capacity to transact through mere delivery, we are unlikely to solve these problems. As an alternative, one may even suggest the use of fingerprints or other biometric elements that, together with the use of private keys, could pass the test of identification, and in turn capacity and consent.

Certainty of Subject Matter

One of the most important questions in determining whether a contract has been formed is whether it is clear to the parties what has been agreed. The Civil Code requires a contractual commitment to be sufficiently certain before it is made binding on the counter party. The question is how should 'certainty of subject matter' be assessed?

As discussed above, a smart contract may be structured in a way so that the terms of a transaction are expressed in natural language with an agreement to execute the performance and enforcement of all or part of the contract using code (smart legal contract). In this scenario and in view of the use of natural language, the requirement of certainty will be assessed no differently from other forms of online and offline contracts.

In the case of consumer contracts, the provisions of the Electronic Commerce Act require service providers to disclose certain basic information about their business and the transaction 'in clear, comprehensive and unambiguous terms', and the terms must be made available in a way that allows the counterparty to store them and reproduce them at a later date' Such information includes (a) the different technical steps that a consumer must follow to conclude a contract, (b) whether the contract will be filed by the service provider and whether it will be accessible, (c) the technical means for identifying and correcting input errors prior to the placing of the order, and (d) the languages offered for the conclusion of the contract[26]. Such terms must be provided in all electronic contracts although in business-to-business transactions, the recipient may waive the right to such information.

In the online context, service providers often contain their terms in a click-wrap agreement on a pop-up screen that users are required to accept without discussion or negotiation should they wish to continue with the contracting process[27]. The ability of such agreements to bind consumers to their terms has been the subject of ongoing debate and many commentators submit that such contracts of adhesion should not be considered legally binding at all[28]. It is expected that smart legal contracts will adopt a similar mechanism to share transaction information with its users and consequently we can expect the debate surrounding the validity of click-wrap agreements to also extend to the natural language aspect of smart legal contracts.

But what if there is no click-wrap agreement and the terms exist exclusively in code? As seen above, a smart contract may be written exclusively in programming language and subsequently compiled on to the blockchain in a way that can only be read by computers (smart contract code). This is the form of agreement under which participants are most likely not to receive enough clarity on the transaction due to the fact that the terms will be written in a programming language with which they are unlikely to be familiar. Will this feature invalidate the agreement?

In the context of consumer contracts, the Consumer Affairs Act, seems to suggest that it will. Firstly, Article 44(2)(m) makes it clear that terms with which a consumer has no real opportunity of becoming acquainted before the conclusion of the contract will be deemed unfair and hence not binding on the consumer unless the contract is capable of continuing in existence without such terms. Therefore, to the extent that the code can only be consulted after the transaction is completed, then that agreement will not be binding. Secondly, the Act requires that where all or some terms offered by a trader to a consumer are in writing, these terms shall be written in 'plain and intelligible language which can be understood by the consumers to whom the contract is directed'[29].

To the extent that smart contract code includes complex programming that is difficult for anyone not expert in the field to understand, this requirement will not be deemed fulfilled and consequently, no contract will be formed. Indeed, it would not be reasonable to expect participants to become familiar with the hundreds, if not thousands, of different programming languages available, all with specialist uses and varying degrees of complexity, popularity and shelf life. Consequently, for these type of contracts, information disclosures required by the Electronic Commerce Act and the Consumer Affairs Act should only be deemed fulfilled if they are contained in a natural language wrapper so that if a party makes a claim on the basis of a complicated piece of code against a party who is a non-expert, and the latter party was not explained the precise meaning of that code, then the non-expert should be able to have the agreement nullified on grounds that the implications of that code were not sufficiently certain.

Of course, this is not to say that all other contracts should also follow this trajectory. Indeed, it is conceivable that simpler non-consumer contract types could indeed be executed in code only. One example of such agreements that is currently being heavily tested is Smart Derivatives Contracts whereby the whole contract process including the contract formation part, will be fully automated with absolutely no human intervention at any point[30].

To this end it should be a matter of policy to clarify what types of contracts should be granted legal validity even though they are expressed exclusively in computer code. Other types of contracts (such as consumer contracts) may be considered unsuitable on the basis that code is not, and is unlikely to be widely understandable by society at large. This lack of user knowledge was identified by the Consumer Affairs Act and the Electronic Commerce Act a key risk factor in the widespread adoption of digital technology. In fact, those enactments are partly based on the assumption that users are more likely to engage in cross-border online transactions when basic information about the transaction and the service provider has been clearly communicated. Such rationale applies equally to smart contracts executed as a hybrid of language and code as to contracts executed in natural language but in a digital environment. Hence there is an argument to say that although the information requirements imposed by the CAA and the ECA might be cumbersome on service providers, they are ultimately designed to benefit the industry by encouraging the speedy uptake of services provided in non-traditional contexts.

It must be noted however that the existing laws are contemplating a world as it exists today that is still largely paper-based, notwithstanding the vast amount of digitization taking place. If we try to fit innovative technology into the current landscape, could we not be running the risk of denying the efficiency and cost benefits of the innovative technologies to the same consumers we are trying to protect?

Consideration (Causa)

The concept of 'causa' under Maltese law is similar to the concept of 'consideration' in continental Europe. Causa defines the actions of the parties and the reasons why they conclude an agreement. Consideration is unlawful if it is prohibited by law or contrary to morality or to public policy[31]. This is an essential element of a contract[32]. In a bilateral contract, the causa of an obligation is linked to the other party's performance of its obligation.

Additional Legal Requirements that Impact the Formation of Contracts

The general legal principles just discussed are not the only requirements that determine whether a legally binding contract is formed as a matter of contract law, and other more particular laws may apply to determine the legality and enforceability of specific types of smart contract deployments or use cases. Space does not permit a detailed consideration of all the additional requirements which may apply, however some examples include:

- In the case of consumer contracts, the Consumer Affairs Act sets out an indicative list of unfair contract terms that will invalidate a consumer contract unless the offending term can be struck out;
- The Electronic Commerce Act contains a list of areas in which transactions cannot take place using electronic communication, for instance transactions in the field of tax;
- Laws governing data privacy apply in the case of almost every transaction where the identity of the parties is known, and the transaction is not completely anonymous;
- Certain contracts must be done by public deed or private writing in order to have effect vis-à-vis third parties, such as the transfer of real estate titles and testamentary instruments.

These examples underscore the need for advice regarding local law on any proposed smart contract to ensure that the deployment and smart contract model chosen meet local law requirements.

Enforceability of Smart Contracts

As discussed previously, a smart contract must be enforceable in some way, either 'by execution of computer code... by ordinary legal methods or by a mixture of both'.

Where the arrangement between the participants amounts to a binding contract, a court will enforce the parties' legal rights under that contract as it would for any other legal agreement, for instance by looking at the intention of the parties at the time, bringing in witnesses or documentary evidence to support a position and finally by making a binding determination on the interpretation of that contract and the appropriate remedy.

Where performance of a smart contract is automated through the use of Boolean logic ('if/then'), it is often argued that the scope of ambiguity within a contract is removed[33], and, with it, the need for a trusted third party such as the courts, to intervene and enforce its terms.

However, even where a smart contract has the ability to auto-perform, events could arise where the parties, the law or even the public may find themselves wanting the contract to be performed differently or not at all. To take the vending machine example, what of those situations in which a coin is inserted and the chocolate fails to comes out? An injured party to a smart contract should also have a remedy in the face of a performance malfunction, or where one or both parties have misunderstood the characteristics of goods to be delivered, or are mistaken as to whether they have capacity or authority to take a relevant action.

Equally, the wording of the contract could contain 'gaps' either because of a situation the parties have not anticipated, or because certain clauses are found to violate mandatory legal requirements such as consumer protection laws. Where technology fails, a trusted third party will need to intervene.

Some commentators argue that even where the outcome of a smart contract was not predicted, the 'code is law' theory demands that such outcome be accepted as a manifestation of the intention of the participants[34]. This was the main argument of the blockchain fundamentalists in TheDAO hack of 2016 when a participant to TheDAO smart contract exploited a feature of code to syphon off funds[35]. This 'hack' raised two competing views on the enforceability of smart contracts. For some, the view was that, as the code in the contract had permitted the breach, the outcome was legitimate by design. TheDAO participants, they said, had agreed to be bound by the smart contract, and were therefore bound to any outcome under that code. The opposing view was that participants had more broadly agreed that TheDAO would only be used to fund agreed projects and that such a strict interpretation of the smart contract was unreasonable and contrary to the intention of the participants[36].

From a legal perspective, the argument that 'code is law' is weak. If someone writes code under which a person is entitled to commit a crime, that crime will not be legitimized on grounds that it is included in code. The power to make rules is vested in the law-making bodies of specific government systems, not in code. Code is not law. One needs also to give some importance to concepts of unjustified enrichment as, if someone benefits from an unintended oversight in the code, such person should surely not seek to keep the benefit. Indeed, suggesting that he should keep it is evidence of abuse in itself. Concepts of fiduciary obligations, such as the ones we find in article 1124A et seq. of the Maltese Civil Code continue to apply.

Which argument ultimately prevails remains to be seen. In the meantime, courts seeking to enforce smart contracts will need to grapple with another challenge, namely how to ensure that the well-honed set of tools available for undoing and altering contracts are to be applied so as to be as efficient and effective in the context of distributed ledgers as they are in an offline environment. This issue will be considered in the following sections.

Issues with Rescission and Termination

In terms of Article 1212 of the Civil Code, 'any agreement which is defective by reason of the absence of any of the conditions essential to the validity of contracts, or which is expressly declared by law to be null, shall be subject to rescission'.

If a court determines that a smart contract is void ab initio, or voidable on grounds of a mistake or lack of capacity, the consequence of such determination would be that a transaction that has already taken place will need to be deleted, and the record of such transaction on the blockchain removed. The aim of this remedy is to put the injured party in the position that he/she would have been had the contract not been entered into. In an offline environment, this could mean for instance that the injured party will return the subject matter of the contract back to the seller, and receive from the seller the purchase price paid.

In the case of blockchain technology, application of the remedy of rescission is not so straightforward. First, DLT technology relies on an append-only data process, which means that information can be added but cannot be removed. Second, public blockchains rely on a distributed data storage system where the same information is recorded by each participant in the entire network. Accordingly, any change requires practically the entire network to agree and implement the change, which is not acceptable because it leaves the injured party with an unpredictable outcome.

One possible solution could be to allow for 'reverse transactions' which seek to restore the parties to the position they would have been in had the deficiency not occurred. In a reverse transaction, the original (erroneous) transaction remains unchanged. A second, inverse transaction will then be recorded so that once executed, the second transaction will have the effect of negating the original one. This simple solution works from an economic perspective in the sense that following the second transaction, the value transferred erroneously under the original transaction will be transferred back, and the error will be seemingly rectified. However, from a legal point of view, this solution is not necessarily satisfactory. For example, in the case of immovable property, there is a legal difference between ownership records showing that there has been a transfer of an asset from Party A to Party B and a 'reverse transaction' thereafter, and the position where, following the transfer of an asset from Party A to Party B, it is determined that this transfer was void from the outset and so the records should show that it never took place[37].

Issues with Rectifying Errors and Gaps

Similarly, if there are errors and gaps in a smart contract resulting, for example, from an incomplete agreement or violation of mandatory legal provisions, these 'gaps' will need to be filled in, in line with the parties' intentions or the applicable legal provisions. This could mean striking out an offending clause and/or stopping its auto-performance. Similarly, where a mandatory provision has been left out, the smart contract must allow such provision to be included.

As seen in the previous section, where the agreement is recorded in code, this will be particularly difficult to achieve. Similar issues will arise where the agreement is in natural language, but the offending clause is one that is linked with the automatic execution of the smart contract. These difficulties call into question whether the legal techniques of striking out an offending clause may be inappropriate for smart contracts. This is because the task is not a simple linguistic one, but would likely require the software engineers to re-code, re-test, validate and re-run the programme. Instead, there may be other techniques that could be used by the parties (or perhaps imposed by a court if the changes required are to reflect a court judgment or mandatory provisions of law) to achieve an analogous outcome.

For instance, the parties could agree to let the smart contract continue to perform automatically in ignorance of the law in question, and for the parties to deal with the consequences outside of its operation. Legally speaking, this can be risky. The consequences of continuing to perform obligations originally required by a contract but that have become contrary to law are not limited to significant economic loss (for example, amounts paid may not be recoverable), but also include potential legal action and penalties (such as for breach of anti-money laundering laws). This would therefore appear to be a sub-optimal outcome.

Alternatively, the courts may, instead of striking out an unfair penalty clause, achieve an equivalent economic result by awarding an appropriate amount of compensation under an action for damages. In fact, in situations where a transaction cannot be stopped or reversed, recovery for damages will probably be the only possible recourse for a counterparty.

Technology could also provide effective remedies such as a built-in right for either party to suspend the automatic performance of a smart contract such as when the contract no longer represents the legal obligations of the parties, or when it is unlawful. This is not suspending the contract between the parties – just its automatic performance. The parties' rights and obligations continue to exist. In fact, there is an argument to suggest that for a smart contract to function properly, there should be such mechanisms embedded within that allow the parties to suspend automatic performance of a contract where absolutely necessary.

The opposite view is equally compelling if one considers the need for trust in automated smart contracts. Without this trust, smart contracts will simply not be relied upon. For this reason, the argument would be in favour of ensuring that no one can ever interrupt a smart contract from operating as coded. Should any issues arise about the outcomes, then they need to be sorted out through remedies based on unjustified enrichment or mistake, with the victim taking the risk of the counterparty going bankrupt in the meantime, blocking any effective remedy on a practical level. The importance of knowing with whom one is dealing for these remedies to be at all possible cannot be over emphasized and in the current stage of development, the identity of the counterparty is a difficult issue to deal with as blockchain operates through private keys that are coded. They do not refer to actors and so it will never be clear who is acting, which is of course the basis of any purported remedy.

An ancillary expectation emerging from the last position described would be that the courts would never seek to stop a smart contract from operating as coded. Injunctions must therefore be unavailable against smart contracts. We find precedents for this in Maltese law in the case of on demand bank guarantees, for example, so extending this to the present context would not be a serious challenge as long as one is clear on the reason for doing so. Is it in the public interest to ensure trust in blockchain systems? Some think this is a non-starter while others think it's a no-brainer.

Issues Arising from Coding Errors

Smart contracts introduce an additional risk that does not exist in most text-based contractual relationships — the possibility of the protocol containing an unintended programming error. In fact, most 'hacks' associated with blockchain technology, mostly relating to exchanges, are really exploitations of an unintended coding error. As with many bugs in computer code, these errors are not glaring, but rather become obvious only once they have been exploited. Understanding who is legally responsible is a major challenge: should liability fall according to culpability, or with reference to the nature of the relationship between the parties? In traditional contracts, the parties would be able to sue the drafting lawyer for malpractice, but in a DLT context there may be no obvious defendant against whom legal action could be brought, particularly where transactions are conducted pseudonymously.

If a dispute arose, how would an aggrieved participant to a permissionless blockchain identify the other party to a smart contract in order to bring legal proceedings against it? The Commissioner of the CFTC explained his belief that smart contract developers could be potential targets for liability if 'these code developers could reasonably foresee, at the time they created the code, that it would likely be used by U.S. persons in a manner violative of U.S. Commodity Futures Trading Commission (CFTC) regulations'[38]. If such a use is foreseeable, Commissioner Quintenz believes that a 'strong case could be made that the code developers aided and abetted violations of CFTC regulations'.

The same would apply to general errors that would cause damage apart from breach of regulatory law. If a developer is negligent when creating a smart contract and then again negligently deploys it, under tort law principles he will be liable for the damages, and could be sued. The problem we have here is that open-source software is generally available for anyone to modify, can go back many years and there may be no link between one author and another, there may be no knowledge of reliance, and no relationship between the software designer/s and the unilateral use of the software by a third party. The emerging distance between the act of design and the use, in time and space, will undoubtedly result in remoteness and failure of causation that will weaken arguments of liability based on tort.

The Case of Augur

Augur, a new blockchain-based prediction market platform, is getting a lot of media attention because people are using it to predict the deaths of celebrities. Apart from a concern that this type of platform could inspire real killings, Augur presents an additional and more fundamental problem.

Augur's open-source software uses smart contracts to let users set up their own prediction markets that automatically pool cryptocurrency bets and distribute winnings without the need for participants to identify themselves. Predictably, the Ethereum-based protocol, has already led to markets for forecasting the demise of Donald Trump, Jeff Bezos, and others. So far, the amounts wagered on this platform have been tiny, making it unlikely that someone would be inspired to engage in foul play. Nevertheless, Augur may already be facilitating illegal activity that could prove far more problematic.

In the US, prediction markets are generally not permitted and certain activities allowed on the Augur website are also unlawful in the US without approval from the relevant authority, the CFTC. In fact, in a similar case in 2012, the CFTC sued an Irish prediction market business (similar to Augur), and eventually a judge blocked the market provider from offering the contracts in the US.

The problem with Augur, is that even if the CFTC decides that Augur is engaging in illegal activity, how will the CFTC enforce that decision? And against whom? Augur's creators claim they have no control over what its users choose to do with the protocol — or the ability to shut it down. The service is decentralized, meaning it is hosted on computers spread around the world with no central authority in charge. In the absence of a concrete intermediary responsible for running the marketplace, how should the law be applied to prevent such activity from occurring? In this case it may be possible to apply the law and penalties to the players as they are using a platform to break the law, as well as the persons who deployed the software facilitating the breach of law by others. The problem will be identifying the persons involved, but that is a problem we already have in many torts. In this case it is made more difficult and perhaps one should consider mandatory disclosure on one end of the scale to mandatory insurance or guarantees/ sinking funds on the other end of the scale, as a condition for allowing platforms to be deployed. If there are no identifiable persons who can cover potential liability then users should be warned in clear language of the circumstances, and reference should be made to the methods of recourse, and the values available under the different options. Smart contracts can then be used to calculate the value of user assets and calibrate it to the amount of insurance cover on a daily basis. Premia would be payable from the cash flow of the platform to ensure they are paid on the cover value on a daily basis as well.

In the face of such challenges, some commentators have started to advocate new standards of liability in cases where defendants can be said to be acting in furtherance of a common purpose[39]. This argument is based on the idea that distributed ledgers are operated on the basis of joint participation of various actors who jointly control the ledger in a way that closely resembles a partnership. While of course the criteria for the creation of a partnership differ from jurisdiction to jurisdiction, it is a common feature of most partnerships, that once created, they confer joint liability on their members. On this basis, there is an argument to suggest that if nodes and developers co-operate in developing and managing a blockchain, they could find themselves tied together by their being jointly liable in relation to third parties. This is, of course, the most dangerous situation for the users, often ordinary consumers, and solutions need to be found to avoid this happening.

General Observations

On the basis of the above, some general observations can be extracted:

- Under Maltese law, unless the requirements in the Civil Code are met[40], a smart contract will not give rise to a binding agreement just because the moniker 'smart contract' includes the word contract in it.
- Whether a smart contract is binding will need to be assessed on a case-by-case basis depending on the type of smart contract,

the counterparties, the factual matrix within which it operates, and the applicable law determining the issue.

- As a general rule, the form in which a smart contract is recorded (e.g. in pure code) should not be determinative of whether it gives rise to legally binding obligations. Consequently, in certain circumstances smart contracts may be considered legally binding contracts under existing contract laws.
- Smart contracts are unlikely to create legally binding obligations in cases where the law requires adherence to particular legal formalities such as the case of the transfers of immovable property and contracts involving consumers.
- The use of smart contracts to support legally binding contracts does not of itself invalidate an agreement that is otherwise legally binding under Maltese law, a position supported by the Electronic Commerce Act[41].
- Where smart contracts do not create legally binding obligations between the parties, they could still create other legal implications both on the parties involved and third parties at large.
- The Augur example highlights the fact that traditional remedies for enforcement could fall short in a decentralized and disintermediated context, and new approaches to regulation and liability will need to be considered, such as the possibility of joint liability for co-ordinated activities on a DLT.
- In some instances, the solution could partly lie in the technology itself, which could help in providing newer, smarter and more flexible type of enforcement mechanisms such as the possibility of creating reverse transactions or suspending automatic performance[42].

Conclusions

Sooner or later it is likely that the legal status of a smart contract will be tested in the courts. Our analysis demonstrates that those who wish to deploy smart contracts in the belief that they can never give rise to contractual relations or tortuous liability between the parties should be wary of accepting that conclusion uncritically. Having said that, although existing legal frameworks may allow for use of smart contracts, parties may face practical challenges in complying with existing legal or regulatory requirements, such as form requirements, and if not addressed, these types of issues could prevent or slow down the widespread adoption of smart contracts[43].

Endnotes

1. Primavera De Filippi and Benjamin Loveluck, "The Invisible Politics of Bitcoin: Governance Crisis of a Decentralised Infrastructure", Internet Policy Review, 5.3 (2016).
2. Lawrence Lessig, Code and Other Laws of Cyberspace (Basic Books, 1999).
3. Gernot Heller, Thomas Escritt and Michelle Martin, "France, Germany Call for Joint G20 Action on Cryptocurrencies", Reuters, 2018.
4. Rakesh Sharma, "More US States May Roll Out Cryptocurrency Regulations", Investopedia, 2018..
5. "Arizona HB2417 | 2017 | Fifty-Third Legislature 1St Regular", Legiscan, 2017.
6. Stan Higgins, "Vermont Governor Signs Bill Clearing Way for Blockchain Companies".
7. "Cryptomonnaies: Le Rapport Landau", Bitcoin.fr, 2018.
8. Nick Szabo, "Smart Contracts: Building Blocks for Digital Markets", Phonetic Sciences, Amsterdam, 1996.

9.   D. M. Levine, "A Day in the Quiet Life of a NYSE Floor Trader", Fortune, 2013.
10. Gideon Greenspan, 'Beware the Impossible Smart Contract' (Multichain, 2016).
11. MDIA Act, art 2(1).
12. The DAO was a 'Decentralized Autonomous Organization' created as a sort of venture capital fund and effected via a smart contract on the Ethereum platform. It had no management; instead, participants would directly agree to fund projects according to the terms of its establishing smart contract.
13. Adam J. Kolber, "Not-So-Smart Blockchain Contracts and Artificial Responsibility", Stanford Technology Law Review, p. 21 (2018).
14. Josh Stark, "Making Sense of Blockchain Smart Contracts", Coindesk, 2016.
15. Maltese Civil Code, art 960.
16. Ibid, art 1233.
17. Said Peter Paul et vs Said Mario et, Reference: 4/2008, 24/07/ 2009, Courts of Malta.
18. Christopher D. Clack, Vikram A. Bakshi and Lee Braine, "Smart Contract Templates", CORR, 2016.
19. The ISDA/Linklaters Smart Contracts and Distributed Ledger – A Legal Perspective paper also distinguishes between two different models of smart legal contracts: the external model and the internal model. In the external model, the coded provisions remain external to the legal contract, and represent only a mechanism for automatic performance of the contract. In the internal model, the provisions that can be performed automatically are included in the legal contract, but are rewritten in a more formal representation than the current natural language form. A computer could take this formal representation and automate performance.
20. EC, Proposal for a EuroParl and Council Directive on Certain

Legal Aspects of Electronic Commerce in the Internal Market (586 Final) p. 25, Brussels, 1998.

21.   Christopher D. Clack et al., "Smart Contract Templates" Alexander Savelyev, "Contract Law 2.0" (SSRN: 2885241), 2016.

22.   Emily M. Weitzenboeck, "Electronic Agents and the Formation of Contracts", International Journal of Law and Information Technology, 9.3 (2001), pp. 204-234.

23.   Smart Contracts: Legal Framework and Proposed Guidelines for Lawmakers, EBRD, 2018.

24.   Max Ganado, chapter 11 of this book.

25.   Electronic Commerce Act, Chapter 426 of the laws of Malta.

26.   Electronic Commerce Act, art 11(1 & 3) & the First Schedule.

27.   Sylvia Kierkegaard, "E-Contract Formation", Shidler J. L. Com. & Tech., 3.12 (2007).

28.   Usually, such form of agreement is displayed in a separate window that the user cannot download or print, thereby calling into question the extent that the requirements in the ECA are being complied with even today.

29.   Consumer Affairs Act, art 47(1).

30.   Whitepaper Smart Derivatives Contracts: From Concept to Construction (ISDA, 2018).

31.   Maltese Civil Code, art 990.

32.   Ibid, art 987

33.   "What's in a Smart Contract", Freshfields Bruckhaus Deringer, freshfields.com.

34.   To our knowledge the discussion dates back to Lawrence Lessig's seminal book Code and Other Laws of Cyberspace p. 24 et seq. where he used the phrase 'code is law' as a metaphor, 'in that the code controls behavior as law might control behavior'.

35.   Dirk A. Zetzsche, Ross P. Buckley and Douglas W. Arner, "The Distributed Liability of Distributed Ledgers: Legal Risks of Blockchain", 2017.

36.   CryptoIQ, "DAO Dilemma: Hard Fork or No Fork", Medium, 2016.

37. Smart Contracts: Legal Framework and Proposed Guidelines for Lawmakers, EBRD, 2018.
38. Brian Quintenz, "Remarks of Commissioner Brian Quintenz at the 38th Annual GITEX Technology Week Conference ", U.S. CFTC, 2018.
39. Dirk A. Zetzsche et al.
40. Like many others, Maltese law has codified the principle of pacta sunt servanda in its Civil Code, whereby Article 992 states that 'contracts legally entered into shall have the force of law for the contracting parties'.
41. Electronic Commerce Act, art 9(1).
42. Under the Electronic Commerce Act, art 10(2) service providers have a duty towards consumers to make 'available to the recipient of the service appropriate, effective and accessible technical means allowing him to identify and correct input errors, prior to the placing of the order'.
43. Blockchain, DLT and the Capital Markets Journey (Hogan Lovells, 2016).

13. Hybrid Programmer-Lawyers: Vital for Smart Contracts

Joshua Ellul, Ian Gauci, Gordon Pace

Perhaps at some point in the future, executable smart contract code will be weaved into legal frameworks allowing for the automation of obligations, and for the partial enforcement of agreements... If such a future were to come to pass, the concept of the hybrid lawyer-developer may indeed need to be revisited if legally valid smart contracts are to be written in an efficient and precise, or subjective, manner as required.

Dr Joshua Ellul set up the Centre for DLT at the University of Malta and is the first chairman of the Malta Digital Innovation Authority, which aims to instil higher levels of assurances into innovative technologies.

A legal expert on the National Blockchain Taskforce, Dr Ian Gauci, is a partner at GTG Advocates, Afilexion Alliance and Caledo Group. Ian is a Blockchain Malta Association board member.

A professor of Computer Science at the University of Malta, Gordon Pace has also worked at in various institutions in Sweden, France and Argentina. He is a leading thinker on the Blockchain Island.

Introduction

Digital automation plays a crucial role in many professions. Whereas until a few decades ago, expertise in the specific domain of the profession sufficed, one now also requires mastering skills to use software systems to perform calculations, automate tasks and take decisions in that domain. Take, for instance, the engineering profession. Until a few decades ago, structural engineers were required to perform manual calculations to approximate forces on planned structures in order to assess their safety. When software systems were designed to automate this analysis process, their speed and accuracy (usually thanks to their speed, computer systems can perform analysis to a finer-grained level of accuracy) far exceeded those of human engineers. The result was that the role of engineers changed, with the new focus now on the design process, and the choice of the proper tools of analysis. More recently, we are seeing the application of machine learning and AI techniques to automate the design process itself, further relegating the role of engineers to that of supervising and using such software of design support.

Despite the automation provided through these digital tools, scripting and querying customization still requires human expertise to maximize their effectiveness. However, some of the skills required to do this no longer lie in the domain of expertise of the professional, but in that of using, customizing and scripting the software systems. As a result, some argue that coding or programming is a new form of basic literacy that professionals (perhaps even the general public) should have[1].

One profession that has lagged behind in automating its processes is the legal one. Perhaps one of the biggest challenges is that this profession is based on the interpretation of natural language texts, and requiring a degree of precision in semantics that rules out the occasional misunderstanding of a phrase or sentence. It was only the past few years that saw the rise of the new field of 'regulatory technology', also referred to as RegTech, covering the use of IT to enable automation in the regulatory domain – from compliance to contract analysis and classification.

However, more recently, a further intrusion of IT into the legal domain appeared in the form of 'smart contracts' on blockchain and other DLT. Smart contracts bridge the notions of legal contracts and computer programs — artefacts that are effectively software systems, but act as legal agreements regulating notions such as ownership and obligations. Developing such an artefact thus demands both coding and legal expertise.

In this chapter, we investigate the skill set required by a professional to be able to develop such smart contracts, since clearly both traditionally trained lawyers and software engineers lack the expertise in one or other of the skills required to code smart contracts. Will an uptake of smart contracts require a new hybrid professional, with a combination of legal and coding skills?

In order to answer this question, we start by discussing the similarities and differences between legal and smart contracts. We then look at different ways of addressing the challenge of smart contract development. We start off by looking at the traditional setup of teams of lawyers working in tandem with software engineers. However, as we shall point out, this approach has its limitations. A better way forward would be that of training legal professionals to a degree of coding literacy. In the context of this chapter, the choice of both the terms 'coding' and 'literacy' is deliberate. The professional with proficiency in both law and software engineering is a chimeric ideal — one to which only a few individuals can aspire. In practice, forming professionals rooted in one domain with secondary expertise in another is a more realistic prospect. Since legal skills are crucial in drafting smart contracts, one question is if we can change the toolsets available to produce smart contracts — moving away from software development to an activity more akin to drafting a traditional legal contract. In practice, current approaches have shown that although useful in specific applications, e.g. financial contracts, such approaches inherently limit the class of contracts that can be written.

The question is thus perhaps that of the feasibility of training legal professionals in programming. More specifically, the question is to what degree of proficiency is programming required as a secondary skill for lawyers. Do they require the skills of a software engineer, able to plan, design, build, maintain and manage a software artefact? Do they need to have the skills of a software developer, or is it sufficient to be literate in programming or coding? In this chapter, we argue that lawyers working in the domain of smart contracts require a degree of programming or coding literacy. In particular, we argue that they should be able to understand what can be done through smart contracts and programming in general, as well as appreciate the challenges and potential pitfalls in building such systems. Hence the use of 'coding' as opposed to 'software engineering', 'software development' or even 'programming', and 'literacy' rather than 'mastery'.

Smart Contracts versus Contracts

Smart contracts were originally proposed by Nick Szabo in 1996[2] as 'contracts [...] robust against naïve vandalism and against sophisticated, incentive compatible breach'. Legal contracts specify ideal, as opposed to actual, behaviour. For instance, if a clause in a contract states that 'the seller is obliged to deliver the ordered items on time or pay the buyer a fine of €1000', nothing stops the seller from delivering the items late without paying a fine. Szabo's vision of smart contracts was that of artefacts ensuring that such divergences were impossible or impractical. In a way, a notary holding €1000 paid by the seller, ready to give them to the buyer if the delivery deadline is exceeded can be seen as the human version of a smart contract. The use of computer systems enabled automation of such smart contracts. However, using either a notary or computer code to effect a contract still allows for 'naïve vandalism' if the notary does not follow the instructions, or the party entrusted with executing the code modifies it or its behaviour. Without a regulatory structure to provide safeguards against such divergences caused by undesirable behaviour from central points-of-trust, one is simply postponing the problem of compliance by a step.

With the rise of blockchain and other DLT it was quickly realized that immutable ledgers and decentralized consensus mechanisms provided a means of doing away with the need for such centralized trust in legal agreements with the party executing the code. The first realization of this form of smart contract was the Ethereum blockchain, which supported the execution of computer code on the so-called 'world computer', the agglomeration of Ethereum nodes, ensuring that the code (i) remains unchanged; and (ii) is executed faithfully.

With such a view of smart contracts, one can see such artefacts as deterministic agreements or even protocols between the participating parties, executed through computer code capable of enforcing behaviour and taking decisions when certain preconditions are met. This offers new ways to formalize digitised relationships beyond the functionality of their inanimate paper-based ancestors.

Such smart contracts represent the fusion of diverse intrinsic factors. In the first instance we have technology, through code, DLT, cryptography, etc., but we also have a social duty, as well as an expression for more certainty by the users, and this is also fused with law, starting from any applicable lex terrae and substantive law provisions, to lex specialis like the one in Nevada or Malta that deal specifically with smart contracts and lex cryptographia. Hence, here we have innovation from the societal, legal paradigmatic, and contractual as well as technological point of view, all this spurred by digital innovation.

From the technological point of view, smart contracts can be seen as one farther step in the evolution of electronic agreements[3] — an extension of 'Electronic Data Interchange'[4] (EDI) format used in many business-to-business and business-to-consumer contracts, and dating back to the 1960s. From its inception, EDI was seen as a killer application for contract formation and execution[5] but suffered from the use of proprietary formats developed by a single firm for exclusive use by its trading partners, thus limiting the exchange of EDI across firms until standards started to appear. In the early days of EDI, legislators gave little to no attention to developing laws to regulate and formalize the basic conditions for the contents of EDI. It was therefore primarily left up to the trading parties to enter into these EDI agreements, with the risk that these exchanges might not have necessarily produced an enforceable contract.

For this reason, international organizations have also focused on recommendations for change to the legal environment in order to facilitate the use of EDI. For example, in 1994, the EC published a Recommendation on EDI that includes a European model EDI agreement[6]. This has been used as a basis for standard agreements at a national level, such as the Standard Electronic Data Interchange Agreement. The UN Commission on International Trade Law (UNCITRAL) also developed a model law on EDI. The UN joint EDI

Committee has developed the EDIFACT international standards (Electronic Data Interchange for Administration, Commerce, Transport).

EDI as a model removed the communication and interface between humans but, while implementing commercial security models, too often they did not cater for the contractual needs and obligations of the parties[7]. To this end, lawyers were usually not even considered in the whole EDI negotiation, drafting and exchange. Furthermore, although EDI addressed computer-to-computer interchange of documentation automating processes between the parties, it was designed to exclude monetary instruments[8], and it focuses on the operations – a request to send an item, rather than a legal statement about the transfer of ownership rights.

In contrast, smart contracts through blockchain technology have the ability to tokenise physical assets, add digital certificates as well as digital identities, all as part of the ledger. This provides a transparent view of the asset's real value, title, permits, transactions etc., and an imbued element of trust. Performance of the legal relationship or elements thereof does not have to be tied to any action in the real world — it is automatic and subject only to the rules established in the smart contract. Operating through smart contracting, in the future ownership can be controlled by digital means, e.g. traded and loaned via blockchain. The blockchain thus becomes a system for recording and managing property rights. Legally, property consists of rights and obligations. One of the rights making up property is the right of ownership, consisting of the right to possess, use and dispose of property. Possession means the right to be in control of property. Usage is the ability to enjoy property in accordance with its purpose. The right to dispose of property is an underlying aspect of the right of ownership since it is this aspect of ownership that enables the transfer of the property, thus making it merchantable and turning property into an asset.

The interaction between smart contracts and legal contracts thus goes beyond EDI and similar earlier technologies in two manners:

1. Since the agreed-upon result occurs automatically and in a guaranteed manner (through consensus, rather than through execution on a machine or server acting as a shared central point-of-trust), uncertainty about performance, and about judicial recognition, disappears.
2. The code is itself the contract, and provisions are laid out in precise terms to a heightened degree as compared to traditional contract language but in a manner that is still directly related to legal notions of ownership, rights and obligations.

On Writing Smart Contracts

Currently, smart contracts are largely deployed as computer programs that automate a process. As a result, practically all development is carried out by software developers leading to a number of shortcomings in terms of looking at them as legal contracts.

Firstly, software developers tend to see smart contracts myopically as a system that has to be built for a client. Considerations taken into account are typically those with which the developers are familiar in the development of typical software systems. Requirements are identified and driven by end users. This does not impart to smart contracts due consideration as executable embodiments of legal contracts. Moreover, it does not take into consideration legal requirements of contracts, such as competence and capacity of the parties. Neither does it take into consideration the necessity for the object and purpose of the contract to comply with the law. The latter is particularly salient since smart contracts typically handle transactions of digital assets and cryptocurrencies, activities that are increasingly regulated by a stringent legal regime. Furthermore, phases of the typical lifecycle of a legal contract are frequently fully or partly omitted. For instance, rarely are all the phases identified by Governatori et al.[9]– negotiation, notarisation, performance, enforcement, modification, dispute resolution and termination – built into a smart contract.

Limiting one's view of smart contracts as software programs brings about an additional problem – smart contracts typically run into hundreds or even a few thousand lines of code, and are thus viewed by software engineers as small systems. The critical aspect of smart contracts arises not from the size and complexity of the code itself, but from the implications of potential misbehaviour or misuse. Furthermore, the immutable nature of such code means that, unless explicitly handled within the smart contract itself, divergences from the expected behaviour will continue recurring. As documented incidents have shown far too many times, developers have built smart contracts with the typical mindset used in software development, particularly for small systems, in which one deploys the system and applies patches as issues become apparent – often with a 'fail fast' mindset. Far too many incidents with smart contracts arise because either full patching is impossible, or because, by the time intervention happens, irreversible transactions have taken place.

These shortcomings with the current state of smart contract writing highlight two observations: (i) the close affinity between smart contracts and legal ones and the fact that such contracts manipulate ownership of digital assets. This means that their design must be supported, shaped and directed through legal knowledge in order to ensure that they do embody legal agreements and that they do not violate legal obligations; (ii) smart contracts are critical systems, and despite the fact that they are typically small in size and contained in complexity, they are to be designed in a thorough manner as is typically reserved for high-risk systems such as financial transaction software or safety-critical systems.

The first observation indicates the need for legal expertise, which may be construed as an indication that lawyers are best equipped for writing smart contracts. In contrast, the second indicates that a sound background in software engineering is required in order to build dependable smart contracts. We now consider the different alternatives through which these requirements may be met.

The Hybrid Developer-Lawyer

Given the current state of the art, it appears that writing smart contracts requires hybrid experts, with a sound basis of both legal drafting and software development. The need for multiple expertise is common in the software development industry – when developing a health system, medical expertise is essential, as is structural engineering expertise when developing systems to model physical structures. These software systems are meant to support experts in professional domains, and the need for domain specific expertise is to embody relevant knowledge into the system. In the legal domain, this is akin to the development of compliance engines as part of software systems, ensuring that legal violations do not occur. However, in all these cases, the expertise is required during the development of the system, which once deployed will be used by domain experts with basic ICT literacy skills, and no need for software development knowledge.

In contrast, smart contract developers will be involved in the development of bespoke contracts handling a variety of legal domains, yet requiring sound software development skills. If anything is to be learnt from the development of compliance engines[10], it is that such systems can only be developed by teams of diverse experts – for instance to develop compliance engines for financial transaction systems, one requires a team of software engineers working in tandem with legal experts and financial instrument engineers. Such systems require teams to develop in a dependable manner, and each individual typically plays a role wearing the hat of expertise in just one domain.

Should smart contracts be developed by teams of software developers working with lawyers? The main challenge in building teams with diverse specializations is one of communication, with terminology and interpretation differing all too frequently between domains. While a software developer may interpret legislation requiring a financial transfer to be performed 'without delay' to mean that there is a hard limit beyond which the transfer would be considered late, or at the very most, a probabilistic distribution indicating how timely a transfer is, a lawyer may highlight that a delay acceptable in a business-to-business transfer is not necessarily so in a consumer-to-consumer or business-to-consumer one. A legal obligation on a user to perform a transfer may be interpreted by a developer as an opportunity to automate the transfer in a smart contract, thus ensuring compliance. Yet, a lawyer may point out that another regulation may prohibit the use of a service if the obligation is not observed, and thus the user should have the choice whether or not to uphold the obligation to make the transfer. While experience gained in working together imparts to developers a better intuition of legal requirements, and to lawyers a better understanding of technological capabilities and limitations, this requires a long-term working relationship between experts in the different domains.

The Code-Literate Lawyer and the Law-Literate Developer

The main challenge in assembling teams for the development of smart contracts from both lawyers and software engineers is that of bridging the two islands of expertise. From a software engineer's perspective, the major challenge is that of understanding the foundational principles of the law, with a basic understanding of various areas of the law, including contracts, torts and companies. Such training is distinct from that aimed at producing professionals that can practise law, who are masters of the legal domain, able to draft legal contracts and understand subtleties in such agreements. In contrast, this training is intended to furnish software engineers with law-literacy: the ability to understand legal terms, read legal texts, follow legal arguments — in effect the ability to communicate with lawyers as part of a smart contract development team. Although in software engineering, some have exalted the virtues of a software developer's domain ignorance[11], particularly since it encourages questioning of the underlying assumptions and brings to light ambiguities, smart contract developers require legal knowledge, not in a single project, but across multiple ones. In such circumstances, ignorance of the legal domain is just as disadvantageous as ignorance of software engineering.

If law-literate developers can simplify one direction of the communication in a smart contract development team, the other direction can be addressed by providing lawyers with the foundational knowledge necessary to appreciate the process of software development, and to understand basic notions of programming languages and coding. Basic code literacy is taken to cover various aspects of software development in order to ensure that such lawyers can direct and support smart contract drafting more effectively. The skills include: (i) the ability to understand basic notions of programming, particularly of smart contracts; (ii) understanding of the design of smart contracts, and the ability to support the writing of specification documents from legal contracts; and (iii) appreciation of sources of complexity and error in software systems.

Teams with both law-literate developers and code-literate lawyers on board will facilitate ease of communication, and enable more streamlined 'writing' of smart contracts corresponding to, and acting like, traditional legal contracts. Achieving the levels of literacy required to achieve this is lower hanging fruit compared to the creation of a polymath specialist with expertise in both smart contract development and law. It also enables professionals already working in the industry to expand their skill set that is required on such teams. However, the question remains as to whether the development teams responsible for the drafting of legal contracts embodied in smart contracts require expert software developers as part of their team, or, as has happened in other industries, it is feasible to provide domain specific languages and tools to permit domain experts themselves to implement the required processes (or smart contracts in this case).

Lowering the Bar in Smart Contract Development

The need for expert developers to build smart contracts stems from the need to write potentially complex contracts. However, some are predicting a trend towards the proliferation of minor variants of a number of standard contracts. A recent study[12] of smart contracts deployed on the Ethereum blockchain confirmed a 'considerable lack of diversity', although it is unclear whether it is 'endemic to smart contracts (or Ethereum itself), or if it is merely a reflection of the relative youth of smart contracts'. In such an ecosystem, the model consists of a minority of template builders for a majority of template users, and the 'role of lawyers might shift to producing smart contract templates on a competitive market, [and] contract selling points would be their quality, how customizable they are, and their ease of use'[13]. If smart contracts are used to model legal agreements, parties can either create template hybrid arrangements that integrate with natural-language contracts or use a standard template within its range of customizability. This would bring significant possibilities for greatly reducing the development effort as well as the legal costs of executing some kinds of contracts while at the same time creating the opportunity for new kinds of businesses and social institutions based on smart contracts or the hybrid forms of contracts. De Filippi and Wright[14] have further emphasized this claim:

"Just as we moved from an earlier era of expensive, highly tailored clothing toward mass-produced garments with limited personalization, with the growing adaptation of blockchain technology and other contract automation tools, we may witness a shift from expensive and bespoke contracts to low-cost and highly standardized legal agreements with limited avenues for customization."

The more distribution and disintermediation, and a network society as described by Castells[15], the more these standardized agreements will be distributed and widespread. Since these are more deterministic in nature, they will likely reduce litigation significantly, as well as the societal role courts have in crafting necessary inputs and levers in formulating and interpreting the law. From this angle, given its utmost importance, lawyers, who know what is legitimate, how laws and what laws should apply to transactions, and also have the experience to mitigate possible contractual conflicts, should form part of the design process of these artefacts, and can understand code, and also write it. The participation of the legal practitioner, therefore, in the development of smart contracts, will serve to place these artefacts on a surer legal footing.

Increasingly, various academic and industrial projects are focusing on the development of smart contract languages that can be used by those lacking expertise in IT. Natural language processing techniques have made huge strides in the past years, but the pipe-dream of interpreting and executing as smart contracts those contracts written in plain English is still a distant objective. The ambiguity inherent in natural language, also present in legal contracts, with such ambiguity giving rise to conflicting interpretations by different lawyers, is one of the major challenges to realizing this objective. Another challenge is the diversity of smart contracts that may be designed to implement a particular legal contract. For instance, a clause requiring a payment within 24 hours of accessing a service may be enforced (1) by performing the payment immediately upon accessing the transfer; (2) by waiting for just under 24 hours to perform the transfer; (3) anything in between such as making the transfer as soon as funds are available after the service is used; (4) to put the choice of time for payment into the user's hands that, however, may lead to a contract violation, and thus provides limited enforcement.

Due to these challenges, many efforts focus on (1) using contract templates allowing for only particular forms of contracts to be specified; (2) building a controlled natural language – a language that looks like a natural one, but allows the use of a constrained vocabulary and syntax in which to specify contracts; or (3) build domain-specific languages, similar to controlled natural languages, but looking and functioning more like programming languages. As one moves from the first to the third approach, one obtains increased expressivity, but at the cost of increased complexity in drafting a contract. When one requires contracts for a particular purpose with little variation, templates may be sufficient, but with more complex contracts one may need to use a domain-specific language that requires basic programming skills. The domain-specificity ensures that certain programming pitfalls can be avoided, but still at a cost of limited expressivity. For instance, Simon-Peyton Jones et al.[16] proposed a domain-specific language for financial contracts that has been used by various banks and payment institutions. The language guarantees that the contracts thus specified not only can be executed, but also analyzed, allowing for algorithmic trading and also contract negotiation. However, the language is limited, allowing no contracts outside the financial scope of the language, or even contracts requiring computational operations not within its algorithmic scope.

Clearly, for a particular class of contracts, one can build tools to support lawyers draft smart contracts directly themselves. However, for a wider domain of application, this is not a viable solution for general drafting. At best, one hopes for lawyers to draft parts of smart contracts using natural language driven tools, leaving the more computationally complex parts for extension by software developers.

Conclusions

Lawyers dealing with the challenges of innovation look at the legal system as a whole and apply the system's foundational principles. The law provides an abundance of generally applicable principles, including the law of contracts, torts, property, partnerships and companies, some of which are enshrined in legislation while others (in particular in common law countries) are in case law that applies in the absence of specific legislation. A lawyer with an appreciation of the technology around him, and the potential of artefacts like smart contacts, can divest his mental process from legacy scenarios and from applying solely functional equivalents, and thus be able to create solutions for future policy and legislation. It is essential for lawyers to keep an open mind given the era of unprecedented technological changes on all fronts and the relentless daily pace of technological innovation.

Future lawyers will also need to diversify if they are to remain in practice. The use of technology to enhance legal practice and process is not new. If blockchain as a foundational technology, with smart contracts as a main lynchpin, can carry the legal industry across the threshold of these technological paradigm shifts that diminish the need for traditional legal service, then lawyers need to extend their capabilities by becoming increasingly multidisciplinary.

Perhaps at some point in the future, executable smart contract code will be weaved into legal frameworks allowing for the automation of obligations, and for the partial enforcement of agreements. Much progress needs to be made on many different fronts to achieve this, and such progress may be slowed down by challenges including technological, constitutional, educational and societal ones. If such a future were to come to pass, the concept of the hybrid lawyer-developer may indeed need to be revisited if legally valid smart contracts are to be written in an efficient and precise, or subjective, manner as required.

Although the long-term goal is that of executing legal contracts as smart contracts, possibly with a human legal expert overseeing or directing the enforcement of different clauses that are to be enforced, there is still much work to be done in natural language processing in order to achieve this. In the meantime, when smart contracts are used to model legal agreements, it appears that the way forward is to have code-literate lawyers working alongside law-literate software developers to design, draft and verify legal contracts embodied in or accompanied by smart contracts, regulating the behaviour between the parties.

Endnotes

1. Annette Vee, Coding Literacy. (MIT Press, 2017).
2. Nick Szabo, "Formalizing and Securing Relationships on Public Networks", First Monday, 2.9 (1997).
3. Kevin Werbach and Nicholas Cornell, "Contracts Ex Machina", Duke Law Journal, 67.2 (2017).
4. Nick Szabo, "Smart Contracts", Extropy #16, 1996.
5. Benjamin Wright, The Law of Electronic Commerce, 1991.
6. "Commission Recommendation of 19 October 1994 Relating to the Legal Aspects of Electronic Data Interchange", Official Journal of The EC, L 338 (1994), 98.
7. Nick Szabo, 1996
8. "Approval of Federal Information Processing Standards Publication 161–2, Electronic Data Interchange (EDI)", Federal Register, 61.100 (1996), pp. 25627-25632.
9. Guido Governatori and others, "On Legal Contracts, Imperative and Declarative Smart Contracts, and Blockchain Systems", AI and Law, 2018, pp. 1-33.
10. Christian Colombo and Gordon J. Pace, "Industrial Experiences with Runtime Verification of Financial Transaction Systems", Lectures on Runtime Verification, 2018, pp. 211-232.
11. Daniel M. Berry, "The Importance of Ignorance in Requirements Engineering", Journal of Systems and Software, 28.2 (1995), pp. 179-184.
12. Lucianna Kiffer, Dave Levin and Alan Mislove, "Analyzing Ethereum's Contract Topology", (IMC'18), 2018), pp. 494-499.
13. Jay Cassano, "What Are Smart Contracts?", Fast Company, 2014.
14. Primavera De Filippi and Aaron Wright, Blockchain and the Law (Harvard UP, 2018). Kindle Locations 1719-1722.
15. Manuel Castells, Rise of The Network Society (Blackwell, 1996).
16. Simon Peyton Jones, Jean-Marc Eber and Julian Seward, "Composing Contracts:", Fifth ACM SIGPLAN International Conference on Functional Programming, 2000, pp. 280–292.

PART IV
SCIENTIA

Knowledge and Application

14. Not 1984: How the Truth Will Set Us Free

Tyron Baron

In this digital age of ours we've passed the privacy event horizon. There is no going back and those who yearn for a return to nature, pristine privacy, and a time before the world wide web are searching for the impossible. A possible solution is to embrace DLT as the next standard of what society needs to base the truth on, and that's what will level the playing field not by hiding but by elucidating.

Tyron Baron is the CEO of InboundMuse working in the realm of A.I. & blockchain for use cases from GDPR to Supply Chain Management and Tokenised Memberships.

Introduction

"Tempora Mutantur, Nos Et Mutamur In Illis"
– "Times change, and we change with the times."
From the moment the author became involved in the industry of innovation, the ethical trajectories have fascinated him and, though some will struggle against the tide, he believes that the traditional notions of privacy as we might have once conceived them are invariably becoming obsolete.

The services we depend on, the accuracy we demand, and the infrastructures they are built on, have irrevocably entwined themselves with our lives and thrive on the paradigms of access we have tacitly assented to, and on the data we have collectively made so freely available. Society is now increasingly compelled to reassess its standards of behaviour with a view to become more open and equitable, rather than policing and oppressive – 1984 need not be a self-fulfilling prophecy.

There are two things to bear in mind at the onset. Of the first part, that the so-called Anthropocene – the Age of Humans – was not brought about by our fierce intellect (as evidenced by some of our individuals), but by the enthusiasm with which we collectively throw ourselves at the endeavour of progress.

Of the second, that ever since Hesiod's Works and Days (c. 800 B.C.), through to the Odes of Horace (c. 23 B.C.), and well into modernity there has always existed this notion of things devolving over time, and yet it is clear from the data that by and large we have never lived through more peaceful and prosperous times.

The Rate of Progress

"Nothing is more responsible for the good old days than a bad memory."

– Franklin Pierce Adams

If everything is great, and as such things have always been this way, what is the commotion all about? There is, in fact, a salient new element that muddles the mixture – The unprecedented cumulative acceleration of progress.

Progress itself, often cited as inexorable, is not inevitable or universal. Not everything becomes better for everyone, everywhere, all the time. It is not a matter of faith or optimism but a fact of human history, and if there is such a thing as progress, as the author argues that there is, what causes it? It is not some mystical force, or a mysterious arc of history tending towards justice. It is the cumulative result of human efforts governed by the ideals of the Enlightenment, that if we apply reason and science, we better our lot. With this we have occupied our minds, thus progress is not spontaneous or automatic, but intensive problem-solving. Problems, which are the inevitable component, and the solutions themselves, create their own problems that have to be solved in turn, and so on.

In 1736 Leonhard Euler invented a new branch of mathematics – Graph Theory – on a whim to provide a rigorous proof from first principles that there was no way one could walk across the then 7 bridges of Königsberg and never cross the same one twice. Within a few centuries, a heartbeat in the history of human civilization – we have already realized the unparalleled benefits of a hivemind – a planet-wide miracle interconnecting the species in a way that has enabled us to ship our minds, our words, and our learning ever faster, to an ever-growing number of contributors, or nodes. This accelerating rate of transmission not only furthers our progress, but exponentially accelerates the rate at which we progress in the vein of Metcalfe's law, which states that the influence of a network is proportional to the square of the number of connected users of the system (n2). From the onset we had crossed an event horizon – we can only ever become more increasingly connected.

In 2019, at the confluence of our obsession with collecting data en masse, our desire to exploit it, and the access to 'artificially intelligent' technologies that can fuel their own improvement from the results they generate in the course of their intended operations, we find the 'critical point' that heralds the runaway chain-reaction towards the scenario in which humans are increasingly able to redirect the requirements of intellectual horsepower to a machine that, given its 'North Star' metrics – its raison d'être – will tirelessly optimize itself and its environment to maximize for this result.

Automation used to mean stupid machines doing repetitive work in factories. Today, they can predict the optimal layout of thousands of supercooled magnets to control a billion-degree plasma in a fusion reactor, model entire galaxies light years away to calculate how much dark matter is present in the system, and more importantly, just like a machine can automate the process of learning chess, by playing more games against itself than a pair of humans can hope to play in a million years, to become a Grandmaster in a few days, it can undertake the same pains to understand the pathways that lead you to buy a new toaster with adverts, in the right place, at the right time, for the cheapest cost.

While even our smartest machines are bad at doing complicated jobs and understanding nuance, they are extremely apt at narrowly defined and predictable tasks. This is why menial, repetitive work is evaporating out of developed economies. But if you look at a complex problem hard enough, and you will only find many, narrowly defined, and predictable tasks done in predictable series, with some decision paths in between – voila, the algorithm.

In the age of information, when we track data about literally everything, we are picking up speed towards the inevitable cliff-edge, the point where we shall be out-competed by machine-learning algorithms. For the first time, these can be provided with the volume of data necessary to be trained (or rather train themselves) to reach and supersede human proficiency in any complex task, whether stocking a warehouse, selling insurance, or removing a tumour.

Tell the machine where you have been, and what you have bought, and soon you will have a new friend that knows you better than anyone else. And it will provide you with just the recommendation for everything you did not know you were looking for – from which retailer, at the best price, from the closest location. We see this daily. Google directs you to a café that has your lactose-free WiFi fix, Netflix recommends to which documentaries you should stay subscribed, and Amazon recommends a list of everything with a power button in descending order of 'cool'.

We vote for the commodification of convenience with our credit cards and our complacency, and there should be no reason to constrain the imagination to our phone or the browser. Even if, through sheer force of will, or masochistic tendencies, one were to recuse oneself from any digital presence, any number of emerging technologies such as networks of smart billboards, making use of computer vision and embedded systems, might be able to catalogue your presence in their space. The computer may not be able to pull a profile of you from some database, but it may just add you as a fresh entry, recognizing the brands you wear, the coffee cup in your hand, the shopping bags you carry, the sentiment on your face, and any other pertinent demographic datum. All this in the name of a conveniently placed ad to activate those all-powerful consumer genes that push our dopamine buttons. All the while, these and many other tactics, while intrusive, will fill every available lacuna in a perfectly legally compliant manner, given that finding 'workarounds' – what lawyers might call loopholes – is the technologist's modus operandi.

Resistance is Futile

It should therefore begin to be appreciable just how automation has led to this hunger for data and its implication for privacy.

This is not to dismiss the more traditional methods that humans with spreadsheets have been employing for the sake of Business Intelligence, indeed since before Munehisha Honma used data and technical analysis in the 1700s to optimize for profit at the Dojima Rice Markets in Osaka. However, it does stress how momentous the removal of the implicit bottlenecks tied to human efficiency is. This, tied to our complacent lethargy, if not wilful ignorance, of how the world around us works, makes us prime targets for the powers that be, and conjures up the classic Hollywood idea of the machine 'take over'. This is of course absurd. There will not be so much a 'taking over' as a 'rolling over'. Less 'Terminator', More 'Her'.

We can now surely imagine some of the implications of what the endgame scenario of this Information Age might look like, and start to well understand how privacy through obfuscation is a futile attempt.

It is not all doom and gloom, however, for defaulting to pessimism is no safeguard against complacency. What is needed is a more stringent requirement for accuracy; to be aware of the dangers, numerous as they are, without resorting to the fatalism of believing that if all our efforts at improving the world have been in vain, then why throw good money after bad? Nor should we resort to the radicalism that if our institutions are beyond hope for reform, we should seek to smash the machine, on the assurance that whatever rises from the ashes is bound to be better than with what we were on a collision course.

The Cultural Role of Blockchain

In a book about blockchain, by the Blockchain Malta Association, one does go on awfully long without mentioning distributed ledger technologies (DLTs) in all this, but one would also argue that such is the point. If the consideration is data, its use, and our privacy, should we not appreciate a reason to research a vast subject for ourselves more seriously instead of trading the nuance for convenience?

Often enough it would be all too convenient to hail an emerging technology, which very few people actually comprehend, and rattle off any number of very impressive sounding use cases, even fewer of which have been implemented to any meaningful degree, but this does the reader and the dialogue itself an injustice.

Blockchain is a truly revolutionary technology that has a part to play but we must be mindful that it is still in its infancy, and it is very definitely no panacea to anything at all.

The greatest enrichment most stand to gain from blockchain technologies is more of a cultural appreciation of how interconnected we are and have yet to become, as well as bringing more people into the discussion. Blockchain has a role to play in igniting an interest if not a passion for technology, in collectively engaging in the dialogue and direction from the points of view of the personal and the political, the ethical and the economical.

Conclusion

At this point, we have established a number of premises. The first is that progress is driven not by intellect, but by problem-solving, often ad hoc, or as one might say, necessity is the mother of invention. The second is that to the contrary of what poets tend to think, we are moving not from the Golden Age to the Iron Age, but from the Stone Age to the Information Age. The third premise is that technology is developing at an exponential rate through a framework of global interconnection. The fourth is that this technology has arrived at the point where progress is taking place on the basis of the collection of vast amounts of data and the automated processing of this data at tremendous speeds.

The consequent of these premises is that no single human being, or even communities of human beings, have a hope of escaping the effects of such data collection and processing. We are all under surveillance on a level of granularity that would turn the T-1000 green with envy. And with the deflationary cost of technology, and its exponential growth, there is no escape whatsoever. A prospect that will appear truly grim to those of us with a dystopian bent.

But though these premises are established, and the consequent deducible therefrom, the conclusion has not yet been resolved. We will have had to update our notions of privacy, yes. But there is another angle of looking at the matter. The end of privacy need not mean the end of the individual's control of himself. For if in the age of data, it is impossible to prevent the collection and processing of data, it may yet be possible to protect it. What technology takes away, technology provides. Privacy is gone. But data protection has taken its place. As it stands DLT, with cryptography at its centre, has the best chance of ensuring this data protection – not only with the technology that it provides, but with the communities it fosters and the dialogue it encourages.

It is said that DLT, though pseudonymous, is public and transparent. It is. But it comes with multiple tools in its arsenal to give control over data to its users. Zero-knowledge proofs allow a user to prove to his peer that he knows a value without disclosing more information apart from the fact that the user knows this value. DLT also comes with second-layer solutions that are off the main chain, allowing users to transact multiple times, while revealing only what they choose to reveal. Interoperability, vis-à-vis Atomic Swaps and the like, are features that appeared early on, and it is not only foreseeable but unstoppable that the blockchain will evolve into a blocknet, a decentralized network that connects blockchains like the internet connects computers. And this blocknet may provide the facility to bridge disparate permissioned blockchains, with user-selectable levels of data protection at each interface.

Privacy as we have known it may be going the way of the dial-up. But, on the other hand, a distributed network takes the control of data away from central authorities and places it directly into the hands of its owners, making it possible for them to select the amount of their personal data that they wish to make public, or rent, or sell – or protect. Instead of losing autonomy through the loss of privacy, these technologies may very well generate new sources of economic and technological value without comprising the individual's autonomy and agency relative to the central powers that that very technology has disenfranchised. Hope is not lost. It is renewed in a different form.

εἰ γάρ κεν καὶ σμικρὸν ἐπὶ σμικρῷ καταθεῖο
καὶ θαμὰ τοῦτ᾽ ἔρδοις, τάχα κεν μέγα καὶ τὸ γένοιτο. –
"For even if you place only one small thing on another/and do this often, it will rapidly become a great thing."
Hesiod, Works and Days, 361-362.

15. How Much Knowledge Is Zero-Knowledge in Blockchain?

Charlene Cassar

Nobody should have access to another person's personal data unless they need it and they have consent for access. Zero-knowledge proofs, such as zk-SNARKs or the newer zk-STARKs, are proof systems that only give access to the required data while keeping remaining data private.

Charlene Cassar works in I.T. focusing mainly on Software Engineering and Data Science related subjects in various sectors, including e-commerce, gaming and banking.

Introduction

DLTs such as blockchain provide several benefits over their centralized database counterparts. Such benefits include transparency, immutability, integrity, and confidentiality. While blockchain is still at the initial stages of development, it is the first step towards a disruptive revolution in recording and transferring data of value. However, in the wake of GDPR[1], there is a raging debate on whether blockchain can still ensure data protection in compliance with this act or not. Currently, blockchain is deemed unsafe, and is perceived to be a technology that is in conflict with the GDPR. Zero-knowledge proofs may be the solution to resolve this conflict.

Distributed Ledgers

Contrary to a traditional centralized system, a DLT stores data in a manner that does not require a trusted third-party entity. The principle of DLTs is that data is replicated at each specific node in the network, and each node can communicate directly with one another. DLTs remove power from centralized entities by using consensus algorithms instead of intermediate entities. Blockchain is a type of DLT in which each block within the ledger stores hashes and uses consensus algorithms to ensure the validity of the blocks.

There are several benefits that DLTs offer. In the first place, DLTs do not require a central, trusted entity for exchanges between two or more parties, and can be ideal for situations lacking trust between two or more parties. Secondly, methods of hashing and encryption guarantee the integrity and safety of the data. Thirdly, since all data is replicated on all the nodes of the network, single points of failure are eliminated. Finally, DLTs ensure transparency since all the users on the network have access to the entirety of data, a feature that can be applied to enhance security settlement systems[2].

Blockchain

Blockchain is the brainchild of Satoshi Nakamoto, who first proposed it as a peer-to-peer, distributed system that eliminates the decades-old, double-spending problem. Blockchain is a distributed ledger that makes use of consensus algorithms to verify transactions. As noted, distributed ledgers have several advantages such as removing control from a central, trusted entity. Blockchain technologies are immutable, require verification through consensus algorithms, are decentralized, transparent, and make use of cryptographic techniques.

The first use case for blockchain, and the reason for its first implementation was Bitcoin. Bitcoin is the first cryptocurrency that made use of the Proof-of-work consensus algorithm. Proof-of-work (PoW) is an algorithm through which miners compete with each other to complete computations in order to verify transactions and add these blocks to the network. PoW was chosen because it offers security from denial-of service (DoS) attacks since it is too expensive in terms of computational power for hackers to launch DoS attacks on a system running such an algorithm. Blockchain has proven to be a disruptive technology revolutionizing several sectors such as healthcare, politics, real estate, law, security, government, rentals, ride sharing, crowdfunding, and education. For instance, in the case of the financial sector, Blockchain can facilitate transactions, money-lending, and risk management offerings among other things.

However, because of blockchain's decentralized nature and cross-border transactions, the technology continues to provoke debate in jurisdictions that have formulated data protection regulations. For instance, when dealing with the personal data of users belonging to EEA countries, GDPR automatically comes into effect, and must be complied to. As may be seen from the extensive list of sectors in which blockchain is expected to have impact, most of these sectors, if not all, make use of data that is of a personal nature. Thus, security and privacy with respect to blockchain technologies need to be dealt with in order for these technologies to become compliant with the GDPR.

General Data Protection Regulation (GDPR)

On 4 May 2016, the Official Journal of the European Union defined the documentation for the legislations Act regarding GDPR. According to these rules, personal data is defined as 'reference to an identifier such as a name, an identification number, location data, an online identifier or to one or more factors specific to the physical, physiological, genetic, mental, economic, cultural or social identity of that natural person'.

Although GDPR is an EU regulation, it applies not just to EU countries alone, but to any person, company or system that stores data of citizens of EU nations, no matter where the company or person holding the data is in the world. GDPR regulations limit access of personal data to third parties by only allowing them usage of data that they need upon given consent by the owner of the data. GDPR protects personal data that identifies the individual even when this data is encrypted. This means that simply encrypting data in a database or blockchain is insufficient for compliance.

Given the definition of personal data, public and private keys that are used in asymmetric cryptography, also known as public-key cryptography, may still fall under the category of personal details. If this is the case, then Bitcoin and Ethereum, which are still using asymmetric cryptography may be in breach of the GDPR.

Zero-Knowledge Proofs

Zero-knowledge Proof Systems are a cryptographic technique designed in the late 80s in order to maintain a high level of data protection and privacy in the system to which they are applied. Zk proof systems offer privacy, integrity and transparency in a trustless communication system. Given that zk proof systems require no centralized trusted entity to act as an intermediary, blockchain is the perfect candidate for their use. Two examples of zero-knowledge proof systems are zk-STARK and zk-SNARK, both of which are described in more detail in this chapter.

Zero-knowledge proof systems are composed of a prover and a verifier. A proof makes use of a prover to prove that a statement is true. There are two types of proofs; interactive and non-interactive proofs, and zero-knowledge proofs can be either. Interactive proofs differ from non-interactive proofs as non-interactive proofs manage to produce a 'true' result in the case of a true statement. However, non-interactive proofs cannot produce a 'false' result in the case of a false statement.

Provers and verifiers form an integral part of cryptographic proofs. In zero-knowledge proofs, the prover's role is to provide proof to the verifier that they know a specific value without exposing more information than strictly necessary. There are two types of zero-knowledge proofs; interactive and non-interactive. The prover and the verifier interact between themselves with the verifier challenging the prover, and the prover providing the necessary proof. Interactive zero-knowledge proofs require a lot of interaction between the prover and the verifier whilst non-interactive zero-knowledge proofs do not require interaction between the prover and the verifier.

Data Protection Issues with Blockchain Technology

Blockchain is a transparent, immutable ledger that stores data in a distributed manner with the benefits of immutability, transparency, and trust among others. Due to the nature of blockchain, caution must be taken with regards to data protection regulations. There are many types of blockchains, public, private, permissioned and permissionless, all of which treat data privacy in different ways.

Public blockchains allow anyone to access the network, which stores a replicated copy of data on every node. Private blockchains gives access to everyone within an enclosed group of members of the network. These networks can also be permissioned or permissionless. Permissioned blockchains allow specific users with specific rights to be able to contribute to the network, giving them rights that include read and write access. On the other hand, permissionless blockchains allow every user within the blockchain to view and contribute to the blockchain. Given the read access rights within a blockchain network, consideration must be taken to ensure that data is protected without restricting the users' rights read access to the data that they require.

Blockchains are immutable ledgers, which means that once data is written on the ledger it cannot be modified or removed. This conflicts with the GDPR's principle of the 'right to be forgotten'. This means that owners of personal data can request that their data be modified or removed after the fact. This presents a serious problem on an immutable database such as a blockchain. There are a set of conditions that must be met for the owner of the personal data to exercise their right to request their data to be rectified or removed. Such conditions include the right of a person to withdraw consent.

GDPR has been conceived for application to centralized networks rather than to distributed ledgers such as blockchain. However, this does not exempt blockchain from data protection laws. There are several different fora that are drawing attention to the conflict between GDPR and the immutability of blockchain, and they are trying to find a solution. The European Commission's EU Blockchain Observatory and Forum was formed with this purpose in mind. This chapter will investigate possible solutions to some of the conflicts between GDPR and blockchain technologies.

Using Zero-Knowledge Proofs for Data Protection

A non-interactive zero-knowledge proof system can be defined by the (P, V) pairing where P denotes a prover and V denotes a verifier. These proofs have three main requirements – completeness, soundness and privacy.

Completeness

The completeness requirement means that if the NP statement is true, in the zero-knowledge proofs system there is a very high likeliness that the prover will be able to prove that it is true to the verifier.

If a statement x belongs to a language L, the proof π must have the property of completeness.
Completeness can be defined as:

$$V(x, \pi) = 1 \dots\dots\dots\dots\dots\dots\dots\dots\dots\dots\dots\dots\dots (1)$$

Soundness

The soundness requirement means that if the NP statement is false, the zero-knowledge proof system, there is a very high likeliness that the prover will not be able to prove to the verifier that it is true. If a statement x does not belong to a language L, the proof π must have the property of soundness.

Soundness can be defined as:

$$V(x, \pi) = 0 \dots\dots\dots\dots\dots\dots\dots\dots\dots\dots\dots\dots (2)$$

Privacy (or Zero-Knowledge)

The privacy requirement means that when the prover returns a verdict on whether the NP statement is true, there would be no other data revealed by the zero-knowledge proof system. This is also known as Witness Preservation.

Applications of Zero-Knowledge Proofs in Blockchain

Zerocash (ZCash)

Zero-knowledge proofs have been adopted in several blockchain applications. One such application is Zerocash. Zerocash was designed and implemented as a better alternative protocol alternative for cryptocurrencies such as Bitcoin. Zerocash is a newer attempt to secure a level of privacy on blockchain technologies by hiding or rather, not exposing the user's origin, destination, or transaction amount when effecting a transaction payment. Being an extension to Bitcoin's protocol, Zerocash includes new types of transactions that do not include this additional information. These are mint transactions and pour transactions.

A decentralized e-cash scheme is used in the Zerocash protocol. In this scheme, a tuple of algorithms (Setup, CreateAddress, Mint, Spend, Verify) are used to define correctness and security properties.

Mint transactions are used to convert non-anonymous bitcoins into zerocoins that reference a Zerocash address. A cryptographic commitment based on the SHA-256 hashing algorithm is embedded into the zerocoin to ensure that personal data is not exposed. A merkle tree is used to store the Zerocash nodes.

Cryptocurrencies were built on Zerocash – anonymous coins are known as zerocoins and non-anonymous coins are known as basecoins. These non-anonymous base currency coins can be converted into anonymous zerocoins and used for transactions. Zerocash makes use of zero-knowledge Succinct Non-interactive Arguments of Knowledge (zk-SNARKs) that is based on the cryptographic method based on zero-knowledge proofs.

Zk-SNARKs

The Zero-knowledge Succinct Non-Interactive Argument of Knowledge (zk-SNARKs) makes use of zero-knowledge proofs. Zk-SNARKs have been adopted by ZCash and Ethereum. Zk-SNARKs have the following properties: completeness, succinctness, proof of knowledge (and soundness) and perfect zero knowledge. The completeness requirement means that if a statement is true, the prover can convince the verifier that it is true.

The succinctness requirement means that the proof must be succinct (small) and verifiable in milliseconds. Non-interactive means that the communication between prover and verifier is limited and only sent once. There is a lack of interactive communication. Argument means that the proof holds the soundness requirement. The knowledge requirement means that there is an additional player in the proof: the witness. Zk-SNARKs satisfy four main components – encoding as a polynomial problem, succinctness by random sampling, homomorphic encoding or encryption and zero-knowledge.

There are several issues with zk-SNARKs. One of the issues is that the trusted setup stage is not secure, and zk-SNARKs are not very scalable. Also, zk-SNARKs are not transparent, nor are they secure against quantum computers. Even though zk-SNARKs have several benefits, due to these issues, a better solution is needed.

Zk-STARKs

Zk-STARKs are a newer type of Zero-knowledge proofs. Zk-STARK is an acronym formed from Zero-knowledge, Succinct, Transparent, Argument of Knowledge. Zk-STARKs promise an improvement over zk-SNARKs by superior scalability without compromising the level of privacy. Much of the motivation for the adoption of zk-STARKs comes from the failure of zk-SNARKs to meet requisite levels of security against quantum computation. Zk-STARKs promise to be a better alternative to zk-SNARKs.

Zk-STARKs do not have a trusted setup stage, thus eliminating the risk factor from the setup stage in zk-SNARKs. Scalability is another issue that has been tackled by zk-STARKs due to the different complexity computations on zk-STARKs versus zk-SNARKs. In the case of zk-STARKs, the arithmetic circuit complexity in zk-STARKs transforms the proof to higher-degree polynomials.

The communication complexity of zk-STARKs grows at a slower rate than zk-SNARKs. However, zk-SNARKs communicate far less after the one setup stage. This actually means that there is a lower complexity in favour of zk-SNARKs. Apart from these, the prover complexity of zk-STARKs makes zk-STARKs around 10 times faster than zk-SNARKs with an increase in computations. The final complexity factor, which shows that zk-STARKs have better scalability than zk-SNARKs, is the superior complexity of the verifier in zk-STARKs.

In zk-STARKs, the complexity grows slightly whereas in the case of zk-SNARKs, there is a linear growth when verifying due to the one setup stage. However, it takes zk-SNARKs less time to verify after the one setup stage. It seems that overall, zk-STARKs perform better until post-setup stage in the case of zk-SNARKs. Post-setup, zk-SNARKs perform better with less complexity with an increase of computations.

In the case of quantum computing, zk-STARKs do not use private-public keys for increased security against quantum computing. Instead, zk-STARKs make use of collision resistant hashing and an oracle model, which makes zk-STARKs a better alternative to zk-SNARKs.

Bulletproofs

Another version of zero-knowledge proofs is Bulletproofs. Similar to zk-STARKs, Bulletproofs do not need a trusted setup stage. Bulletproofs are non-interactive proofs, and have been found to consume more time than zk-SNARKs in the case of verification. Bulletproofs are succinct and manage to diminish a proof from 10 kb to under a tenth of the size. They have been found to be useful in privacy-preserving smart contracts, verifiable proofs and other applications.

Ethereum

The first use case of blockchain was Bitcoin—the first P2P cryptocurrency. Bitcoin was designed with the idea of being a peer-to-peer method of transferring value from one account to another. The Ethereum blockchain introduced the concept of smart contracts as trustless programmable contracts between two or more parties. The main objective of Ethereum was to let developers or users execute their smart contracts in a trustless manner. To use the Ethereum platform, users can use ether tokens or gas, a token which is used to pay miners fees for the purposes of executing transactions.

Ethereum is a transaction-based public blockchain that exposes every transactional detail of the nodes on the platform. This is a problem in the light of privacy-preserving regulations, such as the GDPR. Recently, EY announced that they would apply zero-knowledge proofs to Ethereum. Although Ethereum is on a public Blockchain, EY hope to be the first to present the first implementation of zero-knowledge proofs to Ethereum, and for transactions to be private[3]. As Paul Brody, EY's global innovation leader for blockchain states, 'With zero-knowledge proofs, organizations can transact on the same network as their competition in complete privacy and without giving up the security of the public Ethereum blockchain'.

Hawk

Hawk is a decentralized framework for implementing zero-knowledge, private smart contracts. It was designed by Ahmed Kosba, Andrew Miller, Elaine Shi, Zikai Wen and Charalampos Papamanithou. Programmers can easily implement smart contracts with cryptographic proofs using this framework without any knowledge of cryptographic protocols or zero-knowledge proofs. Hawk is divided in two parts – private and public. The private section accepts data, computes the transaction and keeps the details private. The public section does not deal with the personal data.

There are many security benefits of using Hawk; On-chain privacy, and Contractual security. On-chain privacy means that zero-knowledge proofs are used to keep private, transactional data secure on a public blockchain. Contractual security protects contractual entities from each other. There are four types of contractual security properties that Hawk guarantees: (1) Input independent privacy; (2) Posterior privacy; (3) Financial fairness; and (4) Security against a dishonest manager.

Hyperledger Fabric V1.3

Hyperledgers are a set of open-source projects that combine forces from high-profile members from finance, banking, IoT, manufacturing, healthcare, supply chains and technology. Hyperledgers were introduced in 2016 and governed by 21 members, and the Linux Foundation leaders. Hyperledgers was created with five main goals in mind. The first goal is to create open-source project for business transactional records. The second goal is to create a community with high-profile governance. Hyperledgers aim to create user cases and field trails. Another goal is to inform the general public about blockchain's potential. The final goal is to inform as many people and companies of the public as possible about Hyperledgers and the toolkits' potential. Some of the hosted projects include Hyperledger Iroha, Hyperledger Fabric, Hyperledger Burrow and Hyperledger Indy.

The Linux Foundation developed a Hyperledger project, known as the Hyperledger Fabric. Hyperledger Fabric is a plug-and-play framework that makes use of the Membership Service Providers implementation with Identity Mixer. Membership Service Provider (MSP) provides an abstraction of cryptographic proofs and user authentication. An Identity Mixer is a trust model that has a setup phase (with a public/private key pair), credentials, presentation and verification. Hyperledger Fabric makes use of zero-knowledge proofs to be used on proving credential signatures.

Problems that Zero-knowledge Proofs Cannot Fix

This chapter has shown that although blockchains and the GDPR appear to be incompatible, these can be compatible with each other if the appropriate measures are taken. This chapter has proposed zero-knowledge proofs in blockchain as a way to comply with the GDPR. However, these proofs do not solve all of the issues of blockchain data with respect to the GDPR.

The GDPR requires blockchain applications to keep personal data of people from European countries safe and private, that users may ask for all of their data to be returned to them, and that users have the right to ask for their personal data to be modified or removed. It is important to note that although zero-knowledge proofs can be used to secure and keep private data private, this chapter has not tackled other stipulations of the GDPR, such as the right to be forgotten, personal data to be extracted and returned, and personal data to be edited on request.

Right to be Forgotten

The GDPR clearly specifies that a user in EEA countries has the right to request that his data be modified or removed. Zero-knowledge proofs do not provide for the right to be forgotten, and due to blockchain's quality of immutability, this poses problems. Zero-knowledge proofs ensure privacy of personal data. A solution for the right to be forgotten needs to consider the use of encryption.

By encrypting all data on the network nodes with a private-public key pair, both keys are then needed to decrypt the encrypted data.

When a request from a user for deletion is made, the blockchain application would delete the public key, and thus the encrypted data would not be able to be decrypted. The data will remain on the blockchain but inaccessible to any user to read. However, this approach has several flaws namely the potential security breaches of the keys before they are removed and disposed of.

Another possibility is to store data on another database, and then store the hashes of this data on the blockchain. Upon request from a user for their personal data to be deleted, the hash will remain on the blockchain but the data that is stored off the blockchain would be removed. Unfortunately, the hash on the blockchain is considered to be personal data according to GDPR[4]. This means that leaving hashes of the personal data would not be accepted even if the original data has been removed. One solution to this would be to use a peppered hash, but this has been reported to be unsafe (in terms of preserving privacy) and may not necessarily be secure. A peppered hash is when a random string is added to the data, known as a nonce. It is unknown if this approach would be compliant with the GDPR, and it has been reported to be insecure, and can be compromised if the nonce is discovered.

Copies of Personal Data

A citizen of an EEA country may request for their personal data to be extracted and returned to them. Blockchain does not make it easy to extract all data belonging to a person while not extracting anyone else's personal data. This is a problem since giving a user another person's personal data would be in conflict with the GDPR's privacy preserving clause. The solution for this is the same as the solution for the right to be forgotten – storing data off-chain. By storing data off-chain, the user can request a copy of all of their personal data, and, if using a database, this can be easily queried and returned to the user.

Conclusion

This chapter has shown zero-knowledge proofs can be used to make blockchain work and abide by the GDPR. A part of the GDPR specifies that users have control over their personal data and that nobody without authority should be able to access their data. Nobody should have access to another person's personal data unless they need it and they have consent for access. Zero-knowledge proofs, such as zk-SNARKs, or the newer zk-STARKs, are proof systems that only give access to the required data while keeping remaining data private. This means that by using zero-knowledge proofs in blockchain applications, these applications would be compliant with the GDPR's privacy clause. Several different applications have made use of zk proofs such as Zerocash, which is intended to be used as a more secure version of Bitcoin.

Although zero-knowledge proofs can used to comply with the GDPR's requirement of keeping data private from people who should not have, or do not need, this information, these proofs do not meet the other requirements set out by the GDPR, namely the right to request modification to personal data, to right to be forgotten and the right to receive a copy of personal data that a company or individual may be storing. For these requirements, other solutions, some of which were discussed in this chapter, must be found. By choosing the right technologies and methods, it is possible that blockchain applications may come to be seamlessly compliant with the GDPR.

Endnotes

1. GDPR, Regulation (EU) 2016/679 27/4/ 2016.
2. Enhancing Securities Settlement Systems (Greyspark Partners).
3. Yogita Khatri, "EY Reveals Zero-Knowledge Proof Privacy Solution for Ethereum", Coindesk, 2018.
4. "How Does the EU's GDPR Apply to Hashed Data on the Blockchain?", Global Legal Blockchain Consortium, 2018.

16. Using DLT in a World Built on Trust

Ian Gauci

Today, with the advent of computers, the internet and the development of distributed ledger technologies (DLTs), we are not only seeking better ways of ensuring that trust is maintained, but to place our trust not in the hands of individuals but in having trust inbuilt into the systems we use.

Dr Ian Gauci was the legal expert on the National Blockchain Taskforce entrusted with reviewing proposals and making recommendations to the Government to implement its National Blockchain Strategy.

Trust is essential in society because only through it are complex relationships and progress possible. With rising complexity, trust becomes even more crucial. A foundation of solid trust permits innovation and evolution. Betrayal of trust shatters society to the core.

Innovation flowed with the expansion of communities. Nomads set up villages, and eventually built cities. The growing complexity of trade and relationships required the adoption of reliable methods of communication obligations, especially through the use of dependable instruments. Contract law developed as a result and it shaped the manner that courts and tribunals operate, allowing for such institutions to interpret contracts and the will of the parties as expressed therein, the principle of pacta sunt servanda. Courts and tribunals played a vital role in reducing uncertainty and solidifying trust among, not only the direct parties involved with that specific contract and that are bound thereto, but also among the general population, by showing that individuals could rely on the authority of the courts to enforce agreements in cases of a breach.

Today, necessity is not simply the reason to innovate. There is another factor to consider, and that is the technological possibility to innovate, something that the people preceding us did not have. Thus, as much as historic societies wanted to innovate, they were limited by the state of the art, by the limitations of the knowledge and technology at their disposal. Today, with the advent of computers, the internet and the development of distributed ledger technologies (DLTs), we are not only seeking better ways of ensuring that trust is maintained, but to place our trust not in the hands of individuals but in having trust inbuilt into the systems we use.

The demands posed by the digital economy create a borderless world and create the need for individuals, institutions, and entire organizations from different parts of the globe to trust individuals on the other side of world. This need not only undermines the model of the central seat of power but also reflects a reality in which more than ever we look to a distributed/decentralized model through which one does not need to trust a central system or authority but to trust in the fact that power and decision-making are distributed among many players. By distributing trust, therefore, we increase the reliability of the system.

DLTs have presented themselves as a solution to many industries, and as a model that can regain the trust that individuals have lost in the systems that surround us. After all, it was the 2008 financial crisis that reportedly spurred Satoshi Nakamoto into creating Bitcoin, and thus in applying DLT in a manner through which people could transact without a middleman or other intermediary, crucially removing banks and financial institutions from the picture.

DLT can thus present a solution to trust issues by removing the said middleman in whom trust was to be imbued. Through, for example, smart contracts, obligations can be automatically created on distributed ledger, thus creating a decentralized and distributed model of power, management and execution of obligations.

Smart Contracts

The idea underlying smart contracts emerged in the 90s, specifically in 1997, from Nick Szabo who conceptualized smart contracts as a set of promises that are specified in digital form. These include protocols within which the parties perform on each other's promises.

If one had to draw comparisons between contracts, as used for centuries, and smart contracts, the latter type of contract has the means to guarantee that the outcome of the contract, as agreed upon, is achieved in an automatic self-executing manner due to the coding of the smart contract. Therefore, smart contracts offer the possibility of highly reliable communication about future outcomes, offer more deterministic purposes, and thus allow for certainty of contract performance and penalties in the instance of failure to perform. If contract law exists to facilitate reliance through the ability to opt into predictable future consequences, then smart contracts can serve this function seamlessly.

Smart contracts work in modus ponens logic, namely 'if this than that' logic. In theory, this creates self-executing, self-enforcing and state-contingent contracts. The most 'primitive' analogy of a smart contract would be that of the vending machine, in which all actions that can occur, when inputting money into the vending machine, are predetermined due to its make-up, including the perfecting of the contract, when foodstuff is given out by the machine.

In practice, smart contracts are written in code and deployed on a DLT network, whether private or public, or a hybrid thereof, or between inter-chains. Their trustworthiness is ensured because they are hashed and shared with thousands of nodes or computers. By reason of their encrypted nature, they keep unauthorized persons from amending or accessing the contents of the contract, even if technically these are accessible if deployed on a public DLT.

The smart contract thus ensures that obligations are transparent, traceable and irreversible. En masse smart contracts are more than just an efficient way to execute contracts. They are an evolutionary step in the way that individuals carry out tasks. Smart contracts are not just a solution, nor are they just another process forming part of the trend of computerized technologies. Rather, they have the potential to be an enabler for a higher purpose: an expression and medium for societal evolution.

On an academic level, smart contracts provide us an opportunity to ruminate over centuries of accepted methodologies and traditions in the manner that we draw up contracts, and in the manner that we, as humans, communicate. This will not necessarily change that which is in place but will illuminate any foundational issues in the theory of contract and law that might exist. After all, law is a system that is to be seen from the cultural context from which it emerges, and which is not a hermetically sealed system. The law does not solely evolve following decisions given by courts or amendments promulgated by parliament. The law also evolves within society, and as a product of the way we interact.

Smart contracts can disrupt the manner in which we think and contract, not just for the sake of disrupting such ways but because they have value in fundamentally replacing or reducing litigation, impacting moral values, the court's remit and thus change the social norms and fabric of society, culture and ultimately the purpose of certain legal provisions and future law by removing the need of trust.

There are some challenges that can present themselves when utilizing smart contracts. Complications may arise if parties are left with no choice but to execute the contract by force. This could create issues of validity if such smart contracts are unable to observe the law of the land (lex terrae). For instance, certain contracts like distance contracts and consumer contracts might not be validly constituted if they have an absolute zero tolerance.

To a certain extent, even freedom to contract would not allow an absolute zero tolerance, as the law allows the right in certain cases for individuals to amend, rescind or revoke the contract (such as in consumer contracts). Therefore, while contract law implements a series of safeguards to protect individuals from scenarios that might either invalidate the contract or make it non-enforceable (e.g. information asymmetries, undue influence, unconscionability, and incapacitation), smart contracts operate within their own closed technological framework.

This presents a challenge, but one that needs to be looked upon as an opportunity to understand legal systems and find common ground, rather than one that is simply treated as an obstacle.

DAOs

Going beyond utilizing smart contracts for singular obligations, smart contracts may be utilized in a more complex manner, by ensuring that not only one single task is achieved but more than that, a whole project is executed. This may perhaps be achievable through a 'DAO' – a decentralized autonomous organization.

At a conceptual level a DAO functions in a completely autonomous manner, through a number of smart contracts and consequently in accordance with a set of pre-determined, hard-wired, and self-enforcing rules. Multiple obligations are written into the smart contracts, and performance of such obligations happens in an automatic manner. The DAO can either adopt a role whereby it mediates between different parties involved or whereby it functions completely through algorithms.

The DAO presents certain complexities when regulatory bodies taking action against the DAO may find it difficult to shut down a whole organization due to the manner in which services being offered by the DAO are stored and executed in a distributed manner across an entire network of hashed nodes and computers.

As devices become more autonomous, a DAO may be able to directly interact with individuals, entering into contractual relationships with the same individuals. This may create certain dilemmas of legal consequence, but as services become more automated, the question of how to regulate such contractual relationships should be one for the now, rather than for later. We are heading towards a future when 'algorithmic governance' may reign, and we must be prudent in our approaches, to ensure that in our ambition to achieve, and in our necessity to create stronger systems, we do not create a situation in which due to the extremity of the code, we are trapped in a predicament of our own making, unable to move away from rules that do not make sense and allowing the emergence of the modernized version of a totalitarian regime conflicting with the democratic and egalitarian principles behind the notion of a decentralized democratized society.

Other practical issues that DAOs, and even smart contracts, may present are issues relating to jurisdiction, seeing how difficult it is to determine the jurisdiction of a DAO. The principle of lex situs (law of the place where the property is situated) cannot be implemented and this may be an intricate dilemma should issues of liability arise. However, we must continue to explore legal principles in light of these technologies and in our willingness to use them.

Humans will continuously seek to evolve and to simplify processes, and more importantly to enhance ways in which trust is not questioned, or rather not even necessary. Humans will continue seeking ways not only to move processes from the hands of individuals into those of technologies, but to build trust into the same technologies that we use. In this golden age of technological advancements, we see a new paradigm fuelled by technology, code, and algorithms and we need to make sure that all of us, as we move forward, trust in the systems that surround us, and, failing that, build systems in which we can trust.

PART V
EPILOGUE

17. Art of Disruption

Lida Sherafatmand, Joseph Anthony Debono

The abundance and surplus of nodes strengthen a blockchain, and likewise the abundance of thinkers, researchers, and professionals in Malta strengthen the jurisdiction's potential in this sector.

Joseph Anthony Debono is a noted classicist turned DLT disciple, co-editor of this book and author of chapter 2.

Artist Lida Sherafatmand was born in Khorramshar southern Iran and has been painting since the age of 3. Her image adorns the cover of this book.

At this early stage in the development of DLT, it still has to make its impact on the world of art. However, Lida Sherafatmand is a fine artist based in Malta who does have blockchain experience. The art she drew for the cover of this book reflects the multiple interactions between Lida's philosophy, Malta, DLT and art itself.

War and Peace

Lida Sherafatmand is of Iranian origin, now a citizen of Malta, to where she fled as a refugee from war, revolution and persecution. She is a flourishing artist, writer, researcher, dancer, and poet whose work has been exhibited in over 20 countries, and has won multiple awards and nominations. Her most significant intellectual contribution to art is 'Florescencism', an artistic philosophy advocating the cultural and social flourishment of individuals and civilizations through the expression of floral themes in art. Lida's flight from theocracy, war, political ideologies and territorial interests, have made her a firm believer in decentralization and the empowerment of individuals and diverse communities. Lida's life and philosophy led her to experiment with blockchain as a means to make her art more accessible and more affordable to the man in the street, instead of concentrating solely on the traditional art markets with their generally social and financial elites. To this end, Lida fractionalized pieces of her art on an online trading platform called 'Feral Horses' operating on a blockchain-based title registry called the 'Codex Protocol'.

Fine Art and the Blockchain Book

As a Malta-based artist with actual experience of blockchain, Lida was a natural choice to paint the cover art of this publication. The intellectual challenge was significant. Lida had to unite three basic ideas into her work: (a) blockchain; (b) her philosophy of Florescencism; (c) the Maltese context of this book. The concept she came up with is that of a tree springing from a network of roots immersed in water. At first glance, it may not be easy to work out how this image expresses the three ideas that Lida set out to express, but once the concept is outlined, it does fall elegantly into place. The network of roots expresses decentralization, with each one starting from a single node. These roots are also a metaphor for the different strands of thoughts, and the different authors from their diverse fields represented in this book. The roots also represent the merkle tree in which a blockchain stores the record of its transactions. The roots grow upwards to provide a single record of truth. Together they sustain the tree springing from their collective union in the same way that the different nodes of a blockchain, by competing through game theory, collaborate to guarantee and authenticate a single record of truth that is dependent on nobody but on the underlying network. The water from which the roots are growing symbolizes two ideas. In the first place it symbolizes the essential transparency of the blockchain. There is no hiding the contents of the ledger from anyone with a blockchain. All one needs to do is to download a copy of that blockchain, or to look at a block explorer. In the second place, the water symbolizes the archipelago of Malta in the middle of the sea, the home and hub of all the thinkers and writers who have contributed to this book, and also the ambitious jurisdiction whose innovative and visionary work in the sector has already earned it the epithet of the Blockchain Island.

The artistic syntax of Lida's Florescence is apparent in the multiplication of a floral design, in this case of the roots. It expresses abundance and surplus, and the way they strengthen the whole. Lida observes that the abundance and surplus of nodes strengthen a blockchain, and likewise the abundance of thinkers, researchers, and professionals in Malta strengthen the jurisdiction's potential in this sector. Lida also points out the importance of the water as a symbol of both Malta and transparency. Blockchain brings undisputed authenticity and transparency to data, something acutely needed by the art market, which at times can be obscure to such an extent that it can create scope for market manipulation as well as money laundering. Moreover, the transparency of the water symbolizes the hard work that Malta has done to create a legislative framework for blockchain that is significantly more rigorous, and requires significantly more compliance, than the current best standards around the world. Lida also emphasizes the importance of decentralization. With the art markets traditionally dominated by a handful of elites, decentralization is the best way of opening art to the individual and spreading it beyond private collections to community nodes in every city and region around the world. Blockchain, believes Lida, may very well be as disruptive in art, as it promises to be disruptive elsewhere, and that it is truly a grand new hope, given that this disruption promises to disseminate the benefits of art to a far wider circle than the traditional elites that have hitherto dominated this world.

18. Dotted Lines

Gordon Pace Flores

An inner call to attention from your angel draws your eye towards a girl coming through the door. Another micro-contract has just been signed. And before she even has time to walk over to your table, the waiter brings along a second beer.

Co-author of chapter 13, Gordon Pace Flores is mostly a computer scientist most of the day, most other things most other times. He once designed a board game. Although a scientist by training and profession, Gordon has found himself dabbling in far too many other things over the years: from board game designer responsible for Politicks, a satirical card game poking fun at Maltese politics, to artist, with his work blending contemporary calligraphy, photography and abstract art that has appeared in various exhibitions solo and otherwise. In contrast to his calligraphy, which largely consists of meaningless combinations of alpha-numeric characters creating a texture of haphazard symbols, he has more recently started attempting to string words together in a more coherent manner, of which this story is the first to appear in print.

Dotted Lines

....

A micro-contract dystopia combining all the current buzzwords:
AI, ML, smart contracts, IoT, human-embedded
chips.

You walk through the door. It's your first time in this bar but you find your favourite beer waiting for you in an inner dark corner of the room — just the way you prefer. The beer has already been paid for over the chain. Actually, there's more to it than that. Your Guardian Angel, the nick used for the software supporting your life, has negotiated with the barman's angel a deal. Once you find a place you like, you tend to stick to it, so the deal was that the beer would be 10% cheaper, but with an obligation to drink there at least 5 times over the coming week. If you do not, you will be charged the normal price plus an extra 10% for the beers you have consumed. Not that you know any of this. Your Guardian Angel takes care of you without burdening you with the difficult choices it makes on your behalf. It's your first day in Madrid. It's Madrid isn't it? You checked on the plane's boarding gate screen, but it's not that important, is it? You found a taxi waiting for you that took you to your hotel, one on which you had never laid your eyes before.

An inner call to attention from your angel draws your eye towards a girl coming through the door. Another micro–contract has just been signed. She has been in the city for a whole week and she will tell you all about the places she has been to — her tastes are similar to yours, and you could both do with some company. In return, her Guardian Angel has negotiated that you pay for her beer. And before she even has time to walk over to your table, the waiter brings along a second beer.

Nostalgia. Her name was Rachel, or so the angel says. But the way she held onto the table as she recalled the emotions that engulfed her in front of Goya's depiction of Cronus at the Prado, and her passionate refusal to use the Roman name of the Titan – I will never forget that. Or will I? The burden of memory lifted, yet still weighed down by the doubt shrouding all your recollections. I try to address my angel directly, proposing a contract. "Let me know whether Cronus ever loomed over Rachel at all, whether that evening is nothing but a memory or whether the white tips of her fingers as she held onto the table were really there at the same time as I sipped my beer. Let me know, even if for a fleeting moment, and then resume your duty to safeguard the happiness in my life." Other thoughts flood my brain.

The following days in Madrid were spent at the Prado, staring over Cronus's shoulder willing the muddy blacks to take shape. "If you look long enough, his sister Mnemosyne will emerge." But she never did. Sitting at your table, you stared at the door, willing Rachel to be back. But she never came. You reasoned that if you yearned for her enough, your Guardian Angel cannot but will her back, even if just for the sake of your own sanity. If the stakes were raised high enough, a contract will be able to promise enough in return to make it worthwhile for her to reappear walking through that door. You struggled to keep the deluge of other thoughts contained outside your mind, to rush away from taxis that your angel contracted on your behalf to take you back to the airport. And as you discovered that drink was your only ally against the goodwill of your angel, the pints of beer stopped appearing at the table.

Nothing much else sticks in my memory from that trip. But the black oils smeared on Goya's canvas remain. And with that, her white knuckles on that table. Rachel. Or so I am told her name was. And I still seek her as I sought Mnemosyne in that painting.

A stranger sat at my table just as the waiter left two beers. I barely had time to wonder who paid for the beers, and what the arrangement was when the stranger's conversation turned to the contract with God that humanity has signed. A contract not worth the stone it is carved in, a god not worthy of the worship of its own creators, I thought, as the happiest memories of what I may or may never have experienced fogged my mind. The happiness we signed up for, delivered by His angels, the very happiness with which He has violated our contract. If only I could shave by beard, abandon my faith, default on the Contract.

You wake up in a hospital bed, contract signed. Your obligations pile up as your angel seeks forgetfulness. But in the black slate of your memory, you see the layered brush strokes above His shoulder, and in between those strokes her eyes emerge. Mnemosyne, Rachel, here I am.

Acknowledgements

When I was elevated to the role of Blockchain Malta Association chairman, I had already instigated this book project. Alas, time was tight to complete the task given a parallel need to look after my day-to-day business interests as well!

As to my position as chairman, arriving in office and presiding over a fledgling association with no balance sheet, no bank account and a certain semblance of need to define structure, has made for an interesting year.

Clearly, it was vital to help promote the Association as well as the Blockchain Islands themselves. At the same time, 'operation balance sheet' involves creating a suitable flow of funds to make the Association self-sufficient.

One of the earliest and most enthusiastic contributors, Joseph Anthony Debono has brilliantly stepped into the editorial office and assumed a co-editor role for which I shall be forever grateful. He has a pedigree of exacting standards (more pedantic than my own slightly perverse approach to grammar many might add) while his classical education (a proper one not merely my scraping O' levels in Latin and Ancient Greek) are evident throughout his profoundly thoughtful and detailed work. I have valued Joe's counsel as we created the contributor list and worked on the concomitant manuscript. Furthermore, I hugely appreciate Joe's detail work with contributors and his magnificent ability to deploy classical witticisms as having sinister or at least, motivating, undertones, to ensure we could make this project happen in reasonable time.

We have been able to edit this tome thanks to the work of many folks and indeed at least one key Valletta landmark. I am sure Samuel Taylor Coleridge would turn in his grave to hear that our book was organized within earshot of his former office, but nowadays as the Casino Maltese it is a club that offers a perfect idyll in the historic centre of Valletta. To the President, board, Marguerite and all the staff who have allowed us a perfect environ from which to discuss this book and meet many of the contributors, our profound thanks.

Many of the contributors were Joe's suggestion but before that the whole genesis of this tome took a hugely positive turn when my excellent counsel, BMA Exec committee member and Partner of Ganado Advocates, Leonard Bonello, suggested meeting one Joe Debono as a possible contributor. From there things progressed in many directions, thank you Leonard!

Among our contributors, Max Ganado is a benchmark for the legal industry in Malta and much farther afield. He has achieved the status of elder statesman of the Maltese legal fraternity despite being young at heart and definitively young of mind. Without him, the nation would be much the poorer and his contribution to the Blockchain Island has been simply immeasurable.

Likewise, Ian Gauci of GTG Advocates is the pre-eminent lawyer at the epicentre of technology and the law itself in this country, and his support throughout the process has been enormous, both as secretary of the Association as well as his many contributions and entreaties behind the scenes.

Leonard Bonello, I have already mentioned as a huge supporter of the project who first introduced me to Joe, from which point this book is actually merely a side product of a growing friendship. Moreover, I have to admit that Joe's chapter continues to intrigue me even though it was the first completed for the book and I have already re-read it many many times.

From both our perspectives, we thank all our contributors without whom the book would not have been possible. These are Ramona Azzopardi, Tyron Baron, Leonard Bonello, Diane Bugeja, Christopher Buttigieg, Charlene Cassar, Joshua Ellul, Jean Paul Fabri, Stephanie Fabri, Max Ganado, Ian Gauci, Simon Mercieca, Gordon Pace, Gerd Sapiano, Lara Tanti, Sophia Tillie, Rachel Vella Baldacchino, and David Zammit. Thanks are also due to our cover artist, Lida Sherafatmand. To find a fine artist of international repute based in Malta and with actual blockchain experience satisfied multiple parameters.

However, primus inter pares aforethought, there can be no doubt whatsoever that the addition of such a considered and indeed downright passionate foreword from the Prime Minister, the Honourable Dr Joseph Muscat MP makes this book a very special volume. From my perspective, I am only sorry readers were not able to enjoy the fascinating discussions at the Auberge de Castille, the Offices of the Prime Minister, where the PM's insights into the future of technology, to our minds, clearly set Malta apart from many other rather more analogue nations!

Parliamentary Secretary Silvio Schembri has been a huge supporter of this project but his even greater achievement has been in developing the Blockchain Island strategy and stewarding, in somewhat record time, the three bills in 2018 that created a unique globally leading regulatory system. On behalf of BMA, I have repeatedly thanked Silvio for his remarkable achievements in the past 18 months. However, it is only fair to record in print that all of the BMA board salute the great work done by the Government of Malta, and particularly the Parliamentary Secretary in making the

Blockchain Island go from dream to reality in less time than some nations spend on consultations.

Of course, that speed to market is something that provides Malta with a competitive advantage and we applaud our many contributors for their role in this singular legislative and regulatory achievement.

Beyond the contributors, I would like to thank a series of people both in the blockchain world and outside it – in either case my bon mots are entirely immutable as one would expect of somebody trained under the London Stock Exchange's Dictum Meum Pactum, 'my word is my bond', motto (Latin immutability for the analogue era that preceded ours). First and foremost, my wife Beata the founder of WomenOnIT has been a passionate devotee of the Association, and worked hard on promoting our brand across social media as well as attending countless workshops as she has built her own blockchain expertise. At home, Toby the pug may be snoring with gusto as I type, but his perpetual optimism is an immutable feature of a sweet dog much better known around the streets of Valletta than his owners. My Mum Lucy remains a great supporter who clearly merits plaudits for nurturing my skills while all my excesses and faults are clearly my own omission.

Thoughts, counsel, strategy, and decent glasses of wine have all been provided by a vast array of folk, to all of you our thanks. Similarly, it has been a pleasure to work with Finance Malta on the BlockFinance series – to Kenneth Farrugia, Ivan Grech, Bernice Buttigieg and the Finance Malta team, thank you.

This book will be launched at a reception on May 20th as part of the Malta Business Network meeting whose Chairman Joseph Zammit Tabona remains perhaps the finest Maltese executive, diplomat and entrepreneur in living memory. A gentleman with a passion for Jaguars, his input, like that of Max Ganado, to the fabric of Maltese business is simply enormous and I hugely applaud his Malta Business Network that remains a benchmark organization for Maltese relations with business in the UK and across the world.

Of other individuals who have lent a generous hand to the publication of this tome, one must pay one's dues to Christine Borg, whose moral support and encouragement during the process of editing were priceless, especially during moments of frustration when the pace of work slowed, and even stalled at times. Nick Refalo rendered services so sterling to the publication of the book that he deserves the amplest thanks. Other thanks are due to Juanita Brockdorff and Ruth Felice for advice and support at a critical moment of the publication. Many thanks are due to Keith Schembri for his prompt, kind and efficient assistance whenever we needed it. Finally, I applaud James Farrugia for his wise counsel building the Blockchain Island

In a world that moves as speedily as the DLT-verse, naturally this cannot be deemed as the last word on the subject but we hope that whether you are new to DLT or Malta, you will find it an interesting read while also useful to all those of you au fait with at least one of: this delightful island nation, and the exciting technology of blockchain that leads to all manner of opportunities, not least of which is cryptocurrency and many more immutable wonders.

Happy reading,

Patrick L. Young
Joseph Anthony Debono
Valletta
Malta
20 May 2019

Select Bibliography

Books

Antonopoulos, Andreas M., Mastering Bitcoin, 2nd edn (O'Reilly Media., 2018).

Antonopoulos, Andreas M., The Internet of Money Volume One, (Merkle Bloom, 2017).

Bambara, Joseph J, and Paul R Allen, Blockchain: (McGraw-Hill Education, 2018).

Brafman, Ori, and Rod A. Beckstrom, The Starfish and the Spider (Portfolio, 2006).

Castells, Manuel, The Rise of the Network Society (Blackwell, 1996).

De Filippi, Primavera, and Aaron Wright, Blockchain and the Law (Harvard UP, 2018).

Filletti, Stefano, Towards a European Criminal Law System (Kite Group, 2017).

Hayek, F. A, Individualism and Economic Order (University of Chicago Press, 1948).

Hayek, F. A., The Nationalization of Money (IEA, 1978).

Jolovicz, H. F., Roman Foundations of Modern Law (Greenwood Publishing Group, 1978).

Lessig, Lawrence, Code and other Laws of Cyberspace (Basic Books, 1999).

Schama, Simon, The Embarrassment of Riches. An Interpretation of the Dutch Culture in the Golden Age (University of California Press, 1987).

Vee, Annette, Coding Literacy (MIT Press, 2017).

Williamson, Oliver E., The Economic Institutions of Capitalism (Free Press, 1985).

Young, Patrick L and Thomas Theys, Capital Market Revolution! (FT Prentice Hall, 1999).

Table of Legislation

Acts and Subsidiary Legislation

Malta

Arbitration Act, Chapter 387 of the laws of Malta.

Consumer Affairs Act, Chapter 378 of the Laws of Malta.

Data Protection Act, Chapter 586 of the laws of Malta.

Electronic Commerce Act, Chapter 426 of the laws of Malta.

Innovative Technology Arrangements and Services Act, Chapter 592 of the laws of Malta.

Income Tax Act, Chapter 123 of the laws of Malta.

Investment Services Act, Chapter 370 of the laws of Malta.

Malta Digital Innovation Authority Act, Chapter 591 of the laws of Malta.

Maltese Civil Code, Chapter 16 of the laws of Malta.

Maltese Criminal Code, Chapter 9 of the laws of Malta.

Prevention of Money Laundering and Funding of Terrorism, Subsidiary Legislation 373.01 of the laws of Malta.

Securitisation Act, Chapter 484 of the laws of Malta.

Trusts and Trustees Act, Chapter 331 of the laws of Malta.

Virtual Financial Assets Act, Chapter 590 of the laws of Malta.

VFA Regulations, Subsidiary Legislation 590.01 of the laws of Malta.

USA

"Arizona HB2417 | 2017 | Fifty-Third Legislature 1st Regular"

EU Directives

Council Directive 2006/112/EC of 28 November 2006 on the common system of value added tax.
   Council Directive (EU) 2016/1065 of 27 June 2016 amending Directive 2006/112/EC as regards the treatment of vouchers.

EU Regulations

Regulation (EU) No 910/2014 of the European Parliament and of the Council of 23 July 2014 on electronic identification and trust services for electronic transactions in the internal market and repealing Directive 1999/93/EC.
   On the protection of natural persons with regard to the processing of personal data and on the free movement of such data, and repealing Directive 95/46/EC (General Data Protection Regulation), Regulation (EU) 2016/679 of the European Parliament and of the Council of 27 April 2016.

Consultation Documents and Guidelines

Consultation for the Strengthening of the Malta Financial Services Authority, PS Financial Services, Digital Economy, and Innovation, 2017, mfsa.com.mt/.

Consultation on The Proposed Regulation of Collective Investment Schemes Investing in Virtual Currencies, MFSA, 2017, mfsa.com.mt.

Discussion Paper on Initial Coin Offerings, Virtual Currencies and related Service Providers, MFSA, 2017. mfsa.com.mt.

Guidelines for the Purpose of the Duty on Documents and Transfers Act, Office of the CfR, 2018.

Guidelines for the VAT Treatment of Transactions or Arrangements Involving DLT Assets, CFR, 2018.

Guidelines on the Income Tax Treatment of Transactions or Arrangements Involving DLT Assets, CFR, 2018.

Malta – A Leader in DLT Regulation, PS Financial Services, Digital Economy, and Innovation, 2018, meae.gov.mt.

VFA Rulebook, MFSA: <https://www.mfsa.com.mt/fintech/virtual-financial-assets/rules/>.

N.B. A full bibliography can be found via the Blockchain Malta Association web site: BlockchainMalta.info

About the Blockchain Malta Association

Malta is a sovereign archipelago covering 316 square kilometres situated 93 km south of Sicily (Italy) in Southern Europe and roughly 300 km North from the North African coast, around 12 kms from major international shipping lanes.

With a rich history dating back to pre-Phoenician times, Malta is an active member of the Commonwealth, EU and UN. A common law jurisdiction Malta gained its independence from the United Kingdom in 1964.

The Blockchain Malta Association was founded in 2017 as an industry association for the fledgling Blockchain Island, supporting a coherent strategy for the development of the cryptocurrency and DLT economy locally and internationally.

The Association cooperates with Finance Malta and any stakeholders within the Blockchain Island and beyond interested in advancing a diverse, digital economy.

BMA is chaired by Patrick L Young who can be contacted via email: patrick@revolutionmarket.capital.

The Blockchain Malta Association web site can be found at: BlockchainMalta.info

By The Same Editor

Patrick L Young:
  Capital Market Revolution!
  The New Capital Market Revolution!
  The Promiscuous Investor
  Single Stock Futures A Traders Guide
  The Exchange Manifesto
  The Exchange Invest 1000

As Editor:
An Intangible Commodity
The Gathering Storm

Forthcoming:
Victory or Death!